The Early Church and Today

The Early Church and Today

Volume 1 • Ministry, Initiation, and Worship

Everett Ferguson

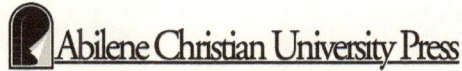
Abilene Christian University Press

THE EARLY CHURCH AND TODAY
Volume One: Ministry, Initiation, and Worship

Copyright 2012 by Everett Ferguson

ISBN 978-0-89112-586-0
LCCN 2012025192

Printed in the United States of America

ALL RIGHTS RESERVED
No part of this publication may be reproduced, stored in a retrieval system, or transmitted in any form by any means—electronic, mechanical, photocopying, recording or otherwise—without prior written consent.

Scripture quotations noted RSV are taken from the Revised Standard Version of the Bible, copyright 1952 (2nd edition, 1971) by the Division of Christian Education of the National Council of the Churches of Christ in the United States of America. Used by permission. All rights reserved.

Scripture quotations noted NRSV are taken from the New Revised Standard Version Bible, copyright 1989, Division of Christian Education of the National Council of the Churches of Christ in the United States of America. Used by permission. All rights reserved. All other translations are by the author.

LIBRARY OF CONGRESS CATALOGING-IN-PUBLICATION DATA
Ferguson, Everett, 1933-
The early church and today / Everett Ferguson.
    p. cm.
ISBN 978-0-89112-586-0
1. Church history--Primitive and early church, ca. 30-600. I. Title.
BR165.F373 2012
270.1--dc23

2012025192

Cover design by Rick Gibson
Interior text design by Sandy Armstrong

For information contact:
Abilene Christian University Press
1626 Campus Court
Abilene, Texas 79601

1-877-816-4455
www.abilenechristianuniversitypress.com

12 13 14 15 16 17 / 7 6 5 4 3 2 1

*To the memory of Dr. Donald Everett Lewis,
my best friend and then brother-in-law; a kind, humble, and
responsible man of integrity; learned chemist;
compassionate teacher, caring for his subject and his students;
loving husband, father, and grandfather;
dedicated Christian and churchman.*

Contents

Acknowledgments 9
Preface 11

Part I: Church and Ministry

1. Four Freedoms of the Church 15
2. The Ministry of the Word in the First Two Centuries 23
3. Ordination According to Acts: Acts 6:1–6 39
4. Laying on of Hands in Acts 6:6 and 13:3 47
5. The Authority and Tenure of Elders 53
6. Church Order in the Sub-Apostolic Period:
   A Survey of Interpretations 63
7. The Ministry in the Apostolic Fathers 87
8. The "Congregationalism" of the Early Church 101
9. Article Review of Dan Williams's *Retrieving the Tradition and Renewing Evangelicalism: A Primer for Suspicious Protestants* 115
10. Women in the Post-Apostolic Church 123

Part II: Baptism and Initiation

11. Baptismal Motifs in the Ancient Church 145
12. Baptism in the Patristic Period 165

Part III: Demonology

13. The Demons According to Justin Martyr 183
14. Origen's Demonology 193

Part IV: Worship and Assembly

15. Justin Martyr and the Liturgy 213
16. "When You Come Together":
    Επι το αυτο in Early Christian Literature 229
17. Τόπος in 1 Timothy 2:8 237
18. Sabbath: Saturday or Sunday? A Review Article 249

Part V: Church Music

19. Jewish Religious Music in the First Century—
    Temple, Synagogue, Home, and Sect 263
20. The Theology of Singing 273
21. The Case for A Cappella Music in the Christian Assembly 277
22. Church Music in Ephesians and Colossians:
    Exegesis of Colossians 3:15–17 283
23. Early Church History and the Instrumental Music Controversy 297
24. Congregational Singing in the Early Church 317

Acknowledgments

The following journals, publishers, and institutions generously gave permission for reprinting my articles:

    Abilene Christian University
    Acta Patristica et Byzantina
    Australian E-Journal of Theology
    Baker Publishing Co.
    Freed-Hardeman University
    Gospel Advocate Co.
    Harding University
    Pepperdine University Press
    Restoration Quarterly
    Scottish Journal of Theology
    Southern Methodist University Press
    Thomas Jefferson University Press
    Trinity Press International
    Western Christian Foundation
    Wm. B. Eerdmans Publishing Co.

Acknowledgement of the original source of publication accompanies each article.

Preface

These articles represent nearly fifty years of my published writings. They are based on scholarly research but were presented to a wider public. Thus they fall between technical writings for an academic audience and popular writings for a church audience.

Ministry and church organization have been a concern of mine since my thesis for the Master of Arts at Abilene Christian University on "Historical Developments Related to the Public Ministry of the Word in the Church of the First and Second Centuries" (1954), supervised by J. D. Thomas, Paul Southern, and Fred J. Barton (summarized in the second article in this collection), and my dissertation for the Doctor of Philosophy degree at Harvard University, "Ordination in the Ancient Church: An Examination of the Theological and Constitutional Motifs in the Light of Biblical and Gentile Sources" (1959), directed by George H. Williams.

Baptism has also received my attention from early in my studies, culminating in *Baptism in the Early Church: History, Theology, and Ministry in the Church of the First Five Centuries* (Grand Rapids: Eerdmans, 2009). The two articles included here, one in print for the first time, summarize some of my conclusions.

The two articles on demonology are expansions, based on fuller research, of my book *Demonology of the Early Christian World* (Lewiston, N.Y.: Edwin Mellen Press, 1984).

Worship is part of my interest in the doctrine and practice of church, exemplified in *The Church of Christ: A Biblical Ecclesiology for Today* (Grand Rapids: Eerdmans, 1996)—now in Korean (1997) and Russian (2005) translations.

I had no idea that research for a paper that Professor J. D. Thomas asked me to give for a workshop at Abilene Christian College in 1971 would lead to so much writing on the subject of church music, somewhat ironic for someone with as little musical ability as I have, but my limitation does not affect a historical approach to the topic. That paper was expanded into a booklet, *A Cappella Music in the Public Worship of the Church* (first edition, Abilene: Biblical Research Press, 1972; now in a third edition, Ft Worth: Star Bible Publications, 1999, and translated into Spanish in 2006). My research soon made it evident that at that time there was little comprehensive assembling of the numerous statements in early Christian literature bearing on the subject of music, which led me to produce numerous scholarly and popular articles in addition to the intermediate articles included in this volume.

For this collection I have made some corrections in the original publications, brought bibliographical references in the notes up to date, and added some observations; but the articles are substantially as they originally appeared. For the most part, I have allowed the conventions for citing references observed by the original sources of publication to stand in these reprints. Since some of these articles would not be easily accessible, these reprints will make the material more widely available.

Part I

Church and Ministry

1

Four Freedoms of the Church

A look at the present religious and social conditions in the world shows much that is discouraging. There seems to be a lack of moral guidance and direction in society, and even the churches are often in confusion. "Conservative" churches do not use the Bible properly and are bound by human tradition or legalism. Liberal (or "worldly") churches have made peace with the world, its standards and ways of doing things. Among Churches of Christ there is much talk about an identity crisis.

In these circumstances I want to lift up our eyes to the vision of the free church. This is a message I took to believers and inquirers in Central and Eastern Europe in the fall of 1991. It is a message relevant to American churches as well.

Since 1967 there has been a series of conferences on the concept of the Believers' Church, that is, churches whose membership depends on a personal confession of faith. It has been my privilege for several years to serve on the Committee on Continuing Conversations for this group, and I spoke at a conference in this series, on the subject of "The Rule of Christ" (church discipline), held at Goshen College, Goshen, Indiana, in May 1992. The designation Believers' Churches is used in contrast to other families of churches—Catholic, Orthodox, and Mainline Protestant. Another term used for Believers' Churches is Free Churches. Although the terms are not equivalent, there is a large area of overlap, and it is those features characterized by the word *free* that I want to emphasize. Our concern should be with the nature of the church according to biblical teaching and not just according to a typology of religious groups. The marks of a free church will provide the structure for this essay.

Freedom from State Control

The first characteristic of free churches from a historical perspective is their practice of the separation of church and state. This is the characteristic that gave the title "free churches" to certain groups. They are free from state control and state involvement. They "give to the emperor the things that are the emperor's and to God the things that are God's" (Matt. 22:21).

In the first three hundred years, Christianity remained separate from the state, until in the fourth century Constantine gave the church the support of the state, thus giving rise to what is known as the Constantinian Church. Constantine may receive more credit, or blame, than he deserves, because it was actually Theodosius who made Christianity the official religion of the Roman Empire. A state church continued as the prevailing pattern in the Christian world for over fourteen centuries and still exists in many places. The arrangements have varied: Sometimes the church has dominated the state; sometimes the state has used the church as a department of religious affairs; and sometimes there has been a mutuality, where church and state were two parts of one society.

Through history, free churches have existed apart from the control of the state. Governmental recognition of a separation of church and state came with the Bill of Rights to the Constitution of the United States. The policy of official separation has been adopted by other countries, but is still not widely followed. Unfortunately for many people in the Western world, freedom of religion means freedom from religion. In Eastern Europe the reactions against the developments of the last fifty to eighty years may mean a return to the state churches of the past. The pope's call for uniting Europe on its Christian heritage may encourage the persecution of dissenters. Those churches in Eastern Europe that maintained their freedom in the face of persecution may still in the post-Communist era not be free from persecution. Coercion is not good, whether it comes from irreligious Communism or from a dominant religion. The free church maintains its independence in the face of persecution.

The vitality of the free churches shows the value of independence, self-reliance, and responsibility. The church is healthier and does its work better when it does not depend on the state for financial and other supports and when it influences society, not by its privileged position, but only by the moral persuasion of its arguments and lifestyle. This aspect of the free church may not seem to be so important to declare in the United States, but even here there may be need for this reminder lest there be temptation to seek greater entanglements with the state or to identify Christianity with government policies.

Freedom from Other External Controls

A free church controls its own affairs. For most free churches this includes the practice of congregational independence. From a biblical standpoint this is the correct position. To be truly free a church must be free from all external control or constraints. There may be coercion and pressure from sources other than government or politics. Three aspects call for comment.

Freedom from Denominational Controls

The Restoration Movement was in part a revolt against creeds, denominational structures, and human organizations. The apostles left no hierarchy to replace their presence but commended local elders to God and his word. "And after they had appointed elders for them in each church, with prayer and fasting they entrusted them to the Lord in whom they had come to believe" (Acts 14:23). "And now I commend you [elders at Ephesus] to God and to the message of his grace, a message that is able to build you up and to give you the inheritance among all who are sanctified" (Acts 20:32).

The local church should be free under Christ to conduct its work, worship, and life according to the instructions of the Bible. There is voluntary cooperation in all areas of concern among believers and churches of the same faith. But they do not create new decision-making organizations. They do not create structures that bind rules for ministry, communion, and fellowship and that come between believers and the Lord. There is cooperation but not control. A free church exercises congregational independence from a denominational hierarchy.

Freedom from Others Regulating Details of Individuals' Private Lives

"Who are you to pass judgment on servants of another? It is before their own lord that they stand or fall. And they will be upheld, for the Lord is able to make them stand" (Rom. 14:4). It need not be a denominational hierarchy that regulates the lives of members. It may be fellow believers who go beyond counsel and admonition and make detailed rules as a basis for communion. There has been in some places a "new monasticism," which gives rules for everyday activities and seeks to regulate the religious activities of members by a strict routine. Such violates the Christian freedom of the individual.

Freedom from Cultural Conformity

"Do not be conformed to this world, but be transformed by the renewing of your minds, so that you may discern what is the will of God—what is good and acceptable and perfect" (Rom. 12:2). The word for *world* in the Latin version of this verse gave English its word *secular*. Secularism is a pervasive influence in our world. Pressures to cultural conformity may come from many sources: in the Western world, from materialism; in Eastern Europe, from communitarian or statist ways of thinking. In our country, selfishness and pleasure-seeking are promoted all around us. The respective dangers are not unique to each, and in all regions there are temptations to throw off biblical, spiritual, or moral restraints.

In answer to a question concerning the greatest dangers to the free churches in Hungary, a pastor of an independent church in Budapest said: "Cultural conformity, materialism, desire for revenge against the Communists, and a lack of cooperation among free churches." With little change, that might be said anywhere.

A free church exercises freedom from demands to conformity, whether from the right or the left, whether political, social, or religious.

Free Choice of Membership

A free church is one in which a person becomes a member by free choice. A free church has a committed church membership, because membership is freely chosen. The combination of the state church and infant baptism has meant for much of the Christian world that birth into a family or a nation is birth into a given church.

Even without infant baptism, there may be family, societal, or cultural reasons for church membership. Churches that practice believers' baptism have their share of cultural Christians and family Christians. Baptism at younger and younger ages may compromise this mark of a free church.

Anything less than membership based on personal faith and commitment is not truly biblical. Succinctly stated in Acts 18:8 is the biblical order of the word, faith, and baptism: "Many of the Corinthians who heard Paul became believers and were baptized."

A free church is a church in which one freely chooses to be a member. That was the situation in the early days of Christianity, and that is the situation today with churches experiencing the greatest growth and vitality. Members of a free church make a voluntary commitment to Christ.

A Freely Chosen Christian Lifestyle

A free church chooses a disciplined Christian life. Freedom does not mean to do as one pleases. Christian freedom requires self-discipline under Christ. "For you were called to freedom, brothers and sisters; only do not use your freedom as an opportunity for self-indulgence, but through love become slaves to one another" (Gal. 5:13). "As slaves of God, live as free people, yet do not use your freedom as a pretext for evil" (1 Pet. 2:16).

Discipline is not a contradiction to freedom. In contrast to the regulations imposed by a religious hierarchy, this discipline is voluntarily chosen. Franklin Littell, one of the foremost spokesmen of the free church, in a recent address said, "Voluntary discipline is an essential element of Christian liberty." "Voluntary discipline"—the freedom comes from the discipline being freely chosen. The discipline is not imposed from outside; it is self-discipline, the self's acceptance of God's discipline.

Discipline is needed in all areas of life. People sometimes think freedom means to do as they please, but as one pundit put it, "When people are free to do as they please, they usually imitate each other." Unlimited freedom to do as one pleases leads to the slavery of selfishness and self-indulgence. A people can be truly free only if they can discipline themselves. Without self-discipline, they will ruin themselves, or someone else will discipline them out of the need for order. It would be a pity for the peoples of Central and Eastern Europe to gain political and economic freedom yet end in moral corruption and spiritual slavery. The danger is not theirs alone. Indeed, a case can be made that moral discipline and spiritual integrity are necessary for political and economic freedom to work.

Where there is undisciplined behavior, freedom is lost. For example, people want sexual freedom, but the greatest freedom in sexual relationships is within the commitment of marriage.

The disciple lives (1) under the Lord, and (2) under the brotherly and sisterly admonition of fellow-believers. And this admonition is practiced mutually, not hierarchically. Freedom is not purely individual. This leads back to the idea of "church," where the individual encourages and is encouraged, admonishes and is admonished. Christians do not use their freedom selfishly, but for the good of the community of believers. A community, a church, requires a commonly accepted standard of conduct, a discipline. The lifestyle is chosen by the community of believers, and the community calls the members to high standards of conduct. The free church, as a community of committed believers, adopts a disciplined life.

Conclusion

The free church as an ideal worthy of guiding religious efforts has the following marks: a church separated from the state, a church free from external control (whether political, denominational, or cultural), a church whose members have freely chosen to identify with it, and a church that practices voluntary discipline.

To summarize another way, a free church cherishes freedom of conscience (where religion or irreligion is not dictated by the state), freedom from coercion (whether from outside or from fellow-believers), freedom of confession (one is not born into it), and freedom of commitment (voluntary obedience to the Lord). The free church means freedom from coercion, freedom of conscience, and freedom for confession and commitment.

*Originally printed in *Restoration Quarterly* 35 (1993): 65–69.

2

The Ministry of the Word in the First Two Centuries

The ministry of the church may be divided into three aspects—the ministry of the word, of benevolence, and of pastoral oversight. One of the specialized meanings of "ministry" (*diakonia*) in the New Testament refers to the dispensing of the gospel. Although some overlapping of functions occurs, the topic of this study is as follows: "Who did the preaching and teaching of the word of the Lord in the early church?"

According to Paul's description of the church as a "body" in 1 Corinthians 12 it is clear that every member was a "minister" (servant) of the whole body. However, the same chapter also demonstrates a place for different types of ministers with their own specialty. Those formally designated for a position of service in the church were spoken of as holding an "office." Filling an office indicated, not the possession of authority, but rather, designation to perform a work; an office was a function, a responsibility.[1] The evidence shows that any Christian man with the requisite ability and knowledge could speak in the public assembly and teach the gospel to others.[2] This study is concerned with those who possessed the necessary "gifts" or qualifications and received formal recognition from the church to do the public work of teaching.

In the New Testament there is a two-fold distinction made with reference to ministers—between local officers and those not bound to a local congregation, and between inspired and uninspired teachers. New Testament congregations passed through three stages of growth: (1) A time when they were served by extraordinary (inspired) ministers; (2) a time when a dual ministry of both inspired and uninspired men were the dispensers of the Word; and (3) a time when the uninspired ministry intended to be permanent in the churches existed alone. Since not all congregations passed through these stages at the same time, many have been able to find a basis for arguing that there was no uniformity in the New Testament in regard to the ministry. As an illustration, an untrained observer on viewing an exhibit of the metamorphosis of a butterfly might conclude that the egg, caterpillar, chrysalis, and butterfly were four different species. However, on reading the description he would learn that he was examining four different stages in the life span of the same insect.

The first public ministers of the church possessed *charismata*, "spiritual gifts" supernaturally given. These are named as "apostles, prophets, and teachers" in 1 Corinthians 12:28. They were called and equipped for their task by the Lord through the activity of the Holy Spirit, they served the church universal, and they filled an office that did not have to be occupied anew after their death.

Although the word "apostles" had a wider meaning of "one sent on a mission,"[3] it had primary reference to the Twelve and Paul,[4] who were distinguished from all others by having a special call from the Lord and by having the gift of plenary inspiration in revealing the will of the Lord to people.[5] In keeping with their special qualifications, their responsibilities included bearing testimony of Christ, revealing the essential truths of the plan of salvation, and enacting all the necessary ordinances for the church.[6]

The New Testament prophets were closely associated with the apostles in revealing the foundation truths of the gospel.[7] They not only revealed the counsels and purposes of God, as shown by Ephesians 3:4f., but 1 Corinthians 14 shows their gift of prophecy also qualifying them to lead in Christian worship, to exhort and edify the church, to unfold the meaning of the oracles of God, and to distinguish the Word of God from the word of men. The point of distinction between the apostles and prophets appears to have been that the inspiration of the apostles was abiding,[8] for they were the infallible and authoritative messengers of Christ; whereas the inspiration of the prophets was occasional and transient.[9] Neither did the prophets have the "care of all the churches"[10] which the apostles had. Part of a prophet's work was in his own community[11] and part was elsewhere.[12]

Whereas the prophet received revelations of the divine will and gave messages in behalf of another, the teacher was closely associated with him[13] in making exposition and application to life of the revealed truth. A careful exegesis of 1 Corinthians 14:6 shows that he who received a revelation was a prophet and he who had "the word of knowledge" was a teacher.[14] The teacher had a rich background in the Judaism of the first century, for the many "rabbis" had the practical, personal task of leading individuals to live their lives in full accord with the will of God. The inspired instructors in the faith fulfilled this purpose (*didaskō*) both by exhortation in the meeting for edification as seen in 1 Corinthians 14:26 and by the class instruction (*katecheō*) envisioned in Galatians 6:6.

Teaching occupied a prominent place in the assemblies of the New Testament church for worship—Acts 2:42[15]; 1 Corinthians 14; Acts 20:7ff.; 13:1ff.[16] Instruction took the form of a single discourse or several shorter messages.

Ephesians 4:11 lists the ministers of the church at a time of transition. Here the reference is to the men who were given to the church; in 1 Corinthians 12 it is to the functions placed in the church. Those who labored in the ministry of the word now included evangelists, who served the church universal,[17] and pastors, who served a local church. These were men whose task did not necessarily require a miraculous gift of the Spirit, and thus it is possible to see the preparation made for the time when the church would function without direct guidance from the Spirit. The pastors are to be identified with those elsewhere in Scripture called elders (presbyters) or bishops, as the Greek of Acts 20:2, 8 and 1 Peter 5:1ff. demonstrates. Very early the apostles began choosing a college of elders to oversee congregations.[18] As soon as qualified men appeared (sooner in Jewish than in predominantly Gentile churches) they were set apart to form the nucleus of a local ministry to guide the churches once the apostles were removed from the scene. Likewise, Paul early began to gather around himself men like Timothy and Titus who were trained to continue the work of preaching the gospel. Second Timothy 4:5 shows that "evangelist" was a technical term for this class of workers in the church. As "bearers of glad tidings" the evangelists were primarily functionaries of the church universal (but could be responsible to one local church), but in laboring to win new converts they both traveled about or settled for a time in one place.[19]

In the letters of 1 and 2 Timothy and Titus there is a description of the last stages of organization through which the churches of Christ passed in New Testament times. This arrangement gave a permanent answer to the needs of the church. At the beginning the functions of oversight, benevolence, and teaching had all been entrusted to the apostles. These activities were now distributed to bishops, deacons, and evangelists, respectively, but not exclusively or categorically. It was necessary for the continuance of the church that the essential functions of ministry be identified with certain offices. That these offices provide for the necessary activities in the church shows their permanent intention and permanent validity as a form of church organization. Other offices—e.g., that of apostles and prophets—requiring a special "gift" ceased when that gift ceased.

The New Testament gives indication of a large number of congregations each under the supervision of a council of presbyter-bishops.[20] The noncanonical literature nearest to the New Testament reveals the same situation.[21] That apostles appointed elders in all the churches, gave qualifications for filling this office, and commanded others to appoint qualified men to the position shows that elders were intended to be permanent in the church. The primary task of these workers as shepherds of men's souls demanded that a large share of the ministry of the word fall on them. Indications of their public teaching role are found in 1 Timothy 3:2; 5:17; Titus 1:9; Acts 20:28–32; and Ephesians 4:11f. Toward the close of New Testament times as the gift of prophecy became less frequent and visits from the missionary ministry less certain, teaching naturally fell more and more to the local leadership.

The evangelistic office likewise exists in the nature of things as long as the church feels the press of the Great Commission. That Paul continued until his death to choose other evangelists and instruct them in the work of preaching further demonstrates that he felt the need of a continuous supply of men prepared for the work of an evangelist.[22] The evangelists' work of preaching the gospel included strengthening the faith of those already converted, refuting false doctrine, instructing the church, and organizing congregations.[23] Their task was preeminently one of teaching and preaching—reproving, rebuking, and exhorting. They might stay for a time with a church fully organized (as Timothy at Ephesus), but Titus 3:12ff. and 2 Timothy 4:10, 12 indicate that apparently Paul saw a value in frequently changing places of labor.

Although bishops and evangelists were the most prominent servants of the Word, the preliminary observations on all Christians as ministers should not be forgotten. Uninspired teachers had a place in the permanent work of the church.[24] Moreover, in keeping with the general freedom of apostolic times, much teaching was done by women.[25] However, this teaching was confined to situations where the woman did not assert herself over men, for teaching in the public assembly was specifically denied to women.[26]

As one moves to the sub-apostolic and second-century literature, one finds that the significant developments in regard to the ministry involved changes in the organization of the church. Three stages of change from the New Testament pattern may be outlined: (1) There was first a decline in the universal or missionary ministry leaving the local officers in control of the entire church; (2) almost simultaneously there emerged a single bishop distinguished from the presbytery; and (3) the monarchial bishop's[27] position was strengthened to meet the challenges of Gnosticism and Montanism. Several factors, some unintentional and some deliberate, contributed to these changes. Before developing them, a survey should be made of the understanding of the second-century church in regard to the functionaries (save elders) already mentioned.

The word "apostle" continued to have occasional use in its wider meaning, including reference to those who were associates of the apostles.[28] However, its overwhelming usage was limited to the Twelve (including Paul)—e.g., in Clement,[29] Ignatius,[30] Justin,[31] and Irenaeus.[32] The second-century evidence confirms what was found in the New Testament: The apostolate died with the Twelve and Paul. Some of their functions were regarded by the early church as having been perpetuated in others, but to what was distinctive about them—the gift of authoritative teaching and the special call by Jesus— no one could succeed. No one called a contemporary, not even the bishops who were regarded as successors of the apostles, by the title "apostle."

The prophetic order was at its peak in the *Didache*, which on the whole gives a picture of the ministry not unlike that found in the New Testament. The prophet presided at the Lord's table, was entitled to have his words obeyed, and was the only person privileged to abide within the community without earning his support by his own labor. Since their gift was for the whole church, prophets might travel or settle as they chose.[33] Ignatius[34] and perhaps Hermas[35] claimed to have the prophetic gift. But shortly after this time prophecy is recognized by the church as a thing of the past. Although Justin[36] and Irenaeus claim that prophets were still present, it was a matter of hearsay with them. The work against Montanism[37] which Eusebius quotes under the name of Miltiades from the second century gives a list of those who prophesied under the new covenant. The writer can give no names beyond Ammia of Philadelphia and Quadratus, who at the latest cannot be placed after the first quarter of the second century.[38] "Prophets" as a class would not have been so regularly used without qualification referring to those of the Old Testament if prophets were a common thing in the writer's own day. Unlike the New Testament usage, when Christian prophets are referred to it is always with some specifying expression. Moreover, the polemic of the church against Montanism's attempt to revive prophecy proceeded on the tacit assumption of the extinction of the prophets. (Likewise the frenzied type prophecy of Montanus was considered false because it did not correspond to the rule of Paul in 1 Corinthians 14:32.[39])

In the second-century literature, teachers do not appear as inspired persons (e.g., in *Didache* they did not have to be tested whether they spoke in the Spirit). A large number of them are favorably mentioned as traveling from place to place, instructing the faithful and preaching to new converts.[40] Most notable of these was Justin Martyr, who included within his activities the establishment of a Christian school similar to the numerous contemporary ones of philosophy.[41] Teachers maintained their position longer than any other group not included within the local organization of a congregation. At Alexandria the institution of teachers survived the longest side by side with the episcopal organization of the churches.[42] The life of Origen (the most illustrious figure of the catechetical school at Alexandria) was the unsuccessful, final struggle of a free "teacher of the word" to keep the ministry of the word from being completely submerged under episcopal domination.

After the New Testament an almost complete blackout hangs over the word "evangelist," until the writings of Tertullian, and his references to the word are not helpful in telling the place of the evangelist in the second century.[43] Eusebius mentions evangelists a number of times as carrying on the activities associated with this class of men in the New Testament, but he is sufficiently vague to indicate that his was not firsthand knowledge.[44] Many of those called teachers also sound like evangelists, so that it is possible that there was a progressive convergence of these terms in the second century.[45]

The apostles had sought to give the church a strong local organization. In the years overlapping the end of the first and the beginning of the second century the church went too far in this direction, at the expense of the missionary ministry. Schismatical and heretical tendencies threatened the church;[46] domestic factions had appeared;[47] and even the presbyters in some cases were falling away.[48] The most serious problem came from the large number of false teachers who were spreading their doctrines under the guise of the revered prophets and evangelists. First John 4:1–6 from the New Testament shows the need for testing, since many false prophets had gone out into the world. The *Didache* and Hermas apply more elaborate tests. This fact alone is evidence of the real challenge from false prophets. The church took two steps to meet this challenge. One is reflected in the *Didache*: The local ministry assumed the place of the prophetic ministry. Every inducement was given to prophets to settle down, and apparently many did.[49] The many false teachers in time caused the whole itinerant ministry to fall into disrepute. No doubt one reason that the church was having so much trouble from false prophets was the fact that the true prophets were beginning to disappear. It appears from the literature's silence that evangelists and teachers had either joined the trend to settle locally or were devoting themselves entirely to laboring in new fields. The *Didache* is significant for the future in representing the honor of the ministry of the word being transferred to the local officers.[50] The congregations looked to those local leaders whom they knew from permanent residence (and in many cases were of apostolic appointment) for sound doctrine. Coinciding with this development was a move in the direction of good order by an insistence on obedience to the local ministry. This is the theme of Clement's epistle.[51] However correct may have been his insistence on obedience in the particular situation at Corinth, the letter represents a type of thinking that was later to make office-bearers actually "generals" and "priests" instead of shepherds of men's souls, and thus there is the beginning of an "institutional" idea of the church.

The next stage through which the ministry of the early church passed was marked by the rise of the monarchial bishop beginning in the early second century. The first step in this process was the beginning of a differentiation of function within the local presbyteries. This may be reflected in some passages in Hermas[52] and would have involved the regular assigning of certain duties to one of the presbyters who was the "overseer" (*episkopos*) of this work. The next step was the full recognition of one man in each congregation as the "bishop" with this name exclusively his. This is the situation in Asia Minor reflected in the letters of Ignatius, the early church's leading proponent of monepiscopacy. This statement in his epistle to the Smyrneans, section 8, is typical: "See that you all follow the bishop, as Jesus Christ follows the Father, and the presbytery as if it were the apostles. And reverence the deacons as the command of God." Ignatius saw the bishop as a necessary symbol of unity in a church threatened by division; for him an office does constitute the church and is necessary for its existence.[53] There has been a mistaken tendency to read into Ignatius the whole episcopal organization of the fourth century. However, the bishop is not yet a distinct order; he is chief of (and not over) the presbyters, a "chairman of the board" as it were whose position was bound up with that of the other office-bearers.[54] The church followed the advice of this fiery preacher as to the way to face its problems posed by persecution from without and false teaching from within. By the mid-century the monarchial bishop was a general feature of the church throughout the Empire. The writings of Hegesippus, Irenaeus, and Tertullian make this certain. It is likely that the "president" of the assembly who preaches the sermon and has charge of alms in Justin's description of a worship service[55] is such a proto-bishop.

The evidence shows that the later bishop was connected with two lines of ancestry—the presbyterial and the apostolic, the former from which he came and the latter whose position he assumed. The second-century bishop had two outstanding characteristics—the right of ordination and the right of giving authoritative teaching.[56] These had been the functions respectively of apostles and evangelists, and of apostles and other inspired men. Although the bishop assumed the duties of apostolic men, the sources point to his having arisen out of the body of presbyters. Irenaeus regularly calls bishops by the name "presbyter."[57] Bishops for some time were regularly chosen from the presbytery and save for ordination the duties of the two largely remained the same.[58] Putting the evidence together monepiscopacy may be connected with the virtual disappearance of evangelists as separate workers in established churches in that wherever the Ignatian type of presbytery prevailed, the local presbytery had itself produced a personal organ with which the evangelist's functions could be combined. An evangelist, prophet, or traveling teacher would settle in a local community. At his death a need was felt for someone comparable, and the place was filled out of the presbytery (see note 58). When the evangelists, prophets, and others of the universal ministry began to lose prominence or fall under suspicion because of the traveling false teachers, it was natural that much of the prestige they held and many of their duties would have gone to the newly developed bishop. A local man was a better guarantee of correct teaching than the wandering ministers with no certain credentials. By its adaptability to the new situation it is understandable that monepiscopacy should have carried the day. Although several factors no doubt contributed to the distinguishing of one man as the bishop, a prominent one would have been the choice of the best qualified man to handle the public teaching. This would fit naturally into the future development that made the bishop's chair "the symbol of teaching."[59]

The final stage of this development was reached at the close of the second century when the position of the single bishop over each church was greatly strengthened by the doctrine of apostolic succession. Once again the change was related to a reaction against a serious problem. The second century was the setting for two great struggles of the church—with Gnosticism[60] and with Montanism. The Gnostic teachers advanced the claim to have received a secret tradition of more authentic Christianity handed down from the apostles through a succession of private teachers. Irenaeus gave the counter-claim of those who were orthodox in doctrine.[61] He emphasized the "succession" of the bishops in the churches founded by apostles as official and authoritative teachers of the true doctrine. Each of these bishops had in turn taken over from his predecessor the same *cathedra* (chair) to impart from it the same teaching. The stability of the doctrine of the bishops in a church was guaranteed by its publicity; its correctness was guaranteed by its consent with the teaching given from the "teachers' chairs" of all other churches. This standard of orthodoxy could be used to supersede an appeal to Scripture, as it was by Tertullian.[62] Apostolic succession at first was from "holder to holder" of the office, not from consecrator to consecrated as it became. With this doctrine it is clear that the bishop now constituted a separate order. He was over the presbyters and was not dependent on them for his position. When Irenaeus wrote, the doctrine of apostolic succession of bishops was concerned solely with the bishop's qualification to act as an authoritative teacher. Teaching seems to have become less and less the duty of presbyters.

Montanism arose as a protest against the growing ecclesiasticism and accommodation of the church to the world. It saw in the recovery of prophecy the way to recover the primitive purity of the church. The church catholic, however, reacted against the extremes of Montanism and went further in the direction of institutionalizing the church. The bishop's position was further enhanced. Having begun as a teacher, he had become a successor to the apostles over against Gnosticism, and now over against Montanism he became a successor to the prophet. The chief significance of this controversy for this study is seen in the fact that the gift of the Spirit was now regarded as the bishop's official (although not personal) possession. Position now validated one's preaching.[63]

All three functions of the ministry—oversight, benevolence, and teaching—were once more centered in the control of one official, contrary to the design of apostolic ordinance.[64]

*Originally printed in *Restoration Quarterly* 1 (1957): 21–31.

Chapter 2 Endnotes

1. 1 Tim. 3:1; Rom. 12:4.
2. Acts 8:4; Rom. 12:6ff.; 15:4; Phil. 1:14; Heb. 5:12.
3. 2 Cor. 8:23; Acts 14:14.
4. Acts 6:2, 6; Rev. 21:14; Gal. 1–2.
5. Luke 6:13; John 16:13; Gal. 1:11ff.
6. Acts 4:33; 2 Cor. 5:18ff.; Matt. 19:28; 18:18.
7. Eph. 2:20.
8. John 20:21ff.
9. 1 Cor. 14:30.
10. 2 Cor. 11:28.
11. 1 Cor. 14.
12. Cf. Agabus.
13. Acts 13:1.
14. Cf. Archibald Robertson and Alfred Plummer, *A Critical and Exegetical Commentary on the First Epistle of St. Paul to the Corinthians* (International Critical Commentary; New York: Charles Scribner's Sons, 1911), 308.
15. Most lexicons take "teaching" in this verse as active, so that it may be paraphrased "They gave steadfast attention to the teaching of the apostles." Cf. a similar translation by F. J. A. Hort, *The Christian Ecclesia* (London: Macmillan, 1897), 44.
16. The *leitourgia* of this verse on the analogy of Rom. 15:16 would include teaching.
17. I.e., their office was not bound to a local congregation; in this respect they were like the apostles and prophets. Such phrases as "universal ministry" and "missionary ministry" have been used to express this concept although it is realized that they are not wholly adequate terms.

The list of officers may be grouped as follows: Apostles and prophets form one category in Eph. 2:20 (as the organs for the revelation of Christ's will they constituted the foundation of the church—personal successors for them were no more needed than a successor was needed for Christ as the cornerstone); evangelists found their place in enlarging the church through the making and strengthening of new converts; pastors and teachers as local instructors are grouped in one category in Eph. 4:11.

18. Acts 11:30; 14:23; 15:6.
19. Cf. Philip who did both—Acts 8 and 21:8.
20. Acts 15:6; 11:30; 14:23; Acts 20:17, 28; 1 Tim. 3; Phil. 1:1; Titus 1:5–7; James 1:1; 5:14; 1 Pet. 1:1; 5:1ff.
21. *Did.* XV:1. "The Teaching of the Twelve Apostles" is a manual of church life, organization, and institutions originating probably in Syria and widely influential in

the early centuries of the church. Its view of the ministry definitely suggests a date not far from the turn of the century.

1 Clem. 42.4. First Clement is a letter from the church at Rome written by Clement to the church in Corinth about AD 96 or 97.

Hermas, *Vis.* III:v. 1 "The Shepherd of Hermas" is a lengthy collection of Visions, Mandates, and Similitudes written by an otherwise unknown member of the Roman church named Hermas. The sections on the ministry would fit a date of about AD 110 for this collection.

Polycarp, *Phil.* 6.

These passages together with the New Testament references indicate the same church organization for Jerusalem, Judea, Syria, Galatia, Ephesus, Asia Minor, Philippi, Crete, Corinth, and Rome.

22. Cf. 2 Tim. 2:2 where Paul has Timothy's equals in mind.

23. 1 Tim. 1:5ff.; 4:6; Titus 1:5, etc.

24. James 3:1.

25. Titus 2:3ff.; 1 Cor. 11:5; Acts 21:9.

26. 1 Cor. 14:34ff.; 1 Tim. 2:12.

27. The term "monarchial bishop" refers to the situation where one bishop emerged at the head of a single congregation. "Monepiscopacy" is also used in the same sense in this article.

28. Clement of Alexandria at the close of the second century, so uses the word in *Strom.* IV:17.

29. *1 Clem.* XLIV.

30. *Tral.* III:1; *Philadelphians* 7.1. Ignatius was "bishop" of Antioch who wrote seven letters while being carried across Asia Minor on his way to martyrdom in Rome about 117.

31. *1 Apol.* xxxix; XLIX; *Dial.* XLII. Justin wrote at the middle of the second century an *Apology* to the Emperor and a *Dialogue* with the Jew Trypho.

32. *Adv. Haer.* II:xxi; II:i; IV:xxiiif. Irenaeus was first presbyter and then bishop of Lyons in Gaul. About 180 he wrote his great work against the heresy of Gnosticism.

33. *Did.* XI, XIII.

34. *Philad.* VII:1.

35. *Mand.* XII:iii:3.

36. *Dial.* LXXXII.

37. In the third quarter of the second century Montanus claimed to have received the Holy Spirit and sought to purify the church by a revival of prophecy.

38. *H. E.* V:xvii:2. Eusebius of Caesarea wrote a *Church History* about 325 valuable for the fragments of earlier literature which it preserves.

39. *H. E.* V:xvi:7.

40. *Dial.* LXXXII: *C. Cels.* III:ix. The latter is an apology written by Origen, active in the early third century and the most learned man in the ancient church.

41. *Acts of Justin.*

42. *C. Cels.* IV:lxxii.

43. *De Praescr.* IV; *De Corona* IX. Tertullian was a prolific writer in Latin in Carthage.

44. *H. E.* II:iii:1ff.; III:xxxvii; V:x:2.

45. This view is suggested by J. Massie, "Evangelist," *A Dictionary of the Bible* (ed. James Hastings; New York: Charles Scribner's Sons, 1908), I:797.

46. Revelation and the letters of Ignatius.

47. Clement and Ignatius to the Philadelphians.

48. Polycarp (early second-century bishop of Smyrna) to the Philippians.

49. *Did.* XIII.

50. "Appoint therefore for yourselves bishops and deacons worthy of the Lord . . . for they also minister to you the ministry of the prophets and teachers. Therefore do not despise them, for they are your honorable men together with the prophets and teachers." Did. XV:1ff.

51. "The apostles . . . preached from district to district, and from city to city, and they appointed their first converts, testing them by the Spirit, to be bishops and deacons of the future believers. . . . They appointed those who have been mentioned, and afterwards added the codicil that if they should fall asleep, other approved men should succeed to their ministry. We consider therefore that it is not just to remove from their ministry those who were appointed by them, or later on by other eminent men, with the consent of the whole Church, and have ministered to the flock of Christ without blame." *Clem.* XLIV. Cf. LIV and LVII.

52. *Vis.* II:iv:2ff.; II:v:1; *Sim.* IX:xxvii:1ff.; VIII:vii:4.

53. *Tral.* III:1; *Eph.* IV:1; *Mag.* VII:1.

54. *Eph.* I, II, XIII:7; *Mag.* II, XI; *Philad.* XI, X: *Smyrn.* IV, XI.

55. *1 Apol.* LXVII.

56. Cf. the *Refutation of All Heresies* I:Pref. and *Apostolic Tradition* 1.9 both attributed to Hippolytus, early third-century schismatic bishop of Rome.

57. *Adv. Haer.* II:ii:4; *Ep. ad Florin.* in *H. E.* V:xx:7.

58. Another influence toward monepiscopacy may have come from the settlement of some prophet or evangelist in a given community. An indication that perhaps not all bishops arose out of the presbytery may be seen in this statement by Origen: "Consider . . . how in some towns where as yet there are no Christians, someone arrives, and begins to teach, works, instructs, leads to the faith, and finally becomes the ruler and bishop of his pupils." *Hom. on Num.* 11:4.

59. Irenaeus's term in the *Demonstration of Apostolic Preaching* II.

60. Gnosticism is a term for a number of different syncretistic religious philosophies which had some fundamental ideas in common. These included a belief that matter was intrinsically evil, the world was created by an evil Demiurge and not by the Father, and the aim of true religion was to bring deliverance of the spirit from the body.

61. *Adv. Haer.* III.

62. *Praesc.* XV, XXI.

63. *Adv. Haer.* IV:xxvi:2; II xxiv:1; *Praesc.* XXXVIII.

64. Cf. the *Apostolic Tradition*.

Selected Bibliography

Bradshaw, Paul, Maxwell E. Johnson, and L. E. Phillips, *The Apostolic Tradition: A Commentary*. Hermeneia. Minneapolis: Fortress, 2002.

Jay, E. G. "From Presbyter-Bishops to Bishops and Presbyters." *Second Century* 1 (1981): 125–62.

Lightfoot, J. B. "The Christian Ministry." *Saint Paul's Epistle to the Philippians*. Reprint. Grand Rapids: Zondervan Publishing House, 1953. 189–269, 349–50.

Lindsay, T. M. *The Church and the Ministry in the Early Centuries*. Second Edition. London: Hodder and Stoughton, 1903.

Milavec, A. *The Didache: Faith, Hope, and Life of the Earliest Christian Communities, 50–70 C.E.* New York: Newman, 2003.

Roberts, Alexander, and James Donaldson, eds. *The Ante-Nicene Fathers*. American Edition by A. C. Coxe. Reprint Edition in 10 volumes. Peabody: Hendrickson, 1994.

Schaff, Philip, and Henry Wace, eds. *Nicene and Post-Nicene Fathers*. Series II. Volume I. Peabody: Hendrickson, 1994.

Streeter, B. H. *The Primitive Church*. New York: Macmillan, 1929.

3

Ordination According to Acts

Acts 6:1–6

Luke often has one full account of an activity and at other times a briefer summary (and occasionally different details) of the same type of activity. Acts 6:1–6 is his fullest account of an ordination—the selection and the setting apart to a public function in the church. Other accounts in Acts are briefer but often include significant details.

Acts 6:1–6 describes an orderly procedure whereby a community of unequal members acts together in choosing and appointing leaders.

1. A need was recognized—"it is not best for us [the apostles] to leave the word of God and serve tables" (v. 2). The apostles were not "too good" to serve tables, nor were they indifferent to the situation of the widows. Rather, there was a work which only they could do, viz., bear witness to the resurrection of Jesus. It was not good for them to leave the ministry that only they could do (the ministry of the word, v. 4) in order to perform a ministry which others

could do just as well (the ministry of tables). A differentiation of function would involve more persons in the leadership of the community, enable more work to be done, and enable it to be done better.

2. Instructions were given concerning the qualifications of persons to meet the need—men from the community "of good reputation, full of the Spirit and of wisdom" (v. 3). Teaching preceded the appointment. The leaders in the benevolent program were to be men who were good examples and who had the qualities necessary for performing the task.

3. The "multitude of the disciples" (v. 2) examined those from their number who met the qualifications—"look out from among you" (v. 3). The method of testing and picking out the right men is not given, but since the community did it, they would already have known the men and recognized them for their ability

4. The "whole multitude" made the selection—"they chose" the seven men (v. 5). Once again, Luke does not record the method of selection—voice vote, show of hands, secret ballot, or some other method—but he does emphasize that the whole congregation did the choosing. The apostles took the lead in calling the whole church together (v. 2) and giving directions about what should be done, but they left the actual selection to the community of believers. The disciples chose men who met the qualifications required to do the work. The apostles presumably held a veto power, but we are not told that, and even if they did, there was no need to exercise it.

5. The chosen men were formally presented before the apostles—"they set them before the apostles" (v. 6). The congregation gave a formal and public recognition of these men who had been chosen by them and so had their endorsement and authorization to serve in the work to which they were appointed.

6. The men were set apart to their work—"they prayed and laid hands on them" (v. 6). It is often assumed that the apostles laid hands on the men. The text of the great majority of manuscripts does not explicitly say this, and although it might be a reasonable presumption, the grammar could be read as continuing the same subject from the beginning of the sentence so that the whole community did the laying on of hands. Even if the apostles did the laying on of hands, they did so as the leaders and representatives of the people

who did the choosing. The men began their work with the benediction of the church and prayer for God's blessings upon them.

The account in Acts 6:1–6 contains several verbal echoes of the Greek translation of Numbers 27:15–23. These parallels make the differences in the two accounts quite striking. In both accounts, there is a command to select a person or persons with specified qualifications to be appointed over a given responsibility, but in Acts 6 the divine choice is made by the people rather than by God directly. In both cases, there is a formal presentation, but in Acts 6 the chosen persons are presented before the apostles rather than before the priest and the whole congregation. In both instances, there is a laying on of hands, but in view of the other reversals, it seems likely that in Acts 6 the laying on of hands is done by the people rather than the leadership (Moses and the apostles).

The Laying on of Hands

The laying on of hands and prayer are mentioned in two of Luke's accounts of appointment to ministry in the church: Acts 6:1–6 and 13:1–3. The imposition of hands was used on many occasions in the Old Testament and in Jewish life. Without examining all these usages at this time, I shall state the conclusion of my study and the arguments supporting this conclusion.

The background for the Christian practice of imposition of hands is the use of this gesture as a sign of blessing, as in the patriarchal blessings (Genesis 48:14). Many lines of evidence converge to indicate that the laying on of hands, especially in reference to ordination, meant an act of blessing.

1. The laying on of hands in Christian usage is always associated with prayer, as in Acts 6:6 and 13:3. The gesture accompanied prayer and indeed can be described as an acted prayer. The prayer was the essential element in Christian ordination. The prayer asked for God's blessings upon the person identified by the imposition of hands, and it specified the kind of blessing desired. The laying on of hands marked out the person as an object of favor.

2. Jesus laid on hands in conferring benedictions. The wording of Mark 10:13–16, the blessing of the children, makes clear the association between touching and blessing. Jesus pronounced a benediction on the children while laying his hands on them. The gesture was apparently common with Jesus, and the practice of the Master was followed by the church. His usage would have been determinative of its meaning for his disciples.
3. Blessing is the one idea that unites the varied occasions when hands were laid on someone. The New Testament refers to the laying on of hands in connection with other events besides the blessing of children: in healings (Mark 6:5; Acts 28:8), in appointment to church office (1 Tim. 4:14), and in imparting the Holy Spirit (Acts 8:14–24; 19:6). Contrary to a common view, the gift of the Holy Spirit was not the only blessing that could be imparted by the laying on of hands. It was only one kind of blessing which could be associated with this gesture. The imposition of hands in every context where it occurs is a symbolic expression of prayer on behalf of someone, and the prayer verbalized the type of blessing intended (cf. Acts 8:15).
4. The church fathers interpreted the laying on of hands in terms of prayer and blessing. This evidence likely carries more weight with me, as a church historian, than it does with you; but I find the writings of early Christian literature a great help in interpreting the New Testament. The interpretation of ordination as an imparting of the Holy Spirit is a secondary development.
5. Early Christian art represented a blessing by depicting a laying on of hands. The nonliterary sources agree with the literary sources in understanding the laying on of hands and blessing as equivalent. Events in the Bible which speak of a blessing are represented in art by a laying on of hands. One example of this is the multiplication of bread and fish in the feeding miracles of Jesus: The text says Jesus blessed the bread and fish (e.g., Matthew 14:19), and the art depicts him placing his hands on the bread and fish.

6. Christian Syriac, a language related to Hebrew, provides a linguistic argument. Syriac developed its technical language for ordination from its cognate word to the Hebrew used for bestowing a blessing rather than from its cognate to the word employed in other occasions of a laying on of hands.

These arguments indicate that in the early church ordination was understood as the community giving its approval and blessing to those chosen for leadership and asking for God's favor upon them.

Other Passages in Acts

Acts 1:15–26 describes the selection of a successor to Judas as an apostle. Some of the same elements found in Acts 6 appear here also. There was recognition of a need to find a replacement for Judas in the ministry (Acts 1:17, 20), a laying down of qualifications for the task (Acts 1:21–22), a formal presentation of two men who met the qualifications (Acts 1:23), and prayer (Acts 1:24). No mention is made of the community's examining potential candidates, but they must have done so, since they narrowed the choice to two men. The process was carried out by the whole community of 120 disciples (Acts 1:15). (The whole community regularly acted and made its own selection in instances involving those who would represent it—Acts 15:22.) Since the appointment of his apostles belonged to the Lord directly, the final choice was left to him by the taking of lots (Acts 1:26), and there was no laying on of hands.

Acts 13:1–3 describes the sending out of Paul and Barnabas as missionaries from Antioch. This is another instance of divine choice: the Holy Spirit made known the divine decision (Acts 13:2; cf. 20:28 for another example of appointment by the Holy Spirit). Even in this instance, the church, through its leaders, was involved in giving its ratification and endorsement to the mission (Acts 13:3). Fasting accompanied the praying and laying on of hands. Fasting was another way of reinforcing prayer. It, like the laying on of hands, added solemnity and intensity to the prayer. The significance of what was done in Acts 13:3 is brought out by 14:26—they were commended to the grace of God for the work they were to do.

Acts 14:23 is a brief summary of the appointment of elders in every church. In part because of the brevity, there are obscurities in the interpretation of the passage. Does the word "appointed" mean that Paul and Barnabas selected the elders or that they set apart for the work those chosen by others? Involved in the procedure were "praying and fasting." As we have learned, prayer was essential to the appointment, and fasting reinforced and supported the seriousness of the event. The appointment meant that the men chosen were "commended to the Lord."

Conclusion

These passages in Acts say some important things about ordination in the early church. It was public and done with the involvement of the whole congregation cooperating together. The selection was made, or at least approved, by the whole body of believers. The ceremony of setting apart was performed with solemnity and seriousness. The persons chosen for leadership were given the blessing of the church and of God, expressed by prayer and symbolized by laying on of hands and fasting.

*Originally printed in *Acts: The Spreading Flame* (Harding University Lectureship; Searcy, AR: Harding University, 1989), 374–79.

Selected Bibliography

Ferguson, Everett. "Laying on of Hands in Acts 6:6 and 13:3." *Restoration Quarterly* 4 (1960): 250–52.

———. "Laying on of Hands: Its Significance in Ordination." *Journal of Theological Studies.* 26 (1975): 1–12.

———. "Ordination in the Ancient Church (IV)." *Restoration Quarterly* 5 (1961): 130–46.

4

Laying on of Hands in Acts 6:6 and 13:3

The narratives of the appointment of the Seven and the sending out of Paul and Barnabas echo the accounts of the appointment of Joshua (Num. 27) and the consecration of the Levites (Num. 8)—the two Old Testament stories in which the laying on of hands is used in setting apart men to God's service.

Acts 6:1–6 shows the following verbal parallels to the Septuagint version of Numbers 27:15–23: (1) Acts 6:3—the people are commanded to *episkepsasthe* ("look about for," a relatively rare meaning) seven men; Numbers 27:16—Moses asks God to *episkepsasthō* ("look about for") a man to lead the people. (2) Acts 6:3—the men are to be "full of the Spirit and of wisdom"; Numbers 27:18—Joshua is a man "in whom there is spirit," which is termed in Deuteronomy 34:9 the "spirit of wisdom." (3) Acts 6:3—the appointment is *epi tēs chreias tautēs* ("over this duty"); Numbers 27:16—the appointment is *epi tēs sunagōgēs tautēs* ("over this assembly"). (4) Acts 6:6—the selected men are *estēsan* ("made to stand") *enōpion* ("before," a common word in Luke) the apostles; Numbers 27:19—Joshua *stēseis enanti* ("shall stand before"; *estēsen enantion* in v. 22) the people. (5) Acts 6:6—they *epethēkan autois tas cheiras* ("laid their hands on them"); Numbers 27:18, 23—Moses *epethēken tas cheiras autou ep' auton* ("laid his hands upon him").

The similarities and differences are interwoven in their significance. The same basic sequence is observable: there is a command to select someone meeting definite qualifications to be appointed over a responsibility, who is publicly presented and then receives the laying on of hands. But the roles are in a measure reversed. The role of the people of Israel is taken by the apostles, and the role of God and Moses is taken by the people of Christ. The people in Acts 6, instead of God and his leadership, select the functionaries who possess the Spirit and lay on hands. Although Codex D gives a reading at verse 6, which has the apostles do the laying on of hands, the best attested text is ambiguous. Unless there is a change of subject in the middle of the sentence (as there is in v. 5), the people do the laying on of hands. The parallel to Numbers 27 strongly suggests that the apostles did not lay on hands, for the role of the apostles is that of the people in Numbers 27, namely the witnesses to a public commissioning before whom the appointees are formally presented ("made to stand") for recognition. Note that in Acts 6 the appointment is over an activity and not over a people.

The verbal echoes indicate that Luke was deliberately alluding to the Old Testament episode. The linking of this first step in organization with the first transmission of authority in Israel (an event which also served as the pattern for rabbinic ordination) was a bold claim that Christians were living in a new age of revelation and were the true heirs of the traditions of the Old Testament. To this doctrinal significance should be added the organizationally significant implication that the new people of God act in the place of God in the appointment of their functionaries.

Numbers 8:5–22 also presents a parallel: the people were assembled together (*sunaxeis*, with which compare the calling together of the disciples, *proskalesamenoi*, in Acts 6:2); the Levites were "presented" (*prosaxeis*) before the Lord; and the people of Israel laid their hands on the Levites (Num. 8:9, 10). However, the events of Numbers 8 seem chiefly to be alluded to in Acts 13. In addition to the occurrence once more of the laying on of hands, the following contacts may be observed: (1) Acts 13:2; Numbers 8:5—the choice in each instance is divinely made. (2) Acts 13:2—Paul and Barnabas are chosen for *to ergon ho proskeklēmai* ("the work to which I have called them"); Numbers 8:11—the Levites are to *ergazesthai ta erga kuriou* ("work the works of the Lord," "of Israel" in v. 19). (3) Acts 13:2—the Spirit makes his will known during a divine service (*leitourgountōn*); Num. 8:22—the Levites after their consecration perform divine service (*leitourgein tēn leitourgian*), and note that Paul considered himself to be a *leitourgos* in preaching the gospel to Gentiles (Rom. 15:16). (4) Acts 13:2—the church is commanded to *aphorisate* ("separate") Paul and Barnabas; in the LXX of Numbers 8:11 the same root is used for the Hebrew "wave offering," as is done commonly in the LXX (cf. further v. 14, where the LXX uses *diasteleis* in order to translate the Hebrew from the root *badal* which is sometimes rendered in the LXX by *aphorizō*).

On first thought, one would expect the pairing of the Levites with the Seven and Joshua with the missionaries. Indeed if the Seven were the first representatives of a diaconate patterned after the Levites, and if Paul and Barnabas received episcopal ordination patterned after rabbinic ordination, then this should have been the pairing. But if the fundamental theological and constitutional implications are as we have suggested, then Luke's pairing is not only appropriate but gives a valuable insight.

The Old Testament allusions indicate that the laying on of hands involved (1) a commissioning and authorization (Num. 27), and (2) a ratification of a choice and creation of representatives who were offered to the Lord for service (Num. 8). These meanings may be regarded as amplifications (present in varying degrees in "ordination" contexts) of the basal New Testament significance of the laying on of hands—the conferring of a blessing or a benediction (Mark 10:16; cf. Luke 24:50).[1] The statements of Acts 6:6 and 13:3 carry the discussion further by specifying that prayer (strengthened in urgency by fasting in the latter instance) was made while hands were being imposed. The expression of human approval is absorbed by the larger idea of the petition for divine favor.

There is no indication that any sacramental power, or more particularly the Holy Spirit, was conferred by the laying on of hands in these passages. Indeed, in Acts 6 the men chosen were already "full of the Spirit"

(v. 3). Although Paul uses *aphorizō* in speaking of his apostleship (Rom. 1:1; Gal. 1:15), he makes clear that his apostleship in the larger sense dates from his conversion (cf. Gal. 1:1; Acts 26:16–18). Although Acts 6 was taken by the later church as the beginning of the diaconate, no special gift seems to have been bestowed. There was nothing more that the community in either case could give than its own blessing (by commissioning or by ratification) and prayer to God. But to say this, when the community functions as the means of the divine choice or in accord with a divine choice, is not to disparage the act but rather to enhance the community which acts.

*Originally printed in *Restoration Quarterly* 4 (1960): 250–52.

Chapter 4 Endnote

1. Compare the extensive study by the writer of "Ordination in the Ancient Church," *Restoration Quarterly* 4.3 (1960); 5.1–3 (1961). More recently, J. F. Tipei, *The Laying on of Hands in the New Testament: Its Significance, Techniques, and Effects* (Lanham, MD: University Press of America, 2009), and my review in *Review of Biblical Literature* (online, posted Feb. 15, 2010).

5

The Authority and Tenure of Elders

The New Testament presents a close interrelationship of three items: abilities, service, and leadership. Within this New Testament perspective a proper understanding of the authority and tenure of elders may be attained.

Qualifications

The gifts which God through Christ bestows on men are the foundation of ministry. "Gifts" is the biblical word; we are more accustomed to speak of "abilities" or qualifications. God's gifts pertain no less to natural abilities than to supernatural endowments by the Spirit. The same word, "gift" *(charisma)*, is applied to both. On the subject of gifts, modern Christians often look no further than 1 Corinthians 12 and the varieties of gifts from the Spirit listed there. Even in this chapter, however, it should be observed that among those appointed by God in the church are "helpers" and "administrators." Christians should also look at Paul's list of gifts *(charismata)* in Romans 12:6, 7—prophecy, service, teaching, exhortation, contributing, giving aid, and doing acts of mercy. Of these, only prophecy requires a special inspiration by the Spirit. The other activities we regard as "natural." They are nonetheless gifts, and God does not bestow them on everyone. A special talent or ability is involved in being a teacher or an exhorter, in having money to give, and in being able effectively to perform acts of benevolence. In 1 Peter 4:10–11, the gifts received from God's grace are summarized in two categories—those of speaking God's word and those of rendering service. God is the source of one's special aptitudes—of whatever kind.

The keynote of New Testament teaching about human abilities is 1 Corinthians 4:7: "What have you that you did not receive? If then you received it, why do you boast as if it were not a gift?" This thrust at the Corinthians' pride in their spectacular gifts from the Spirit cuts the ground from under all human boasting. A natural talent such as musical ability may illustrate the point. My parents gave me violin lessons and later cornet lessons. I spent many hours practicing. Finally, my last year in high school I became second chair cornet in the school band—after everyone else but one had graduated. My lack of musical ability is evident to all who have to sit beside me in church or the college chapel. My friends on the faculty are those who are still willing to sit with me during chapel singing! I do not have the "gift," and no amount of human effort would make me a concert performer. Those who have the talent have the prerequisite for their attainments apart from anything for which they can take credit. Of course, on the other hand, one must train, use, and develop his talent. No amount of talent will make one an outstanding musician without his effort. As the concert pianist explained: "If I do not practice for one day, I can tell the difference; if I do not practice for two days, the critics can tell the difference; if I do not practice for three days, everyone can tell the difference." Abilities given by God, as they are developed, become qualifications for a given activity.

Service

God's gifts are given to be used. This introduces the second point—service. The New Testament teaches that abilities or gifts are to be employed for the common good: 1 Corinthians 12:7, "To each is given the manifestation of the Spirit for the common good." 1 Peter 4:10, "As each has received a gift, employ it for one another, as good stewards of God's varied grace." Ephesians 4:7–12 explains that Christ's gifts to the church of "apostles, prophets, evangelists, pastors and teachers" are for "the equipment of the saints . . . for building up the body of Christ." And Romans 12:6 says, "Having gifts that differ according to the grace given to us, let us use them." Thus "qualifications" are for the sake of service.

Leadership

Service or ministry in the use of one's gifts brings one to a position of leadership in the church. This is the third item in the New Testament teaching. Leadership in the New Testament is based on service. Hebrews 13:17: "Obey your leaders and submit to them." Because of the office they hold? Because of authority given to them? Not at all, but because of the ministry they perform—"For they are keeping watch over your souls." 1 Thessalonians 5:12: "We beseech you, brethren, to respect those who labor among you and are over you in the Lord and admonish you, and to esteem them very highly in love." Why? "Because of their work." Then 1 Corinthians 16:15ff.: "Now, brethren, you know that the household of Stephanas were the first converts in Achaia, and they have devoted themselves to the service of the saints; I urge you to be subject to such men and to every fellow worker and laborer." Paul says, "Be subject to such as devote themselves to the service of the saints." Who are the natural leaders in a congregation? They are those who do the work, those who are active in service, doing things for others. This is how potential elders are identified. One emerges as a leader because of his doing things that need to be done.

Out of this principle specific offices arise. The nature of the service determines the office, whether of evangelist, deacon, teacher, or elder. To summarize, gifts lead to service and service results in leadership. Preaching is necessary to make one an evangelist; caring for needs to make one a deacon; teaching, a teacher; and pastoral care, an elder. Prerequisite for filling an office, therefore, are three things: necessary qualifications (abilities), the use of these which shows that one can and will do the work (service), and recognition (or acknowledgement) of the leadership by the members of the congregation among whom the work is done.

Authority

The above perspective brings the subject of an elder's "authority" into sharper focus. An elder's service or ministry is that of "pastoring" (a shepherd), of oversight (a bishop), of management (a steward), of judgment and example (an elder on the pattern of Jewish elders). The church, in order to be a community and in order to function smoothly, has need of such leadership.

Jesus' principle concerning leadership among his followers is stated in Matthew 20:25–28: "You know that the rulers of the Gentiles lord it over them, and their great men exercise authority over them. It shall not be so among you; but whoever would be first among you must be your slave; even as the Son of Man came not to be served but to serve, and to give his life as a ransom for many." Jesus uses the same word that Peter uses in 1 Peter 5:3 in admonishing elders to lead by example and not to domineer or "lord it over" the flock.

The kind of authority that is denied to the elder may be seen from the use of this word in other contexts. It refers to man's dominion over the earth (Gen. 1:28); Israel's rule over Palestine (Num. 21:24); dominion of sin over humans (Ps. 19:13; cf. Rom. 6:14); death's rule over man (Ps. 49:14; cf. Rom. 6:9); the rule of a king (Ps. 72:8); the authority of the law over a person (Rom. 7:1). Paul renounced the position of "lording it over" the faith of his converts (2 Cor. 1:24). Jesus' words "exercise authority" express the rule of Solomon over other kingdoms (1 Kings 4:21); the authority of governors over the people (Neh. 5:15); the authority of kings (Eccl. 8:4; Neh. 9:37); a man's control over his earthly goods (Eccl. 2:19; 6:2); and one man lording it over another (Eccl. 8:9). Thus Paul declares, "All things are lawful for me, but I will not be enslaved by [brought under the authority of] anything" (1 Cor. 6:12).

Jesus' illustration pertained to government officials. Elders do not have coercive authority—political, military, or legal. This is demonstrated by the fact that words expressive of such authority are absent from New Testament texts about elders. They do not have controlling authority *(exousia)* or power *(dynamis);* their position is not that of a master *(despotes)* or ruling official *(archon)*.

The words that are used of elders and of the congregation's responsibility to them give a different picture from this type of authority. Hebrews 13:17

refers to "leaders." There may be some doubt whether elders specifically are meant, but the teaching of the verse presumably would include them (cf. v. 24). The word is used in the literature of the time for military commanders and high officials (cf. Luke 22:26), but the basic meaning of the word is "leader" or "guide," and it is in this capacity that such officers are so termed. Its basic meaning may be seen in Acts 14:12 of Paul as the "chief speaker" and in Acts 15:22 of Barsabbas and Silas as "leading men" among the brethren. It indeed appears to have been used by Christians, especially of prophets and teachers, because those who spoke the word of the Lord were the men who were the primary leaders in the church (cf. Heb. 13:7). Hebrews 13:17, accordingly, refers to leadership in speaking the word.

First Thessalonians 5:12 refers to "those over you in the Lord." It seems most unlikely that the church at Thessalonica already had elders at this time; but once more we may consider the principle applicable to elders, for the same word is used explicitly of them in 1 Timothy 5:17, "rule" well. The translations "be over" and "rule" seem particularly unfortunate. The word literally means, "to be out front," "to be at the head of," and so "to manage." Thus it is used of a father managing his household (1 Tim. 3:4, 5, 12), but even here in parallel with "caring for." The word was used especially in the sense "to care for" or "give aid to," as it is translated in Romans 12:8. The development in this direction is emphasized by the sense "to be concerned about, to be engaged in," in Titus 3:8, 14. The surrounding terms in 1 Thessalonians 5:12, "labor" and "admonish," definitely suggest the meaning "care for"; and the parallel description in 1 Timothy 5:17, "preaching and teaching," indicates a ministry of the word and pastoral care rather than rule. A derived noun, translated "helper," is used of Phoebe in Romans 16:2. This word referred to a patroness or protector of others. others. One should not claim that Phoebe was the ruler or had the authority in the church at Cenchreae which is claimed for elders. The conclusion, therefore, is that 1 Thessalonians 5:12 and 1 Timothy 5:17 refer to those who are "out in front" in their care for the spiritual needs of the church. Once more, leadership and service are intertwined, and the leadership is that of service.

When the words for the congregation's responsibility are examined, once more there is little indication of the kind of obedience which one gives to governmental authorities. The word translated "obey" in Hebrews 13:17 is literally "be persuaded by," "take the advice of," or "to follow." Note Acts 5:36, "who followed him"; 18:4, "persuaded"; 23:21, "yield to"; 27:11, "paid more attention to." The word "submit" occurs only in Hebrews 13:17 in the New Testament and means "yield" or "give way to." The word translated "be subject to" in 1 Corinthians 16:17 and 1 Peter 5:5 literally means "to rank oneself under." It is a stronger word, used of subordination of a child to parents (Luke 2:51) and a wife to her husband (Eph. 5:22; 1 Pet. 3:1, 5; Titus 2:5), but also of subjection to rulers (Rom. 13:1; Titus 3:1).

What authority, then, does an elder have? The most important kind possible in the Christian system. It is the "moral authority" of service, of example, of spiritual knowledge and experience, of spiritual maturity. When such qualities are pooled in the collective judgment of the eldership, it carries great weight with Christian people. Christians voluntarily subject themselves to mature leaders. They readily follow the example of a concerned eldership which has proved its leadership by unselfish devotion to the cause of Christ, by sound spiritual insight, and by good judgment. As children follow a father who cares well for them, so church members follow their shepherds (1 Tim. 3:4ff.).

The position of elder is a ministry in the church—a way to serve God and build up the church. This ministry of oversight (supervision) extends to all areas of the church's life—worship, preaching and teaching, benevolence, and discipline.

Christians should not select or approve a man as elder unless they are willing to yield to him in matters of judgment. They should appoint only one whom they respect as a spiritual leader and whom they are willing to follow. After the man is appointed is the wrong time to express reservations or declare misgivings. Recognition of a man as an elder is a declaration that he is a spiritual guide and that one defers to him in matters of opinion. Decisions have to be made. The elders are the ones to make those decisions. It is not "bossism" to expect the congregation to follow those decisions. Even as there is no justification for an eldership exercising arbitrary authority, there is no place for a congregation being rebellious at a whim or considering the eldership as an executive to carry out its wishes and to be dismissed if it does not.

Appointment

The congregation does have a crucial role in the appointment of elders. Simply possessing the qualifications does not make a person an elder; nor does one become an elder, even though he has been doing much of the work of an elder, until he receives congregational recognition.

There is a principle of joint participation evident in New Testament accounts of appointment to functions in the church. No matter who took the lead in the selection, the ultimate decision was one in which all interested parties concurred. Thus the selection of the Seven in Acts 6 was made by the church in Jerusalem but was confirmed by the twelve apostles (Acts 6:6). The choice of Barsabbas and Silas in Acts 15:22 was made by "the apostles, and the elders, with the whole church." Even when choices were made by the Holy Spirit, the church gave its confirmation and blessing. So the church at Antioch laid hands on Barnabas and Saul and sent them forth after the Holy Spirit had called them to missionary work (Acts 13:1–3), and the presbytery laid hands on Timothy and commissioned him to his work as an evangelist after prophetic utterances had designated him for this work (1 Tim. 4:14; cf. 1:18). Accordingly, even Holy Spirit-made elders (Acts 20:28), that is, elders appointed in accord with Spirit-inspired revelations, would not have become elders until they received the authorization and blessing of the church. The approval of the congregation is implied in 1 Timothy 3:10 when it says of deacons, after discussing bishops, that these "also" must be tested before being appointed. The first century practice is summarized by Clement of Rome in AD 96 when he refers to "men who have been appointed by the apostles and afterward by other eminent men with the consent of the whole church" (*1 Clem.* 44).

The congregation among whom a man has lived his Christian life knows best his qualifications, and those whom he will lead must indicate their willingness to follow or his ministry will be ineffectual. If the congregation does not recognize the authority of a man's Christian character and leadership, the elder has no other to appeal to. He may be admirably qualified and the congregation too unspiritual to recognize it; but if no one will follow, he cannot lead.

Tenure

An elder's term of service is determined by the same things which made him an elder in the first place. If a man loses his qualifications, ceases to serve, or no longer has the support of the congregation, he can no longer be an elder. "Once an elder, always an elder" has no biblical support. It is proper to admit charges against an elder and rebuke him, provided appropriate procedures are followed (1 Tim. 5:19ff.). As the approval is given by all, so the rebuke is "in the presence of all." That implies that the congregation which gave its approval may also withdraw that approval. Obviously, this must be for a good cause. On the other hand, as long as a man is qualified, continues to serve, and is a recognized leader, he should continue to function as an elder.

This brings up the question of assigning stipulated terms (in the manner of political offices) to elders. The interest in such a practice is perhaps the result of bad experiences with the exercise of arbitrary authority or the feeling of being "stuck" with men who showed promise but then did not develop as anticipated. On the other side, elders themselves whose energies have been drained are sometimes interested in an orderly method of retirement. I know of no biblical or early historical precedent for such a procedure, nor do I recognize any biblical principle which would be violated in such an arrangement. I am open to further instruction in the matter. I would consider it a matter of judgment, if both the congregation and the prospective elders reach a mutually satisfactory understanding in advance.

As a matter of personal judgment, I would offer this opinion: If a man is still growing spiritually and doing a good job, he should be a better elder the longer he serves. The increased experience and the added time for spiritual development should make the man a more valuable spiritual guide. Since the work of an elder is not an exercise of power, safeguards are not needed in this regard. Neither does one become too old to be an elder, provided he maintains his mental alertness. In a collective leadership, burdens can be distributed according to needs at given times. We might think of the eldership on the analogy of the Roman Senate under the Republic, or a modern judicial board, where the reservoir of wisdom and experience is one of the chief assets of a collective leadership. It is not necessary that every elder remain physically vigorous; each may bring certain special talents to the council of the whole.

Conclusion

The ancient world was familiar with at least three kinds of organizational structure and three different conceptions of the nature of office. Three kinds of constitution of which ancient theorists spoke were these: the monarchic (exemplified by the Roman empire), the democratic (represented by certain Greek city-states), and the oligarchic (rule by a few). The church in its earthly organization does not seem to fit any of these. There was another conception, known among the Jews and other peoples, which best fits the working of the early church. This sees the body made up of unequal members but with each given his place and all functioning as a unit.

The Roman pattern of office was to elect or appoint officials and then turn authority over to them. The Greeks, on the other hand, viewed authority as remaining in the will of the people, so officials were elected to carry out the decisions of the people. The Jewish conception was that officials were honored men whose wisdom was respected and with whom the people cooperated and to whom they voluntarily submitted. It seems to me that this last, as might be expected from the Jewish origins of the church, best corresponds to the New Testament injunctions to the people to follow their leaders and to the leaders not to lord it over the people. Although I have exaggerated the characteristics, I think the presentation of alternatives in this form helps to sharpen our thinking about the organizational nature of the church and particularly the authority of leaders in the church.

*Originally printed in *Restoration Quarterly* 18 (1975): 142–50.

6

Church Order in the Sub-Apostolic Period

A Survey of Interpretations

As with many other things, the second century was the time when the form of the ministry assumed the shape which was to become traditional in church history. From the end of the second century, with the acceptance of the doctrine of apostolic succession, it was believed that the apostles committed the churches to single bishops whose successors continued to the present.[1] This view finds strong expression in the *Apostolic Constitutions* (late fourth century):

> We [the apostles] distributed the functions of the high priesthood to the bishops, those of the priesthood to the presbyters, and the ministration under them both to the deacons.
>
> He that believes is not presently appointed a priest, or obtains the dignity of the high priesthood. But after His ascension we offered, according to His constitution, the pure and unbloody sacrifice, and ordained bishops, presbyters, and deacons.[2]

Even within this "dogmatic" interpretation of the rise of episcopacy a variety of explanations was possible. A novel view was that of Theodore of Mopsuestia (d. 428):

> At the first the same officials bore the name of "presbyters" as well as that of "bishop".... Those who had the power of ordination and are now called "bishops" were not appointed to a single church but to a whole province, and bore the name of "apostles." Thus St. Paul set Timothy over all Asia, and Titus over Crete.... [Later men] deeming it therefore a burden to assume the title of "apostles," they distributed the other titles [which had hitherto been synonymous], leaving that of "presbyters" to the presbyters, and assigning that of "bishops" to those who possessed the right of ordination, and who were consequently entrusted with the leadership over all the church As time went on, however, bishops were ordained not merely in towns, but also in small districts.³

Jerome gave a different view of the historical development:

> The presbyter is the same as the bishop, and before parties had been raised up in religion by the provocations of Satan, the churches were governed by the senate of the presbyters. But as each one sought to appropriate to himself those whom he had baptized, instead of leaving them to Christ, it was appointed that one of the presbyters, elected by his colleagues, should be set over all the others, and have chief supervision over the general well-being of the community.... Without doubt it is the duty of presbyters to bear in mind that by the discipline of the Church they are subordinated to him who has been given them as their head, but it is fitting that the bishops, on their side, do not forget that if they are set over the presbyters, it is the result of tradition, and not by the fact of a particular institution by the Lord.⁴

Except for occasional glances at the "historical" process, the "dogmatic" interpretation without reflection on the means of transmission prevailed through the Middle Ages. The Reformation, and in particular seventeenth-century

England, brought a clash between episcopalian, presbyterian, and congregational interpretations of church organization.[5]

Modern historico-critical study of church order arose in the nineteenth century.[6] The ancient interpretations continue to find representatives. In order to give focus to our survey we concentrate on the crucial period from AD 70 to about 150 and on the question of the origins of a singular bishop.[7] Considering the diversity of theories, which would surpass the fluidity and variety in the sources, it is well to note what to this writer are some fixed points:[8] (1) The New Testament witnesses to the establishment of a local ministry by the apostles (Acts; Pastorals; and compare the testimony of the *Didache* and *1 Clement*).[9] (2) This ministry was plural or collegial.[10] (3) There was community election or approval.[11] (4) The terminology was interchangeable. (5) The first appearance of monepiscopacy is found in the letters of Ignatius, and this form of church organization had become general by the end or probably the middle of the century.[12]

Moderate Episcopal Views

J. B. Lightfoot's "Essay on the Christian Ministry"[13] was the starting point for the modern English inquiry on strict historical principles into the origins of the church's ministry. Lightfoot shows that the terms bishops and presbyters were "synonyms" in the apostolic writings and other early Christian literature.[14] He concludes, "the episcopate was formed not out of the apostolic order by localization but out of the presbyteral by elevation" (196). Episcopacy, he surmises, arose in Asia Minor under the supervision of John in the period after 70 in order to counteract dissensions and false teachings. John gave "permanence, definiteness, and stability" to the presidency of the council or college of presbyters. The pattern was the church of Jerusalem, which presents the earliest instance of a bishop in the person of James (205–8). Although episcopacy was not to be found explicitly in scripture, Lightfoot reasoned on historical grounds it had apostolic sanction. Episcopacy rapidly consolidated itself in the early second century because of its usefulness for the needs of the churches now lacking apostolic supervision (210–34). The early development of episcopacy is connected with the names of Ignatius, who advocated the bishop as the center of unity; Irenaeus, who put forward the bishop as the depository of apostolic tradition; and Cyprian, who urged the sacerdotal view of the bishop (234–44).

All of Lightfoot's work is a model of historical scholarship, with all the evidence available judiciously argued and presented. When the *Didache* was later discovered, Lightfoot did not feel that the new evidence required any modification of his argument but only filled in information where there had been a blank. One can hardly quarrel with his arrangement of the evidence, and his conclusions are reasonable enough. But it is precisely at the crucial points where explicit evidence is lacking. James was not called a bishop until such time as episcopacy had become common in the church.[15] The rather exceptional position James occupied may easily be explained by his personal qualities and relationship to Jesus. Again, no evidence connects the beginning of monepiscopacy with John.[16] The two strong points in Lightfoot's reconstruction remain one, the fact that the threefold ministry is first attested in Asia Minor (and Antioch) at the beginning of the second century, and two, the argument that the widespread acceptance of this system would indicate that the development was not revolutionary but had some authority behind it. Nevertheless, the evidence from the West shows that the development was not so uniform and rapid. Moreover, free and independent societies which have close ties with one another often show remarkably parallel developments without any authoritative enactment.

The same line of approach is represented by W. Telfer, *The Office of a Bishop*,[17] with the exception that monarchical episcopacy is derived not from any action of the Twelve or of apostles in any wider sense, but from the office shaped by James the Lord's brother (72) transferred to Antioch.[18] Telfer states his thesis in this way:

> It will be the argument of this book that the office of bishop arose in relation to the maintenance of Christian communities in the revealed pattern of life, and that therefore bishops, so far from being direct successors of the apostles stand in antithesis to them.[19] There is no *a priori* ground for laying to the account of the Twelve the imposition of any form of ministry upon the communities of believers. Rather it would seem that while the

apostles were engaged upon their primary task, the original company of believers in Jersualem began to work out the social implications of the revealed pattern of living. (xii)

In Jewish Christian congregations, government by presbyters who came to office by seniority developed spontaneously (27–30, 39ff.), and in Gentile churches of the Pauline tradition a well-chosen board of presbyter-bishops was installed by authoritative appointment (33–40).[20] The church at Rome had its own life from the beginning of Christianity. There the presbyter-bishops had a consecrated ministerial character (55). The presbyterial board was not a group of co-regents but a collective subject (as a senate), but the growth of external relations created a principate within the "senatorial" oligarchy (61). This occurred by the time of the *Shepherd,* which was written when there was a monarchical bishop at Rome but whose author knew that at Clement's time there was not. Old customs persisted and the presbyterial oligarchy continued to be named the government of the Roman church even when everyone knew its president enjoyed a measure of sovereignty (90).

The pattern of episcopacy in the Eastern churches is represented by Ignatius, who gives no hint that it was the work of the apostles. To arrive at the uniformity implied by Ignatius suggests that an event of sufficiently cogent nature made the monarchical pattern appear simultaneously to these churches as an immediate necessity. Telfer suggests that the crisis was the fall of Jerusalem (69). Each church adopted monarchical episcopacy at that time because of its need to become autocephalous in view of the loss of the guidance and support of the mother church. Perhaps James had suggested that this step be taken if the worst befell. The principal aim was to safeguard right doctrine. Yet there was nothing transmitted to a bishop which gave him a guarantee of truth. Papias certainly did not think that because he was a bishop he had received all that was necessary for teaching the apostolic faith (85). Antioch would have tried to replace Jerusalem as the mother church, and Ignatius reproduces the figure of James (70). Although west of the Aegean there was no monepiscopacy at the beginning of the second century, before the last quarter of that century the East had imparted this organization to the West (81). The presbyterial boards had looked for authority outside themselves—in the East to the mother church of Jerusalem and in the West to leaders in the Pauline tradition. Thus the growth of monepiscopacy came easy. The *Didache* has a theory as to how collegiate episcopacy came to be replaced by monarchical: a resident prophet became "high priest" and received the first fruits (86). In the early days a church needing a new bishop had all the actual power necessary to fill the vacancy (87).[21]

Telfer offers many stimulating suggestions and brings to bear a rich amount of source material. Certainly if episcopacy were of divine origin, it would be natural that it should appear first at Jerusalem. Yet if the historical development had been otherwise, one cannot help wondering if James's position would ever have been thought of as other than exceptional. Nevertheless, my quarrel with Telfer does not emerge so much at the historical level as at the dogmatic. Is historical development the authority? If it is, one cannot, as Edwin Hatch says, make one particular historical development the standard and give it finality.[22]

The High Episcopal View

As historical study challenged the traditional "catholic" view of the ministry, two massive works sought to supply a divine authority for episcopacy on a higher ground than historical development. At the beginning of this line of development we may place Charles Gore's *The Church and the Ministry*.[23] Gore attempted to give the doctrinal basis for his view of the ministry in the opening chapters, which argue that Christ founded a visible church and that the apostolic succession is grounded in the incarnation.

Gore then invoked the witness of church history (mainly third century and later) for the following six principles of the catholic ministry: (i) Christ instituted in his church by succession from the apostles a permanent ministry as indispensable to her life. (ii) While there were three different offices in the ministry, it belonged to the bishops alone to perpetuate the ministry in its several grades by transmission of the authority received from apostles.[24] (iii) Ordination was sacramental and was conferred by the laying on of hands. (iv) The effect of ordination was indelible, maintained on the basis of the distinction between valid and canonical ordination. (v) The conception of the ministry involved a sacerdotal principle, though the use of sacerdotal terms was of gradual growth. (vi) The ministry possessed "exclusive powers."[25]

Gore next looks at the New Testament, where he claims to find the intention that the apostolate be permanent (196–209). In the New Testament there is no clear information on limitation of functions (except that only apostles could impart the Holy Spirit) and on the exact form the ministry of the future was to take (240ff.).

Only at this point in his argument is Gore ready to fill in the links which connect the apostolic ministry with the episcopate of church history (242–97). The possible hypotheses are (1) that the succession was continued by colleges of presbyter-bishops, so that monepiscopacy replaced a diffused episcopate; (2) that the bishop was included in the presbytery, which served as an inclusive name; or (3) that the gradual localization of apostolic men provided the link.[26] The last, against Lightfoot, is Gore's preference (294–302). Gore does not oppose in principle a succession through presbyter-bishops (which he calls a poly-episcopacy with the absence of the later presbytery), and this may have been the case at Alexandria and Philippi. But the evidence of James at Jerusalem, of the *Didache* (where the higher authority of the Word and sacraments remained with itinerant apostles superior to the local bishops = the later presbyters), of Ignatius, and of Clement and Hermas (where the "distinguished men," who continue the "apostolic" power of ordination, or "rulers," are distinct from the local bishops), are taken to be evidence of the last process in most places.

Gore tries to justify the approach of first explaining what he is looking for and then proceeding to look for it (55ff.). The result goes no further than an explanation of how the evidence can be explained if his theory is so, but offers no positive early evidence for the theory. The entire explanation is dependent on the theory that there was a peculiar apostolic prerogative of ordination to be transmitted through a special ministry. This is nowhere to be found in the first two centuries. The early writers appealed to for principles (i) and (ii)—Irenaeus, Tertullian, Hegesippus—support the succession idea but not the crucial claims of (ii). Indeed it seems probable that Irenaeus himself did not receive episcopal ordination.[27] The singular absence of references on (iii) is compensated by an appendix (340–49), but the second-century silence can be penetrated only by putting together things not together in the writings and assuming one concept implies all that is related to it in the theory.

The Apostolic Ministry, edited by K. E. Kirk,[28] created quite a stir, but one does not hear so much about it in these days of ecumenical realities. The editor himself laid down the theological programmatic for the work: there are an essential ministry and a dependent ministry (7–14). The essential ministry was "apostolic," and apostolic men had authority over the local elders whom they appointed. Local churches came under the supervision of resident "successors to the apostles" so that the second-century bishop succeeded to the role of the first-century apostle. The terminology was fluid, but soon the word "bishop" was reserved to the essential ministry alone. The *shaliach* (Hebrew for "apostle") duties of the Lord's plenipotentiaries were handed on. Through all changes, one function was kept by the essential ministry exclusively for itself—commissioning new members to the ministry.

Gregory Dix contributed the crucial historical essay "Ministry in the Early Church" (185–303). He is able to begin his sketch of the historic episcopate at about AD 200 because Hippolytus's *Apostolic Tradition*[29] had been identified. As he begins to work back, he states that apostolic succession was only a new emphasis on the long established custom in the church that the bishop preached on Sunday. Irenaeus added the insistence that the bishop was an ordained teacher whose sacramental charisma was a guarantee of authentic apostolic teaching.

For the period of origins (AD 30–150), the treatment of *1 Clement* is Dix's most original contribution (253–66). He states that the interpretation of *1 Clement* is not a question of whether there was a transmission of apostolic authority to the episcopate in the second century but only of the date and mode of that transmission. Although the argument does not depend on the interpretation offered of *1 Clement* 44, Dix suggests that grammatically the succession provided for is to the ministry of apostles and not of bishops. Who were these immediate successors? Timothy and Titus are typical of these men who were distinct from the local episcopate and exercised a kind of regional authority.

For his summary on the period of origins (266–74), Dix concludes that in the East on the pattern of Jerusalem *episkopē* was exercised by one man;

elsewhere *episkopē* was by the presbytery as a college. The office of *shaliach* continued as a personal commission (and this was unaffected by mon- or plural episcopacy). What we do not know is what happened to the office of *shaliach* in the second generation after the apostles, in the first third of the second century. What emerges in the *Martyrdom of Polycarp,* Hegesippus, Irenaeus, and Hippolytus is that the *shaliach* is given a relation to the elders by an identification with the monarchical bishop.

Although the methodology of working back can be useful, I fear that the obvious danger of letting the later evidence control the interpretation of the earlier has not been avoided. Later studies successfully contradict details in *The Apostolic Ministry.* It has been shown that in Judaism a *shaliach's* commission was not transferable.[30] Irenaeus' charism of truth was "truth as a gift," not a sacramental gift.[31] The interpretation of *1 Clement* 44 would occur to no one without an episcopal theory, according to Hans von Campenhausen,[32] and it has nothing to do with what Clement says and with the purpose of his letter.

It may be that the Anglicans are historically right but theologically wrong. The settling of inspired men and evangelists may have been more significant in the rise of the single bishop than has commonly been accepted by non-Episcopalians, but the other factor of a rise from the presbytery (Lightfoot ,196) was operative too. It seems that episcopacy means more to Anglo-Catholics than it does to Roman Catholics (for a good part of whose history bishops were an administrative distinction within the priesthood) and Greek Catholics (for whom a general council of the church theoretically could change the canons about episcopal organization). Thus, they set out in search for something elusive that has no name in the early sources and was not enough of a concern to be recorded by anyone; yet, it is on this that the essence of the church depends! Therefore a dogmatic explanation must be brought in to supply continuity. There may be precedent for a reality without a fixed name, but the reasoning employed would permit one to find anything he wanted hiding under the fluid terminology of the early years. The episcopal position has an apparent strength from its emergence at the same time the canon and apostolic kerygma were being given definiteness (indeed the episcopate has a priority in time).[33] But the parallel is largely superficial. In the formation of the canon and creed, the second-century church was testifying to what it had received and the testimony is even stronger when features of that testimony were against its own practice. Even when Irenaeus was testifying to apostolic succession, it was not so much to a specific form of church order, for he includes presbyters in the succession.[34]

Liberal Episcopalian Views

Edwin Hatch's Bampton Lectures of 1880 launched the sociohistorical inquiry into *The Organization of the Early Christian Churches*.[35] Hatch understood the offices of the Christian communities as comparable to the senates in municipalities and the committees in associations. They were a plural governing body known by names in current use (38ff.). The work which overshadowed all others was the administration of church funds, so that when a single head emerged, the title which clung to him was the one relative to the administration of funds—bishop (39–41). The Jewish communal council was in harmony with Gentile government by council and respect for seniority (56–64), so the presbyterate in Gentile churches had a spontaneous origin independent of Jewish churches, and this accounts for the variety of names in use for the governing body (56–66). Polycarp shows that the presbyters had supreme oversight of all matters of administration (67).

How did the single bishop come to exist? All the councils in the surrounding world had a presiding officer, and the practical considerations tending in this direction must have been at work in the churches (84–87). Moreover, there were specifically Christian factors operative: the settlement of an apostolic man or one with special powers in a community gave him a personal supremacy; and the Ignatian epistles give evidence of a theory of the church which saw each community as a reflex of the whole church and so in need of a head who represented God in it (86–90). These factors account for a permanent president. The relation of primacy changed into a relation of supremacy in the third century as a result of the Gnostic controversy.

Hatch's conclusions were that the development of the organization of the church was gradual and that the elements of which that organization was composed were already existing in human society (213). This view would diminish some of the controversies respecting ecclesiastical organization, because it calls in question the premise that all that was primitive was intended to be permanent (261ff.). The early church changed its form from a democracy to a monarchy, and the circumstances of the present suggest the question whether the constitution which was good for the past would be, without modification, good for the future (219–22).

Hatch had insisted on the necessity of observing distinctions of time and locality in the use of the evidence (9–12), but he was guilty of not observing these distinctions himself, and later studies have been concerned to speak with more precision as to circumstances at definite localities and specific times. The financial interpretation of early church officers has not been borne out by studies of word usage or by the early descriptions of their activities.

An influential statement of the liberal position comes from B. H. Streeter's *The Primitive Church*.[36] His thesis is that there was an evolution in church order in the New Testament and that at the end of the first century there existed in different provinces different systems of church government so that Episcopalians, Presbyterians, and Congregationalists can each discover the prototype of the system to which he adheres. Streeter cites *Alice in Wonderland*, "Everyone has won, and all shall have prizes" (ix).[37] Streeter argues that the uniform church organization of AD 200 displaced an earlier diversity. In the New Testament, the church at Jerusalem with James provided a primitive monepiscopal system, the church at Antioch had "prophets and teachers" as its leaders, the Pauline churches developed a plurality of elders or bishops as their shepherds, and in the letters of John we have the culmination of the evolution of church order in the New Testament with "The Elder" exercising a kind of archepiscopal responsibility (ch. 3).

Turning to a geographical analysis, Streeter begins with Asia. The Pastorals (ch. 4) are taken as evidence for no later than 110. Remembrance of the benefits of individual rule under Timothy contributed to the monarchical system prevailing in Asia. Historic fact forbade the author to describe Timothy and Titus as bishops, but they are depicted as exercising the functions which at the date of writing were those of bishops.

The *Didache* was contemporary with the Pastorals and *1 Clement*, c. 95, and comes from Antioch. It marks the stage when the system of prophets and teachers as the natural leaders of the churches was breaking down and gradually being replaced by bishops and deacons. When a prophet, who controlled the offerings and celebrated the Eucharist, settled in a local church, he became *de facto* something like a monarchical bishop (see the same suggestion in Gore, 250). Ignatius was such a prophet. The indications are that the threefold ministry championed by him was a recent development at Antioch (ch. 5).

Hebrews, James, *1 Clement,* Hermas, and Polycarp afford evidence that the church order at Rome, Corinth, and Philippi was collegiate (ch. 6). How can this be reconciled with the second-century lists of bishops for Rome? If the church at Rome was organized like a synagogue with a "ruler of the synagogue" in charge of divine worship, such an individual might emerge as a "managing director" of the board of presbyters.

Until well into the third century the bishop of Alexandria was elected and consecrated by the twelve presbyters. For a long time other churches in Egypt had no bishops, so the bishop of Alexandria was at the same time a kind of patriarch (ch. 7).

An appendix to *The Church and the Ministry* (391–409) reviews Streeter's book with the observation that he succeeds in finding only episcopacy in the canon—congregationalism is represented only by the *Didache,* and the argument for presbyterianism from the Pauline churches leaves out of view the authority of the apostle himself. There is certainly hardly anything like modern presbyterianism or congregationalism in the New Testament, but the same goes for episcopacy. Streeter hardly makes out the case for variety in the same terms in which he first framed his thesis. There was fluidity and variety, but this feature is easily exaggerated (see introductory comments on fixed points). There must have been some controlling features at the beginning for the result to be uniform. The diversity Streeter exalts is enhanced by an isolation of evidence which treats what is said by a given author in one place as the whole of what he would have to say. Although one must beware of interpreting one document by another, he must also beware of supposing that fragmentary evidence gives the whole picture. Streeter is bold and imaginative; many of his reconstructions (or better, guesses) may very well be right. But so much depends on critical assumptions about the date and authorship of the New Testament documents that he does not inspire confidence in details.

German Historico-Critical Views

Adolf von Harnack's influential views are most conveniently available to English readers in *The Constitution and Law of the Church in the First Two Centuries*.[38] This particular work was a critique of Rudolf Sohm's essay "Wesen und Ursprung des Katholizismus."[39] Sohm's theory was that the essence of Catholicism consisted in making the actual visible church, regarded as a legal entity, equivalent to the Church of Christ, and in the claim to regulate by ecclesiastical law the life with God.[40] Thus the "Spirit" is guaranteed to an individual *ecclesia* only by fixed forms; this appears for the first time in *1 Clement*. Harnack rather defines the Catholic Church as the "Church of the apostolic tradition fixed as law" (246) and sees this development as accomplished only at the end of the second century.[41]

In contrast to the depreciation of the *Didache* by our high episcopal representatives, Harnack found in it the starting point for his theory of two "hierarchies" in the primitive church: one charismatic and itinerant—the apostles, prophets, and teachers; the other institutional and local—bishops, presbyters, and deacons. Although there was freedom and a "mild and spiritualized anarchism" about the primitive church (23), there was a multiplicity of absolute authorities—Jewish ordinances, the Old Testament, sayings of Jesus, and the position of the Twelve. Jerusalem soon moved to a monarchical office (31–37), where James corresponded to the high priest.[42] The importance of blood relatives led Harnack to postulate the presence of a caliphate principle in Jewish Christianity.[43]

In the second century, the distinction between clergy and laity became established (112–17). By the end of the second century, the monarchical episcopate was everywhere in the church. The epistles of Ignatius are proof of its existence as early as 115 in Antioch and Asia Minor (83–105). The individual community is presented as a reflection of the community as a whole; therefore, the bishop is in the place of God and the presbyters of the apostles. Ignatius's church order was not on a firm canonical basis, nor does other evidence permit us to say that his firm terminological distinction extended to Asia Minor. What Ignatius found was an individual who bore the name "bishop" (but was perhaps not the only one so called) who conducted divine service. The single bishop at Antioch may have been a copy of Jerusalem or, more likely, was due to special conditions there.

Harnack's summary of the period 70–140 marks the following points as certain (87–96): (1) Until past the beginning of the second century the organization of the individual community did not possess the importance which it afterwards acquired. (2) The community as a whole was governed on strictly monarchical lines as respected the authority of Christ. (3) There was a democratic equality based on charismata, but we must accept with the greatest caution (as against Hatch) theories that trace Christian institutions to heathen religious societies. (4) From the beginning the natural division between older and younger was authoritative for the inner life of the local communities, and, out of the former, officials would be appointed who bore various names. (5) From an early period the names bishops and deacons were applied to the presbyters,[44] because of their diaconal functions. (6) In *1 Clement,* what has been essentially a spiritual community became an entity resting on the officials in charge of worship with an ecclesiastical law in the proper sense. The factors leading to the monarchical office were the following (96–99): Where the monarchy of the leading apostle, prophet, or teacher in a local community lapsed, a president of the presbytery emerged; when public worship assumed fixed forms, leadership came into the hands of an individual; communication with other bodies required a single representative; in protecting the communities from Gnostic errors, emphasis was laid on a single authoritative teacher. The putting forward of lists of bishops shows a single individual stood out in the presbyterial college from an early period, but even after the bishop became monarchical he acted in the same way as before, as a fellow-presbyter along with the college.

Harnack's germinal studies have not sustained favor for his distinctive ideas. In particular his theory of the charismatic triad seems too rigid.[45] The failure adequately to relate the two "hierarchies" gave the Episcopalians the opportunity to press their own view of how they grew together.

The concerns of German historical scholarship on the question at hand have found masterful expression in von Campenhausen's *Kirchliches Amt und Geistliche Vollmacht in den Ersten drei Jahrhunderten.*[46] His special contribution is to take the "power of the keys" as the focus for the development of ecclesiastical office.[47]

We may summarize von Campenhausen's conclusions (323–32) before looking in more detail at the treatment of the period chosen for this review. Rightly ordered office and free spiritual power were not originally identical in the church. Neither the authoritarian "catholic" nor the liberal Protestant conception of the church stands before the actuality of early Christianity. Church order did not begin with the institution of an office by Jesus; even less was the beginning a chaotic freedom of the Spirit. The strong correlation in which the Spirit stood from the beginning with the concept of word and witness makes an absolutizing of Spirit versus Tradition impossible. There is a line from *Urchristentum* to *Katholizismus*. A full concurrence of official and charismatic power appeared only once, in Jesus himself (ch. 1). The apostles were neither charismatics nor official persons in the usual sense of the words (ch. 2). The Apostle Paul developed a church concept for his communities in which there was no "office" apart from the quasi-office of his own apostolate (ch. 3). There were only functionaries whose position came from the exercise of gifts and not from office (ch. 4). There developed at the same time the Jewish Christian presbytery-led communities (ch. 5). The mixing of the Pauline and Jewish-Christian forms began early. The officeless, charismatic church order of Paul was unable to hold out after the disappearance of apostolic authority. The grounding of an "apostolic office" in Clement, Ignatius, and the Pastorals was to preserve the proclamation, but the proclamation began to lose its original sense of evangelical power (chs. 6 and 7). With Cyprian and Origen, the development of two different doctrines of office reached a certain conclusion with the former's principle of the unique authority of the bishop (ch. 11) and the latter's view of the spiritual man outside "orders" (ch. 10).

In Judaism and Christianity, presbyterate was a "worth" (83ff.). Luke knew it as normal for a Christian community. The thought of a permanent and universal office could be grounded in elders as bearers of the Christian tradition (85ff.). In *1 Clement,* the Pauline tradition was linked with the un-Pauline presbyterial constitution, as in Acts 20 and 1 Peter, and here as there the patriarchal element had precedence over the pneumatic. Clement's church concept is legal-constitutional, and the presbyterial office stands as apostolic and carries a definite authority (99ff.). In Ignatius there is a cleat gradation within the clergy into three ranks. His church concept is "cosmic-mystical," "a living mystery"

(105ff.). There is a cultic-pneumatic concept of the bishop, who as the head embodies the spiritual ideal of the church (113ff.). The Pastorals are placed by von Campenhausen in the first half of the second century and are seen as representing another way in which the Pauline-episcopal tradition was fused with the presbyterial constitution (116ff.). Timothy and Titus are the pattern of true church officers, and the genuine substance of office is sound doctrine (118ff.). The grace of office is not charismatic, nor magical, but related to an ordination on which one can look back and by which one was consecrated to the task of teaching (125–28). In Clement, Ignatius, and the Pastorals one may almost see, von Campenhausen suggests, the pre-forms of Roman Catholic, Greek Orthodox, and Lutheran elements of office: the bishop as the privileged cult officer of the community, as the spiritual pattern and sacral middle point, or as the ordained preacher of apostolic doctrine (130ff.). In all three cases the patriarchal constitution of elders was the starting point with the Pauline tradition continuing to work as a spiritual corrective.

Von Campenhausen does not suffer "from the German view that the only competence for ministry recognized in the primitive church was the competence of the inspired,"[48] but his treatment is still ruled by the preoccupation with spiritual versus institutional which has dominated German studies on church order. Typically "German" is the narrow view of Paul, and one can easily fault von Campenhausen for his late date on the Pastorals; yet one notes that it is the pre-form of the Lutheran conception which he finds in the canon. No adequate presentation of the fusion of the three sub-apostolic traditions is offered.

A Roman Catholic View

Roman Catholics have not been prominent in historical studies on the origin of episcopacy, perhaps because the means of apostolic succession has been of less concern to Catholic dogmatics. The French scholar Jean Colson has entered fully into modern studies, and some of his points are similar to those urged by Episcopalian scholars, but his "Pauline" tradition differs appreciably from von Campenhausen's.

Colson in *L'Évêque dans les communautés primitives*[49] states that the history of the origins of the episcopate cannot be founded solely on vocabulary: the church possessed hierarchic functions before reserving precise names for each (13). There were in the origins of the episcopate two hierarchic conceptions of the church—one Pauline and Western and the other Eastern, inaugurated by James and propagated by John (14).

In the Pauline conception every function is an operation of the Spirit. In his churches, presbyter and bishop were synonymous; the colleges were acephalous, because the apostle himself was the bond of the community's life (39, 47ff.). Paul used "apostle" for collaborators who partook of apostolic powers (55). Thus in the Pastorals Timothy possessed a power of order equal to that of Paul himself and which carried the transmission of apostolic charisma (60). The presbyterial or episcopal colleges were incomplete without itinerant delegates of apostles.

First Clement shows the same kind of Pauline *ecclesia* as a hierarchic body. The episcopate is no other than the college of presbyters (69). The "other eminent persons" who performed ordinations were successors of those whom Paul called "apostles," e.g., Timothy and Titus (70).

In the book of Revelation appears the Johannine notion of episcopacy which recalls the role of James as center of the college of presbyters and incarnation of the community. The "angel" of a church is the celestial image for a terrestrial reality. The angel was the chief responsible for the church, a residential bishop (81ff.). Whereas Paul, Clement, and Hermas accent the community of which offices are the organs, for John the unity of the church is incarnate in its "angel." Missionary apostolate has become local episcopate in Asia. It is difficult to determine when this occurred, but likely John, after the fall of Jerusalem, came to Asia and organized the monarchical episcopate (89). In Ignatius, the bishop represents Christ and is the image of the Father; he is the organ of tradition, center of unity, and the incarnation of the community (93ff.).

There was a period of transition where coexisted two systems of organization—a resident "bishop" (Ignatius) and a presbyterial college dependent on an "eminent man" who itinerated or resided temporarily (as Clement himself—71). In the second century there was a confusion and fusion of the Pauline and Johannine traditions (Polycarp—111ff.). In Irenaeus, the two vocabularies and two traditions were united (115ff.). He was the first writer in the West to use bishop in its monarchical sense, but the bishop was also a "presbyter" by his function of guarding apostolic tradition. Thus the two conceptions of the church are seen as complementary.

In an appendix, Colson suggests a late second-century date for the *Didache* as aiming at a Catholic-Montanist compromise (125ff.).

A more recent work by Colson, *L'Episcopat Catholique: Collégialité et Primauté dans les trois premiers siecles de l'église*,[50] applies his studies to the concerns of Vatican II and emphasizes the collegiality of the episcopate within the hierarchic structure. For much of Roman Catholic history the papacy has tended to absorb the whole episcopate of the church into itself, but with Vatican II the Roman church has become a more "episcopal" body. The apostolic charge was transmissible (26–29). The second generation "successors" of the apostles were essentially itinerant but continued to exercise the charge in collegiality. Among the third generation successors, Eusebius[51] names only Ignatius and Clement. They were fixed in a church, but their mission extended beyond that church (31ff.). In the second century, the episcopal function of presidents of presbyteries comported to that of successors of apostles. The *potentior principalitas* of the first church at Jerusalem was transplanted by Peter and Paul to Rome (61ff.). The apostolic tradition was guaranteed by the succession of all bishops.

Colson writes with clarity. He incorporates both lines of succession suggested by Episcopalian authors. Nevertheless, finding canonical and apostolic (Johannine) support for episcopacy in the "angel" of Revelation 2–3 remains highly questionable. That the "apostolic delegates" succeeded personally to apostolic functions is not demonstrated, and the argument for their sharing the name "apostle" in the desired sense is tenuous. Colson slips into certain Catholic habits of thought at points: Clement's effacement in the community so that he writes in the name of the church and not of himself is explained as fitting Paul's theology of a united body (*L'Évêque*, 73); Ignatius's address to the Roman church is applied to the bishop of Rome (*L'Episcopat*, 43, 47); the "church at the center of the world" in Irenaeus is interpreted as Rome, rather than as seems more likely Jerusalem (61).

Conclusion

The patterns of interpretation (e.g., the tendency to see Clement and Ignatius as typifying West and East) and the options in accounting for episcopacy (e.g., from James, through apostolic delegates, etc.) show clearly in the books surveyed. Full details of the historical development cannot be known in the present condition of our sources, but actually we are far better informed than some writers would seem to admit. There is remarkable agreement on the facts, and the differences largely arise in the interpretation of their meaning. It still seems possible to make a consistent story and give full weight to the available evidence by following the line sketched by this writer in the first issue of this journal.[52]

*Originally printed in *Restoration Quarterly* 11 (1968): 225–48.

Chapter 6 Endnotes

1. Irenaeus, *Adv. Haer.* III.iii.1-3; Tertullian, *Praesc.* 32. Eusebius constructed his *Ecclesiastical History* in part around such succession lists. See C. H. Turner, "Apostolic Succession," in *Essays on the Early History of the Church and the Ministry*, ed. H.B. Swete (London: Macmillan, 1918), 93ff. Arnold Ehrhardt, *The Apostolic Succession* (London: Lutterworth Press, 1953), saw the pattern for episcopal lists in lists of Jewish high priests and their origin in Jewish concern for successors of James, the Christian counterpart of the high priest. The succession, however, in Christianity was of authoritative teaching.

2. VIII.xlvi. Cf. VII.xlvi.

3. *Comm. on 1 Tim.* 3:8. Theodore was followed by Theodoret, *Comm. on 1 Tim.* 3, and his view has been substantially revived by Anglican writers, as in the work of K. E. Kirk, cited in footnote 26. Theodore's whole passage is cited by Harnack, *The Expansion of Christianity in the First Three Centuries* (London: Williams & Norgate, 1904), 64ff. along with a thorough refutation of its dogmatic points.

4. *Comm. on Tit.* 1:7; cf. *Ep.* 146. A similar view is in "Ambrosiaster," *In Eph.* 4:11; *In 1 Tim.* 3:10. See the references assembled by Gore (n. 24), 335ff.

5. John J. McElhinney, *The Doctrine of the Church: A Historical Monograph with a Full Bibliography of the Subject* (Claxton, Remsen & Haffelfinger, 1871).

6. A full survey is in Olof Linton, *Das Problem der Urkirche in der neueren Forschung* (Uppsala, 1932).

7. Because they deal mainly with the theology of the ministry and are primarily on the New Testament, I omit Eduard Schweizer, *Church Order in the New Testament* (London: SCM, 1961) and A. T. Hanson, *The Pioneer Ministry* (London: SCM, 1961). Because their communion has a special interest in our topic, a disproportionate number of the books selected come from Episcopalians.

8. The evidence is given in the author's paper "Il Ministero nei Padri Apostolici," *Richerche Bibliche e Religiose* 4 (1969): 79–94; English translation the next item in this collection. See also his article in *Restoration Quarterly*, Vol. 1:1, 21–31.

9. When the form of the ministry changed to monarchy, the apostolic claim was transferred to this changed form, but it was already traditional to view ministry as an apostolic appointment. See A. F. Walls, "A Note on the Apostolic Claim in the Church Order Literature," *Studia Patristica* II (*Texte und Untersuchungen,* 64 [1957]): 83–92.

10. A popular presentation of the evidence in the writer's "The Plurality of Elders in the Early Church," *Firm Foundation,* Sept. 11, 1962, 579.

11. See the writer's "Ordination in the Ancient Church," *Restoration Quarterly*, Vol. 5, Nos. 1, 2, and 3.

12. It has been well argued that Justin's "president" in *1 Apol.* 67 was a monarchial bishop—T. G. Jalland, "Justin Martyr and the President of the Eucharist," *Studia Patristica* V *(Texte und Untersuchungen* 80 [1962]): 83–85.

13. *Saint Paul's Epistle to the Philippians* (London: Macmillan, 1878). Page numbers to the works under review will be cited in the text.

14. Ibid., 95–99, gives the evidence in a separate note.

15. Apparently first by Clement of Alexandria, as recorded by Eusebius, *H. E.* I.i.3; cf. the Pseudo-Clementine *Ep. Pet. ad Jas.* and *Ep. Clem. ad Jas.*

16. The oft cited testimony of Clement of Alexandria, *Quis div.* 42, that John appointed bishops in Asia Minor, occurs in a passage where bishop and presbyter are used interchangeably (cf. the usage of *Strom.* viii.1, but contrast the distinction made in vi.13 and *Paed.* iii.12) and where bishops are in the plural. Tertullian, *Adv. Marc.* IV.5 about the Asian succession going back to John is of a piece tracing Rome's bishops to Peter (n. 1).

17. London: Darton, Longman & Todd, 1962.

18. Telfer notes that in the Eastern church James of Jerusalem was commonly regarded as first holding the office of a bishop. Since in the Western church every line of consecration was traced to an apostle, the discrepancy between James as the first bishop and the doctrine of apostolic succession was reconciled by identifying the Lord's brother with the apostle James of Alphaeus. Telfer prefers the idea that the church at Jerusalem made James its leader as it sought the best fulfillment of its corporate life (xvi).

19. In contrast to Harnack (see below), Telfer stated that "the main dividing line is therefore to be drawn not between the itinerant and the settled, but between the bearers of the apostolic message and the edifiers of the congregations" (xi).

20. See the summary of New Testament evidence, 40–42, for the presence of a board of presbyter-bishops as the local governing authority elsewhere than at Jerusalem.

21. W. Telfer has given an impressive argument for the case that Alexandria's presbyters elected and consecrated their own bishop in "Episcopal Succession in Egypt," *Journal of Ecclesiastical History,* Vol. III (1952), 1–13.

22. Of course one may do so by invoking the Holy Spirit, as does A. C. Headlam ("The form and order of the ministry of the Christian Church inspired, as we believe, by the Holy Spirit") in *The Ministry and the Sacraments* (London: SCM, 1937), 342. Even so, those who seek a change in the form of the ministry, whether to or from episcopacy, invoke the guidance of the Holy Spirit for their proposals.

23. Successively enlarged up to the final edition revised by C. H. Turner (London: SPCK., 1936)

24. Gore offers the evidence in detail for episcopal ordination in all geographical areas (109ff.). He finds the evidence unfavorable to the report of Jerome and others that originally the presbyters at Alexandria appointed their bishop; but he reasons that this report is not inconsistent with the principle of succession, for one ordination could have made a man a presbyter and a potential bishop, pending selection by his fellow potential bishops (115–30).

25. Tertullian's view to the contrary (*Exh. cast.* 7) is attributed to his Montanism and refuted by his earlier catholic declarations (196ff.).

26. Another possibility has been put forward by W. Lockton, *Divers Orders of Ministers* (London: Longmans, Green & Co., 1930), and accepted with modifications by E. J. Palmer in *The Ministry and the Sacraments* (n. 22), 368ff. In Judaism there were two kinds of elders, of the Great Sanhedrin at Jerusalem and of the local Sanhedrin. So in the church there were two ranks of elders, the elders of the great church who alone could ordain and the local elders who were supervised by them. The theory flounders on the claim that the Great Sanhedrin alone ordained members of the local councils. Not even Palmer accepts the curious identification of prophets = elders. The differences between the church's apostolate and the Great Sanhedrin are not favorable to this effort to establish two separate orders of continuing ministry from the first.

27. So concludes Einar Molland, "Irenaeus of Lugdunum and the Apostolic Succession," *Journal of Ecclesiastical History* I (1950): 12–28, and accepted by Telfer, *Office of a Bishop,* 87, 94ff., 119.

28. London: Hodder & Stoughton, 1946.

29. Dix's own important edition of this work has been issued in a revised edition by Henry Chadwick (London: SPCK., 1968).

30. T. W. Manson, *The Church's Ministry* (Philadelphia: Westminster Press, 1948), 35ff., especially 43 for the summary of the Jewish evidence. Manson argues against the view that the church is an extension of the incarnation, suggesting rather that it continues the ministry of Christ.

31. Molland, *loc. cit.*

32. Page 97 of the work cited, note 46.

33. Kirk, *op. cit.,* 12–14; Gore, *op. cit.,* 391ff.

34. See my contribution on "The Conception of Apostolic Succession" in *Great Events from History,* Ancient and Medieval Series, ed. E. G. Weltin (Englewood Cliffs, NJ: Salem Press, 1972), Vol. 2, 742–44.

35. London: Rivingtons, 3rd edition, 1888.

36. London: Macmillan, 1929.

37. From a more conservative standpoint, Bo Reike has claimed a combination of the three classical forms of polity for the early church and a counterpart for this in the organization of the Qumran community—see his article in Krister Stendahl, *The Scrolls and the New Testament* (New York: Harper and Brothers, 1957), 143–56.

38. London: Williams and Norgate, 1910. Cf. also *The Expansion of Christianity in the First Three Centuries* (London: Williams and Norgate, 1904), Vol. I, 398–461, and Vol. II, 46–114. His basic work was *Die Lehre der zwölf Apostel* in *Texte und Untersuchungen* 2 (1884), 93–158.

39. In *Abhandlungen der Philo.-Histor. Klasse d. K. Sächs. Gesellsch. d. Wiss.*, Vol. XXVII, part iii (1909), a fresh presentation of his *Kirchenrecht* (1892).

40. Pages 175–258 of Harnack's work are a statement and refutation of Sohm's thesis.

41. He adds that the religious conception of the church still prevailed in spite of the legal forms, and indeed all the main features of third-century Catholicism resulted from lifting the Christian preaching out of its original environment and plunging it into Hellenistic modes of thought (254).

42. That James bore the title "bishop" is open to doubt, but he possessed the powers which afterward belonged to the Gentile monarchical bishop. His exalted position may have led to the conception of some sort of universal episcopate, but whether it aided the formation of the monarchical episcopate is questionable.

43. This suggestion is refuted by Hans von Campenhausen. See footnote 46 below.

44. This has been a widely adopted view. It was developed in his interpretation of *1 Clement* by Friedrich Gerke, *Die Stellung des Ersten Clemensbriefes innerhalb der Entwicklung der altchristlichen Gemeindeverfassung und des Kirchenrechts,* in *Texte und Untersuchungen* 47 (1931), especially 34ff. His views are available in English in a packed article "The Origin of the Christian Ministry" in *The Ministry and the Sacraments*, 343–67. On the other hand, the official use of "presbyter" seems too firmly established, and there is no unambiguous instance of deacons included in the term presbyter.

45. As an example of tension between the universal and local forms of organization Harnack takes 3 John; this is unfortunate, for the representative of the missionary organization is "the Elder"! *The Expansion of Christianity,* 94ff.

46. *Beitrage zur Historischen Theologie* 14 (Tübingen: J. C. B. Mohr, 1953). English translation *Ecclesiastical Authority and Spiritual Power in the Church of the First Three Centuries* (London: Adam & Charles Black, 1969).

47. Chapters 6 and 9.

48. Telfer, *The Office of a Bishop,* viii, in reference to Schweizer, op. cit.

49. *Unam Sanctum* 21 (Paris, 1951).

50. *Unam Sanctum* 43 (Paris: Du Cerf, 1963).

51. *H. E.* III.xxxvii. Eusebius does not indicate in what way these evangelists and shepherds succeeded the apostles other than temporally.

52. "The Ministry of the Word in the First Two Centuries," *Restoration Quarterly* 1.1 (1957): 21–31; reprinted in this collection.

Selected Bibliography

Burtchaell, J. T. *From Synagogue to Church: Public Services and Offices in the Earliest Christian Communities*. Cambridge: Cambridge University Press, 1992.

Dassmann, E. "Zur Entstehung des Monepiskopats." *Jahrbuch fuer Antike und Christentum* 17 (1974): 74–90.

Jay, E. G. "From Presbyter-Bishops to Bishops and Presbyters." *Second Century* 1 (1981): 125–62.

Maier, H. O. *The Social Setting of the Ministry as Reflected in the Writings of Hermas, Clement, and Ignatius*. Waterloo: Wilfrid Laurier University Press, 1991.

Sullivan, F. A. *From Apostles to Bishops*. Mahwah, NJ: Newman, 2001.

Ysebaert, Y. *Amtsterminologie im Neuen Testament und in der Alten Kirche: Eine lexikographische Untersuchung*. Breda: Eureia, 1994.

7

The Ministry in the Apostolic Fathers

I asked which of several approaches to take in this paper: (1) a general historical survey of the development of the ministry in the apostolic fathers, which might be useful for our participants who do not have a detailed knowledge of the documents arbitrarily grouped as "apostolic fathers"; (2) a study of the doctrine of the ministry reflected in the apostolic fathers, which might bypass the historic divisions of Christendom over institutional questions and get at the theology of ministry; (3) a practical look at the activities of an early second-century bishop, which might be the most ecumenically satisfying, for on the practical level of church life the differences between priest, pastor, and minister are less obvious; or (4) a polemical presentation of the ancient church as viewed by a member of the Church of Christ, which might be the most revealing about the author and quickly get to the issues confronting us in the seminar. The result is somewhat of a composite of the four approaches. There should be less difficulty on your part than on mine in identifying when I am doing what.

Perhaps it is due to the historians' glasses, but I see things in terms of continuity, not discontinuity. There is change, as I hope to show, but the account some people have given of the first century makes it difficult, if not impossible, for me to read the second century. Theologically, institutionally, literarily, but not inspirationally, the apostolic fathers belong to the New Testament era. The church acted wisely in recognizing the limits of the canon, but for historical investigation there is a continuum of church life from the New Testament to the apostolic fathers. If one does not have myopia, derived from the old liberal distrust (not without cause) of institutions, the documents of early church history show considerable concern for the organizational or institutional (for lack of a better word) aspects of Christianity. The ministry bulks large in our sources, and this paper cannot do justice to all aspects.

The later documents of the New Testament and the earlier extra-canonical writings present a fairly uniform picture of church organization. The leadership of the local churches over a wide geographical area was in the hands of a plurality of presbyter-bishops, assisted by (less frequently mentioned) deacons:

> Jerusalem-Judea—Acts 11:30, 15:2–6; James 5:14
> Syria—*Didache* 15
> Galatia—Acts 14:23
> Asia Minor—1 Peter 5:1ff.; (perhaps Revelation 4:4 and passim)
> Ephesus—Acts 20:17, 28; 1 Timothy 3:1ff.; 5:17, 19
> Philippi—Philippians 1:1; Polycarp, *Epistle to Philippians* 6
> Corinth—*1 Clement* 44; 47.6; 54; 57
> Crete—Titus 1:5–7
> Rome—*1 Clement* 42–44; *Shepherd of Hermas, Visions* II.iv.2f.; III.v.1; *Similitudes* IX. xxvii.1f
> Alexandria—Jerome, *Epistle* 146; Severus of Antioch (Brooks II, 213); Eutychius of Alexandria (PG CXI, 982).

In several of the above sources, both terms "presbyters" and "bishops" are used, and in such a way as to suggest that the same persons were being talked about. Indeed the terms had a certain interchangeability through the second century—Hadrian to Servianus in Vopiscus, *Vit. Saturn*. 8; Irenaeus in

Eusebius, *Eccl. Hist.* V.xx.7; xxiv.14; *Against Heresies* IV.xxvi.2–4; Clement of Alexandria, *Miscellanies* VI.xiii.106f; III.xii.90; VII.i. Even after the distinction between bishop and presbyter had been firmly established, it was possible to call a bishop "presbyter," although not vice versa.[1]

It has become common to suggest that even from early times "presbyter" was a general term, including bishops and deacons,[2] or that even as late as *1 Clement* it was a nontechnical term for the older spiritual leaders.[3] I find these explanations unsatisfactory. "Presbyter" or "elder" was a term in use in Judaism for an office, and the distributions in the sources whereby "elders" more commonly occur in Jewish contexts and "bishops" in Gentile contexts are too suggestive. Certainly, there was a broader, "nonofficial" use of the term "elder" (Papias in Eusebius, *Eccl. Hist.* III.39; Irenaeus, *Against Heresies* II.xxii.5; V.v.l). The Jewish synagogue, especially in the Dispersion, may have had an "executive committee," and a single "ruler of the synagogue" presided at services.[4] The word "bishop" was singular in its connotations, and this may account for the usage of the Pastoral Epistles (1 Tim. 3:2; Titus 1:7). The ancient church's view of Timothy and Titus as themselves "bishops," continued in some modern interpretations,[5] ignores the distinction preserved in the letters between the addressees—called "evangelist," "minister," "man of God" (2 Tim. 4:5; 1 Tim. 4:6; 6:11)—and the bishops (elders) about whom instructions are given (1 Tim. 3:1ff.; 5:ff.; Titus ff.).

Since "bishop" was the natural term for a singular capacity, when a single executive or president of the presbytery emerged, this was the term adopted—or was it the other way around (use of the word singled out and in time elevated one man previously distinguished from his fellows by a separate function, e.g., presiding at worship, administering benevolent funds, representing the church to others)? Monepiscopacy is first attested in the first or second decade of the second century for Antioch and the churches of Asia Minor by the letters of Ignatius of Antioch. A single bishop at the head of each local church was a general feature of the church by the mid-second century, as evidenced by Justin Martyr's "president" (*1 Apol.* 67), Hegesippus and Irenaeus's episcopal lists (Eusebius, *Eccl. Hist.* IV.xxii; Irenaeus, *Against Heresies* III.iii), and the correspondence of Dionysius of Corinth (Eusebius, *Eccl. Hist.* IV.xxiii).

Three documents among the apostolic fathers offer considerable information on the ministry: the *Didache, 1 Clement,* and the Ignatian correspondence. These three sources reflect three stages in the development of the ministry.

The *Didache,* or "The Teaching of the Lord through the Twelve Apostles to the Nations," is a manual of church order of uncertain date, perhaps late first or early second century. It most likely emanates from rural Syria and reflects a strong Jewish background.

The *Didache* shows a transition stage from an itinerant prophetic ministry to a local episcopal ministry.

> But every true prophet who wishes to settle among you is "worthy of his food." Likewise a true teacher is himself worthy, like the workman, of his food. Therefore thou shalt take the firstfruit of the produce of the winepress and of the threshingfloor and of oxen and sheep, and shalt give them as the firstfruits to the prophets, for they are your high priests. (13)

> Appoint therefore for yourselves bishops and deacons worthy of the Lord, meek men, and not lovers of money, and truthful and approved, for they also minister to you the ministry of the prophets and teachers. Therefore do not despise them, for they are your honorable men together with the prophets and teachers. (15)

The firstfruits that, as Jews, the people had been accustomed to reserve for the priesthood are to go for the support of the Christian prophets. The implication is that the same practice is to pass over to the bishops and deacons of the community. The bishops and deacons are to perform the ministry of prophets and teachers. The emphasis is on "speaking the word of the Lord" (4.1; 11.1). But in addition to teaching, the prophets and then the bishops are expected to lead in worship (10.7; cf. 14–15). Here we see a prophetic and priestly imagery of the ministry merging.

The *Didache* reminds one somewhat of the New Testament teaching that those possessing gifts of grace are to use these in service and in so doing assume leadership (cf. 1 Cor. 12; Rom. 12:1ff.; Eph. 4:7ff.). But the *Didache* originates in an area plagued with false prophets; hence, there is more emphasis on testing the prophets and the community's acknowledgement of its teachers (11–13). Also prophets are rarer, so they are set apart into a separate class not so much for their practical benefit to the community as for who they are as spiritually gifted individuals.

There is a turn to the local, noncharismatic ministry as reliable and free from risk. Mutual reproof and edification are possible to and incumbent on the whole church (4.2; 15.3). Still there is a need for a special ministry. In summary, we note that there is to be a plurality of bishops, they are to be chosen by the community, and they are to possess certain spiritual qualifications that are in harmony with the requirements of the Pastoral Epistles.

Speaking the word is the predominant concept of the ministry also in *Barnabas* and *2 Clement*. The author of *Barnabas* is an early second-century teacher (perhaps at Alexandria) who disclaims his position (1.8; 4.9; 6.5) but stresses the importance of correct teaching (9.9; 19.10; 21.4, 6). *Second Clement* is a mid-second-century sermon from someone who may not be in the circle of presbyters (who also have the duty of teaching—17.2–5). The ministry of the word is not in these writings exercised by the one with the gift of prophecy but with the gift of knowledge (*Barnabas* 1.4f.; 18.1; 9.9) or of exhortation (*2 Clem.* 19.1).

The document known as *1 Clement* is a letter from the church at Rome to the church at Corinth, dated AD 96. The attribution in the manuscripts to Clement (who varies in the early lists of Roman bishops from first to third) as the actual author receives second-century confirmation from Dionysius of Corinth (Eusebius, *Hist. eccl.* IV.xxiii) and Irenaeus (*Against Heresies* III.3). The letter is prompted by the Corinthians being "up to their old tricks again." The disorder this time was the removal of certain worthy (in the view of the Romans) presbyters from office.

Boards of presbyter-bishops are in control of the local churches, but apparently not so firmly in democratically minded Corinth. We hear nothing in the letter of a prophetic or charismatic ministry, even in decline. Clement gives no indication of motives other than jealousy and pride at work in the deposition of certain Corinthian presbyters. Clement can use the word "presbyters" in a nonofficial sense of the older men (1.3; 21.6), but the word may be deliberately chosen with a view to the official meaning to be given later (47.6). There does not seem to be any difference between this official usage and the term "bishops."

First Clement strengthens the New Testament statements of apostolic appointment of presbyter-bishops in the churches (Acts 14:23; 1 Tim. 3; Titus 1:5ff.; cf. the instructions of *Didache* 15 in a document purporting to give the teaching of the apostles):

> The Apostles received the Gospel for us from the Lord Jesus Christ, Jesus the Christ was sent from God. The Christ therefore is from God and the Apostles from the Christ.... Having therefore received their commands, and being fully assured by the resurrection of our Lord Jesus Christ, and with faith confirmed by the word of God, they went forth in the assurance of the Holy Spirit preaching the good news that the Kingdom of God is coming. They preached from district to district, and from city to city, and they appointed their first converts, testing them by the Spirit, to be bishops and deacons of the future believers.... (42)

He further claims an apostolic enactment that such a ministry be permanent in the church (the continuation of the offices of bishops and deacons may fairly be considered the intent of the Pastoral Epistles and *Didache* 15):

> Our Apostles also knew through our Lord Jesus Christ that there would be strife for the title of bishop. For this cause, therefore, since they had received perfect foreknowledge, they appointed those who have been mentioned, and afterwards added the codicil that if they should fall asleep, other approved men should succeed to their ministry. (44)

The succession in the ministry is not sacramental, but a matter of good order. Deacons are in Clement's "succession," as well as bishops. Although the offices of bishop and deacon are grounded in apostolic appointment, their existence is given a Scriptural sanction by a citation of Isaiah 60:17, according to a text otherwise unknown (42.5). The actual selection was made with the approval of the whole church (44.3). Gregory Dix has argued that the "approved men" succeed to the apostles' function of appointing to office and not to the function of bishop.[6] Although this interpretation is grammatically possible, it does not seem to fit what Clement is talking about and has not gained much favor.

Clement's ruling concern is good order through obedience to duly appointed leaders. Natural law, the Roman army, and the Old Testament priesthood serve as illustrations enforcing the need for submission.

The use of the Old Testament pattern of priesthood and sacrifice (40–41) as analogies for the Christian ministry is indicative of the way liturgical leadership was viewed as the chief function of the episcopate (44.4). The presbyters' "liturgy" was especially the "service" or "ministry" of public worship (44.6). Christ is the high priest (36; 61; 64), bishops are the priests offering gifts (44.4), and presumably the deacons are the Levites. In the Old Testament all was to be done at the proper time and place by the proper individuals; even so, God has a law of worship for his new chosen people, and their bishops and deacons have a sacred character. The invoking of the Old Testament pattern was to be pregnant for the future development of the ministry, when the priestly and apostolic terminology would be combined into something more than imagery.

First Clement is important for its testimony to the following points: the offices of bishop and deacon and their first occupants were of apostolic appointments; the apostles intended these positions to be permanent in the churches; bishops and presbyters are interchangeable terms for the same men; there was a plurality in each church; appointments were made with the approval of the whole assembly.

The Shepherd of Hermas, compiled at Rome during the first half of the second century, shows ambition for the chief seats in that church too (*Visions* III.ix.7–10; *Similitudes* VIII.vii.4). Hermas indicates some other things about Rome to which Clement gives no hint. Prophets and teachers still spoke at this time in the church at Rome (*Mandates* XI). Episcopal duties included the extending of hospitality and benevolence (*Similitudes* IX.xxvii.1f., but cf. the stress on hospitality in the early chapters of *1 Clement*).

The seven genuine Ignatian letters were written within a few weeks of one another (c. 115) while the bishop of Antioch in Syria was on his way through

Asia Minor to martyrdom in Rome. The threefold ministry of bishop, presbyters, and deacons is taken for granted and obedience to these officers is strongly insisted on as a means to unity in the face of false teachers.

> Be zealous to do all things in harmony with God, with the bishop presiding in the place of God and the presbyters in the place of the council of the Apostles, and the deacons, who are most dear to me, entrusted with the service of Jesus Christ.... Let there be nothing in you which can divide you, but be united with the bishop and with those who preside over you. (*Magnesians* 6; cf. *Ephesians* 4; *Trallians* 3; *Philadelphians* 7; *Smyrnaeans* 8; but his letter to the church at Rome is silent about that church's organization.)

Ignatius's bishop was still congregational and functioned in close unity with his presbyters, yet (unlike *1 Clement*) he is clearly differentiated from the presbytery. There is no overtly priestly language, no claim for apostolic appointment of the ministry, and no "apostolic succession" of the bishop. The presbyters are the type of the apostles in the church (*Philadelphians* 5). Ignatius claims to speak by the Spirit in urging submission to the threefold ministry (*Philadelphians* 7), so that he unites in himself the charismatic and official ministries. The prophet's role is played by the bishop.

Episcopacy for Ignatius is grounded in the nature of things. An official view of the ministry is based on the order of salvation, related to God, Christ, and the apostles. The bishop is the representative of God (*Ephesians* 5.3; *Trallians* 3) and the image of Christ (*Trallians* 2). The Ignatian bishop holds the place of God not by virtue of preaching the word of the Lord (cf. the *Didache*) but in his own right as an official person. The silent bishop (*Ephesians* 6.1) is especially to be revered, so it is not by virtue of his activities that he claims his position. Nevertheless, Ignatius's bishop, as the father of his people, exercises all the functions and authority in the church that a *pater familias* did in Greco-Roman society. He is the sacred center of the community, and all activities in the church revolve around him (*Smyrnaeans* 8).

The activities of the Ignatian bishop may be illustrated from what is known of the pastoral work of Polycarp, bishop of Smyrna in the first half of the second century (although this is not to say that Polycarp had the same self-estimate of his position as Ignatius enunciates). Leaving aside von Campenhausen's view that Polycarp was responsible for the Pastoral Epistles,[7] a hypothesis which I can only regard as fanciful, we still are well informed about Polycarp's activities from Ignatius's letter to him, his letter(s) to the Philippians (the instructions to the elders in chapter six may be a self-portrait), and later remembrances (especially in his church's early contemporary account of the *Martyrdom of Polycarp* and Irenaeus; and with much reservation, the fourth-century *Life of Polycarp*).

Polycarp was accustomed to preside at public worship. Ignatius exhorts him to have more numerous meetings of the congregation and to seek out the members by name (*Polycarp* 4.2). These congregational assemblies might be for business as well as worship. Thus Ignatius asks Polycarp to "gather a council" and elect a representative to visit the church at Antioch (7.2). Polycarp would preside (cf. *Smyrnaeans* 8.2 and *Magnesians* 6). The appointment would be made by the congregation (*Smyrnaeans* 10), but in a related situation Polycarp could say, "I send" (*Philippians* 13). Ignatius instructs that nothing is to be done without Polycarp's approval (*Polycarp* 4.1). The similar instructions about a bishop in other letters (*Magnesians* 7; *Trallians* 2; *Philadelphians* 7; and especially *Smyrnaeans* 8) indicate that liturgical leadership included the Lord's Supper and Agape, public prayer (cf. *Ephesians* 5.2), and baptism. These activities are confirmed by later evidence about Polycarp as a leader in worship. He was invited to celebrate the Eucharist on a visit to Rome (Irenaeus in Eusebius, *Eccl. Hist.* V.xxiv.16). The prayer placed on the lips of Polycarp in his *Martyrdom* 14 reflects the common form of public prayers in the church; this was the type of prayer (in mode of address and structure) which the church at Smyrna remembered Polycarp praying (cf. *Philippians* 12; *Life of Polycarp* 5; 23; 32). Perhaps the designation of Polycarp as "father" in *Martyrdom* 12.2 refers to his part in Christian initiation, as understood by pagans. Polycarp was also to give his approval to marriages and resolves of continence (*Polycarp* 5.2).[8]

Related to presiding at worship but broader in scope and important enough to deserve special attention is preaching and teaching. Ignatius exhorts Polycarp to "make a discourse" against false teachings (*Polycarp* 5.1). It was as a teacher that Polycarp was invited to write to the Philippians (ch. 3–4). Perhaps it was Ignatius's own preoccupations with division that caused him to give more attention to public worship, for it was primarily as a teacher that Polycarp was remembered in his own church ("teacher of Asia," "apostolic and prophetic teacher," "famous teacher"—*Martyrdom* 12.2; 16.2; 19.1; cf. *Life* 22f.; 28). Such also was Irenaeus's reminiscence (Eusebius, *Eccl. Hist.* V.xx.5–7).

Polycarp was, furthermore, responsible for the administration of benevolent funds. Ignatius refers to him as the protector (or guardian, trustee) of widows (*Polycarp* 4.1). There seems to have been a separate order of widows at Smyrna (*Smyrnaeans* 13; cf. *Philippians* 4; for Polycarp's care of widows, see *Life* 4; 8). Slaves also come in for special mention by Ignatius, as "not to seek to be set free from the common fund" (*Polycarp* 4.3). Polycarp's administration of church finances would also have included hospitality to travelers (*Smyrnaeans* 10; cf. *Magnesians* 15). Polycarp, *Philippians* 11, refers to an unworthy presbyter, removed from office for misuse of funds.

Polycarp represented his church in correspondence and in the sending and receiving of messengers (*Polycarp* 8). The church at Smyrna had the facilities for extensive correspondence and supplied Ignatius's needs in this regard (*Smyrnaeans* 12). The Philippian church requested from Smyrna copies of Ignatius's letters and entered into correspondence with Polycarp (*Philippians* inscr.; 1; 3; 13). The church at Smyrna produced the *Martyrdom of Polycarp*. Irenaeus recalled Polycarp's activity as a correspondent (Eusebius, *Eccl. Hist.* V.xx.8; cf. *Life* 12 which places this work during the time Polycarp was a deacon).

Ignatius's exhortations to Polycarp reflect the heretical challenge at Smyrna, so he stresses the role of the bishop in the public assembly. This agrees with the importance ascribed to heresy in the development of monepiscopacy, but the institution of a president-bishop was already there. Teaching was where Polycarp made his impression. Correspondence, a feature of episcopal activity neglected by scholars,[9] gave him a wider influence and determined the way others viewed the situation at Smyrna. Often more important than how a congregation regards its organization is the way others regard it.

These functions of Polycarp may be paralleled in later references to activities of bishops: (1) Leading in worship, especially at the Eucharist—Justin,

1 Apology 67; Polycrates in Eusebius, *Eccl. Hist.* V.xxiv.3; Tertullian, *Exhortation to Chastity* 7; Hippolytus, *Apostolic Tradition* 3–4; (*Apostolic Church Order* 18). (2) Teaching—Justin, *1 Apology* 67; Hegesippus in Eusebius, *Eccl. Hist.* IV.xxii; Irenaeus, *Against Heresies* IV.23.8; Hippolytus, *Refutation of All Heresies* I pref.; *Apostolic Church Order* 16. (3) Administering funds, including hospitality—Justin, *1 Apology* 67; Dionysius of Corinth in Eusebius, *Eccl. Hist.* IV.xxiii.10; Tertullian, *Apology* 39; *Apostolic Church Order* 16; 18. (4) Corresponding—Eusebius, *Eccl. Hist.* IV.xxiii; note how many of our second-century writings are from bishops and are letters; the *Apostolic Church Order* prefers a literate bishop (16).

This Ignatian-type presbytery was combined with Clementine ideas of apostolicity to produce the "historic episcopate." Of the activities of the bishop known from the beginning of the third century (cf. Hippolytus, *Apostolic Tradition* and the *Epistles* of Cyprian), only discipline and ordaining find no direct confirmation in our second-century sources. In view of this considerable exercise of functions by bishops as the second century progressed, we may speak of the depression of the presbyterate rather than the exaltation of the bishop.

*Prepared for the faculty seminar on the Development of Early Catholic Christianity. Published in Italian translation, "Il Minestero nei Padri Apostolici," *Ricerche Bibliche e Religiose* 4 (1969): 79–94.

Chapter 7 Endnotes

1. J. B. Lightfoot, "The Christian Ministry," *Saint Paul's Epistle to the Philippians* (reprinted at Grand Rapids: Zondervan Publishing House, 1953), 230.

2. Adolf Harnack, *The Constitution and Law of the Church in the First Two Centuries* (London: Norgate & Williams, 1910),69ff.; 89ff.; John Knox, *The Ministry in Historical Perspectives*, ed. H. Richard Niebuhr and Daniel D. Williams (New York: Harper, 1956), 21f.

3. Friedrich Gerke, "Die Stellung des Ersten Clemensbriefes innerhalb der Entwicklung der altchristlichen Gemeindeverfassung und des Kirchenrechts," *Texte und Untersuchungen* 47 (Leipsig: J. C. Hinrich, 1931), 31–37, a work to which I am otherwise much indebted; also his contribution to *The Ministry and the Sacraments*, ed. Roderic Dunkerley (London, 1937), 343ff.

4. On Jewish synagogue organization see Samuel Krauss, *Synagogale Altertümer* (Berlin: Harz, 1922), 114–56; Jean Juster, *Les Juifs dans l'Empire Romain* (Paris: Geuthner, 1914), 439–55.

5. *Apostolic Constitutions* VII.xlvi. With modifications by Charles Gore, *The Church and the Ministry* (London: Longmans, Green, and Co., 1919), 222.

6. In *The Apostolic Ministry*, ed. K. E. Kirk (New York: Morehouse and Gorham Co., 1947), 258ff.

7. Hans von Campenhausen, *Polykarpos von Smyrna und die Pastoralbriefe* (Heidelberg, 1951).

8. There was not an order of virgins at this time, but individuals took vows of continence—Minucius Felix 31; Justin, *1 Apol.* 15; Athenagoras, *Plea* 33.

9. But see P. Nautin, *Lettres et Écrivains Chrétiens des IIe et IIIe Siècles* (Patristica II; Paris, 1961).

Selected Bibliography

Colson, Jean. *L'Évêque dans les communautés primitives.* Paris: Du Cerf, 1951.

Ferguson, Everett. "The Ministry of the Word in the First Two Centuries." *Restoration Quarterly* 1 (1957): 21–31.

Gore, Charles. *The Church and the Ministry.* New edition revised by C. H. Turner. London: Longmans, Green, and Co., 1919.

Harnack, Adolf. *The Constitution and Law of the Church in the First Two Centuries.* London: Norgate & Williams, 1910.

Lightfoot, J. B. "The Christian Ministry." *Saint Paul's Epistle to the Philippians.* London: Macmillan, 1913.

Lindsay, T. M. *The Church and the Ministry in the Early Centuries.* 2nd ed. London: Hodder and Stoughton, 1903.

Schweizer, Eduard. *Church Order in the New Testament.* Studies in Biblical Theology 32. London: SCM Press, 1961.

Telfer, W. *The Office of a Bishop.* London: Darton, Longman, & Todd, 1962.

von Campenhausen, Hans. *Kirchliches Amt und geistliche Vollmacht.* Tübingen: J. C. B. Mohr, 1953; English translation *Ecclesiastical Authority and Spiritual Power in the Church of the First Three Centuries.* London: Adam & Charles Black, 1969.

Williams, George H. "The Ministry of the Ante-Nicene Church." *The Ministry in Historical Perspectives.* Edited by H. Richard Niebuhr and Daniel Williams. New York: Harper, 1956.

8

The "Congregationalism" of the Early Church

"All politics is local." So said "Tip" O'Neill, at the time representing Massachusetts in the United States Congress and serving as Speaker of the House of Representatives. All church life, too, is local. This paper addresses some aspects of the early church's emphasis on the local congregation of believers. Professor George Williams of Harvard, while lecturing on ancient church history, made one of the casual asides that university teachers sometimes make. He referred to the "congregationalism" of the early church.[1] Since he came from a Congregationalist/Unitarian background, the remark may have reflected that perspective. However, the comment stuck in my mind, and now, over forty-five years later, I have occasion to explore it. I do not present my development of the theme as reflecting Professor Williams's viewpoint; in fact, all I remember is the impression his remark made on me, so I cannot claim to represent what he had in mind.

A feature of free church polity has been a basically congregational church organization. This is often modified in practice by synods or conventions, but even these extracongregational bodies are typically not structured in layers as they are in more hierarchically organized churches. With this emphasis on the local congregation, free churches have been suspicious of the church that emerged in the early centuries. They have viewed it as dominated by a clergy understood in priestly terms, as ruled by bishops, and as developing according to a strictly hierarchical model. This, however, is not a wholly accurate picture. There are several elements worth noting of "congregationalism" in the early church, that is, viewing the church essentially in terms of the local congregation of believers.

Professor Williams's comment was to the effect that the congregationalism of the early church had no structure for solving interchurch conflicts. When a conflict was larger than the local congregation, representatives of one congregation went to another congregation to discuss the problem. This was what occurred in Acts 15, when the church at Antioch was troubled by representatives from Jerusalem insisting on the circumcision of Gentile converts to Christ. This meeting became the scriptural basis appealed to as a precedent for church councils, but what took place was essentially a meeting of representatives of one church with another church. Such consultations continued to occur. When there was dispute between the churches of Asia and the church of Rome over the date for observing the Pasch, Bishop Polycarp of Smyrna went to Rome about the year 155 to consult with Bishop Anicetus in an effort to resolve the conflict.[2]

The failure of this meeting to reach agreement on a common observance of the Pasch resulted in the parties agreeing to disagree, both maintaining their own practice but preserving fellowship. In the words of Irenaeus later, "The disagreement on the day of fasting confirmed the agreement in the faith."[3] This disagreement in practice was a factor in the development of regional councils of bishops. When Bishop Victor of Rome (ca. 189–ca. 198) no longer followed the peaceful policies of his predecessors but pushed for a common paschal observance in the churches, "synods and assemblies of bishops were held on this point."[4] There survived to Eusebius's day (ca. 260–ca. 339) letters reporting practices on this question sent by bishops who assembled in various provinces—Palestine, Rome, Pontus, Gaul, Osrhoene, and Corinth.[5]

Regional meetings to deal with a common problem had begun a few years earlier. The first notice of such gatherings relates to the outbreak of the New Prophecy called by its opponents the "Phrygian Heresy" and better known today as Montanism. One of its early literary opponents, Apollinaris of Hierapolis, writing about 180, says, "The believers in Asia coming together many times and at many places" rejected the Montanist heresy "so that they were driven out of the church and excluded from fellowship."[6] Tertullian, a few years later, mentions mandates by bishops in regard to fasting and councils of the churches in Greece that "handled deeper questions for the common benefit."[7]

From such ad hoc meetings developed the practice of regular, usually annual, synods of bishops in a province or region. The correspondence of Bishop Cyprian of Carthage indicates that by the mid-third century synods of bishops in North Africa were highly developed institutions. Some of the letters in his correspondence were written on behalf of councils of North African bishops.[8] Provincial synods provided a precedent for Constantine to call together bishops from the territory under his control to consider problems threatening the peace of the churches—at Arles in 314 to deal with Donatism and at Nicaea in 325 (the first "ecumenical" council) to deal with the teachings of Arius.

Even ecumenical councils did not have inherent authority. The frequent councils of the fourth century that drew up competing creeds show that Nicaea did not receive general acceptance for some time. The authority of the councils depended on their reception by the churches, and conciliar decisions had to be accepted and implemented by Christians. One of the principal sources of information about the Council of Nicaea in 325 is the letter of Bishop Eusebius of Caesarea, the church historian, to his home church. The letter is a justification of Eusebius's part in the proceedings at the council. In an effort to win support from his home church, he offered an extended explanation of key terms in the creed that was adopted.[9] Eusebius needed to make this explanation because the terminology of the creed and the conceptual basis for it did not correspond to the teaching he and presumably his congregation had previously supported. His orthodoxy was already under suspicion in several circles, and his agreeing to accept the creed of his opponents would now jeopardize his position with his previous allies. The emperor and over 200 bishops[10] carried a lot of weight (and Eusebius makes the most of the emperor's endorsement of the creed and of explanations that would put the most favorable light on it in the eyes of potential critics). However, even such an assembly did not automatically have the authority that would be accepted without examination.

Reception by the church at large has remained an important part of the Eastern Church's theory of conciliar authority.[11] The councils of the early church were not canonical institutions but rather "charismatic events," and "no council was accepted as valid in advance."[12] The so-called Robber Council of 449 was an impressive gathering summoned by the emperor, but it was rejected by a majority of the churches. The ancient church developed no theory of reception in regard to conciliar authority; the consensus of the faithful in fact determined the acceptance of doctrines. Reception of conciliar decisions may justly be regarded as an expression of congregationalism that lingered in churches not usually thought of as "congregationalist."

Another indication of the congregationalism of the early church is found in its correspondence. The earliest noncanonical Christian letter is from "the church of God that sojourns in Rome to the church of God that sojourns in Corinth" (*1 Clem.* 1.1). The document is accurately named *1 Clement*, but we know the name of the actual writer not from the document itself but from the manuscript tradition and the testimony of Dionysius of Corinth less than a century later.[13] The letter presents itself as the writing of one church to another. If Clement was something like what would later be called a bishop, he does not present himself as such and speaks with the collective authority of the church, not personal authority. Clement's role was that of secretary for the church, and he writes in the name of the church, not his own name.[14] The letter was written with authority and is expected to be heeded, but no hierarchy of individuals or churches is appealed to, only that the message is what the Holy Spirit would have said in the situation (*1 Clem.* 63.2). A few years later Ignatius wrote six letters to churches and one letter to a fellow bishop, Polycarp. The latter is a personal letter to Polycarp, although the contents were intended for the church as well.[15] Ignatius sent a separate letter to the church at Smyrna, where Polycarp served. The significant fact is that churches were communicating with churches, or an individual was communicating with churches; bishops were not communicating with churches primarily through their bishops.

The two most important early accounts of martyrdom were letters from churches. The *Martyrdom of Polycarp* (probably about AD 156) is actually a letter, employing the same phraseology as *1 Clement*, from "The church of God that sojourns in Smyrna to the church of God that sojourns in Philomelium and to all the communities of the holy and catholic church in every place" (pref.). The account of *The Martyrs of Gaul* (AD 177) comes from two churches and is more broadly worded in its address. It is a letter from "The servants of Christ who sojourn in Vienne and Lyons in Gaul to the brothers and sisters in Asia and Phrygia who share with us the same faith and hope of redemption."[16] Again, churches are writing to churches. In both of these cases, the bishops had died in the persecution and so could not write; nevertheless, the point is that the churches did not write to bishops but to other churches or Christians in order to inform them about events.

The collection of letters of Dionysius of Corinth available to Eusebius included letters to churches and letters to bishops intended for the churches.[17] These letters may represent a transitional stage. By the mid-third century Cyprian's correspondence to people outside of Carthage was with bishops, if there was an occupant of the episcopal chair of the church at the moment.[18] When there was no bishop or if the bishop was guilty of misdeeds, he wrote to the other clergy. Even letters to his own church in Carthage, apart from the letters to martyrs, are for the most part addressed to the clergy. Bishops were now writing to bishops and other clergy instead of directly to churches. Cyprian, furthermore, pioneered the idea of bishops being bishops of the church at large and not simply in a church (on his view of bishops, more following). This is carried further in the large collections of letters of Basil of Caesarea and Gregory of Nazianzus in the fourth century, where the bishop addresses individuals in many churches.

In regard to organizational matters, we should note that in the early history of Christianity there was congregational selection and commissioning of ministers. Our earliest notices refer to election by local congregations. There was precedent for this in the New Testament, as in the choice by the community of believers of the seven servants of the church at Jerusalem in Acts 6:1–6 and the commissioning by the church in Antioch even of those chosen by the Holy Spirit in Acts 13:1–3. Our earliest postcanonical documents reflect local choice. *First Clement* 44 referred to bishops appointed "by eminent men with the consent of the whole church." And *Didache* 15 instructed Christians "to elect for yourselves bishops and deacons." The church orders continued to describe procedures involving election by the local congregation. "Let the bishop be ordained being in all things without fault chosen by all the people. And when he has been proposed and found acceptable to all, the people shall assemble on the Lord's Day together with the presbytery and such bishops as may attend" (Hippolytus, *Apostolic Tradition* 2.1–2). This statement is typical of instructions in the church-order literature, both in the expectation of popular election and in the description of the public nature of the ordination. Not only the selection but also the appointment occurred in the gathering of the church in which one was called to serve.

Election of their bishops by the local churches continued to be the norm in the third century and at many places for some time later.[19] Bishops in turn selected the lesser clergy, as the *Apostolic Tradition* indicates, sometimes even the presbyters,[20] but in this case with the approval of the congregation.[21] A congregation's selection of its own ministers was a firmly established principle of the early church, and that is a distinctly congregationalist principle.

The *Apostolic Tradition*, possibly from the beginning of the third century, assumes the presence of bishops from other churches at the ordination. Canon law later required the presence of three bishops at the ordination of a bishop.[22] This requirement related the appointment of a bishop to the universal church through the presence of representatives of other congregations. The involvement of other bishops in ordination led to the initiative in the selection of the bishop moving outside the congregation, either to the other bishops of the area or to the metropolitan bishop, who at least had to give his approval, but local consent to the choice remained crucial.[23]

During the fourth century, imperial involvement in the selection of bishops, especially at important churches, became an increasing problem. Nevertheless, the older sentiment remained strong. Western bishops at Sardica in 343 wrote to Emperor Constantius II that each community should be allowed to choose its own bishop.[24] A vivid account of popular election in a situation complicated by competing ecclesiastical parties concerns Ambrose of Milan.[25] There was disturbance in Milan after the death of the Arian bishop Auxentius, and Ambrose as governor of the province went to the church to restore order between the Arian and Nicene factions. When he was addressing the people, the voice of a child called out, "Ambrose bishop." The people took this as a divine sign and, although Ambrose was not even baptized yet, both catholics and Arians agreed on his election. Ambrose was reluctant to accept the call but, finally persuaded, was baptized and ordained.

A corollary of congregational election was that a person was a minister in the church where chosen to serve and only in a limited sense a minister in the universal church. The implications of decisions made at Nicaea concerning the status of clergy from schismatic groups reconciled to the Catholic Church have not attracted sufficient attention.[26] When followers of Melitius, Novatian, and Paul of Samosata who held clerical office came into the Catholic Church, they were entitled to the same position in the Catholic Church that they had formerly held in the schismatic or heretical community but they first had to receive a new ordination.[27] Their previous ordinations were not recognized, although the baptisms of the Melitians and Novatianists (but not those of the Paulianists) were recognized. This practice suggests the possibility of a new ordination when a clergyman moved from one Catholic Church to another. Such might be the implication of a canon adopted at Nicaea: "If anyone shall dare surreptitiously to carry off and ordain in his own church a man who belongs to another church without the consent of that person's bishop from whose clergy list he was separated, the ordination will be void" (Nicaea, can. 16). Since in most cases this involved a promotion, a new ordination would have been to the new rank in the ministry and so this canon may not be indicative of a repeated ordination. We lack details about what was done when the same function was accepted at another congregation. However, since normally somebody is doing what is forbidden, some significance attaches to the following decree from the late fourth century: "If any bishop, presbyter, or deacon receives a second ordination from anyone, let him be deprived, and the person who ordained him, unless he can show that his former ordination was from the heretics; for those that are either baptized or ordained by such as these, can be neither Christians nor clergymen" (*Apostolic Canons* 68). This prohibition of a second ordination (to the same rank in the clergy) was an important step toward viewing ordination as a permanent endowment, a result achieved in Augustine's doctrine of the indelibility of orders.

When Polycarp, bishop of Smyrna, visited Bishop Anicetus of Rome (discussed above), "Anicetus, showing his respect for Polycarp, allowed him to celebrate the Eucharist in the church."[28] This was a particular favor and sign of fellowship, and it was referred to by Irenaeus of Lyons later as a demonstration of peace and intercommunion. Polycarp had no inherent right to preside at the Lord's Table in another church. One was originally viewed as a bishop in a particular church, not a bishop "at large" or a bishop in the universal church, although one church honored the leader of a sister church. It was only in the mid-third century with Cyprian that another theory of church office was promoted. In his view, the bishops were not simply bishops of individual churches but jointly shared an episcopate over the whole church.[29] Such a view gave a theoretical basis for what was already taking place, that is, bishops in council speaking for the churches they represented.

The expectation of the early church was that a person would remain in the church for which he was ordained. One was not ordained to be a clergyman at large, but for ministry in a particular church.[30] The attitude is summed up in the canons of the Council of Chalcedon in 451:

> Neither presbyter, deacon, nor any of the ecclesiastical order shall be ordained at large, nor unless the person ordained is particularly appointed to a church in a city or village, or to a martyrion, or to a monastery. And if any have been ordained without a charge, the holy Synod decrees, to the reproach of the ordainer, that such an ordination shall be inoperative, and that such a person shall nowhere be allowed to officiate. (Can. 6)

The principle was much older than Chalcedon. An important reflection of the view that the clergy were identified with a particular congregation was the position that there was to be no translation of bishops from one church to another.

> On account of the great disturbance and discords that occur, it is decreed that the custom prevailing in certain places contrary to the canon, must wholly be done away, so that neither bishop, presbyter, nor deacon shall pass from city to city. And if any one, after this decree of the holy and great Synod, shall attempt any such thing, or continue in any such course, his proceedings shall be utterly void, and he shall be restored to the church for which he was ordained bishop or presbyter. (Nicaea, can. 15)

The practice of transferring from one church to another was thus applied to presbyters and deacons as well as bishops, but it was the translation of bishops that drew frequent prohibition in the canons of various councils.

> A bishop may not be translated from one parish to another either intruding himself of his own suggestion, or under compulsion by the people, or by constraint of the bishops; but he shall remain in the church to which he was allotted by God from the beginning, and shall not be translated from it, according to the decree formerly passed on the subject. (Antioch [341?], can. 21)[31]

The feeling was strong that a minister must remain in the place where he was ordained. At a time when the hierarchy of bishops and synodal procedures were being institutionalized, the church preserved a basically congregational consciousness of its organization and ministry.

Whether the initiative was with a person who tried to transfer to another church (Nicaea, can. 15, above), with a church that tried to carry off someone from another church to serve them (Nicaea, can. 16), or with bishops trying to strengthen their party by placing someone of their persuasion in a given church, the canonical legislation opposed the moving of ministry from one place to another. A person certainly had the rank of his office wherever he went, and he did not lose the right to exercise his ministry with the permission of the bishop of the church where he was visiting, but canon law sought even the limitation of the period of time a clergyman could visit another church.[32] The primary conviction was that the minister was considered wedded to the church where he was ordained.[33] His ministry was to be for a particular people at a particular place.

The frequently repeated prohibition of translation from one church to another shows, however, that the practice was common and was not eliminated by conciliar canons. Churches wanted proven men from other churches, and ambitious men (and probably others who sincerely felt called) wanted advancement to larger or more prestigious churches. The troubled ecclesiastical conditions caused by the doctrinal conflicts of the fourth century created situations that encouraged "clergy at large" without assignment to a particular church. One of the canons adopted at Antioch (usually assigned to the council of 341 but probably from another council) pointed to the kind of situation that could (and did) arise:

> If any bishop ordained to a parish shall not proceed to the parish to which he has been ordained, not through any fault of his own, but either because of the rejection of the people, or for any other reason not arising from himself, let him enjoy his rank and ministry; only he shall not disturb the affairs of the church which he joins; and he shall abide by whatever the full synod of the province shall determine, after judging the case. (Can. 18)[34]

The fourth century saw increasing occasions when one party in the trinitarian disputes of the age covertly ordained someone of their persuasion and tried to force that person on a given church. Such a divorce of ordination from the local church is illustrated by a comment by Jerome, defining the Greek word for ordination, *cheirotonia*: "That is, the ordination [*ordinatio*] of the clergy which is accomplished not only at the verbal prayer but at the imposition of the hand (lest indeed in mockery someone be ordained ignorantly to the clergy by a secret prayer)."[35] Jerome refers to the two principal actions in ordination—prayer and the laying on of hands. His comment shows that prayer was the central element of the ordination and the laying on of hands an accompanying circumstance.[36] He offers a practical reason why the laying on of hands was also necessary. His explanation in regard to the possibility of secret ordination may be hypothetical, but his very entertaining of the thought shows that what would have been inconceivable in an earlier period, when ordination was done in the context of the assembly of the church for whose service one was being ordained, was now conceivable.

The attitude that would forbid the transfer of bishops (and other clergy) from one church to another was more strongly affirmed in the East, where it still obtains, than in the West. For instance, Gregory of Nazianzus had to resign as bishop of Constantinople on the charge that his appointment was illegal since he had been ordained as bishop of Sasima (although in fact he never served there). A basis for modification of the legislation against transfer of bishops was already present in Cyprian's theory of the episcopate belonging to the whole church, and the premise of the old view was changed by Augustine's view of ordination as a permanent possession not tied to the action of a local congregation.[37]

A modern Benedictine, in introducing his translation of a work by a Father of the Greek Church, Maximus the Confessor (580–662), expressed the viewpoint of the Greek Church in a statement that those of a congregational polity would also endorse: "The Church is not made up of the sum of its parts, but all of it is present in each of its parts."[38] A modern Greek Orthodox theologian defines the church in terms of the local eucharistic community, each in full unity with other communities by virtue of the whole Christ represented in each.[39] Congregational church polity has attempted to carry out consistently the implications of this insight.

Free churches have things to learn from the ancient church, as other essays in this collection will argue. From the perspective of this essay, it is also true that much in the ancient church is congenial with or even supportive of emphases found in free churches. These include the local congregation as the basic organizational unit of the church, the local congregation as the essential decision-making body, congregations related directly with one another and not through their leaders, and the right of the local congregation to choose its own ministers. The convictions and practices of the early church remind all church communions to focus on the church, not only as an institution, but as the gathered community of believers.

*Originally printed in D. H. Williams, ed., *The Free Church and the Early Church* (Grand Rapids: Eermans, 2002), 129-40.

Chapter 8 Endnotes

1. George Williams's detailed account of the organizational development of the early church (and much more) is found in his two articles, "The Ministry of the Ante-Nicene Church (c. 125–325)" and "The Ministry in the Later Patristic Period (314–451)," in *The Ministry in Historical Perspectives* (ed. H. Richard Niebuhr and Daniel D. Williams; New York: Harper and Brothers, 1956), 27–81; 290–301.

2. Eusebius, *Ecclesiastical History* (= *HE*) 4.14.1.

3. Quoted by Eusebius, *HE* 5.24.13 and 16.

4. Eusebius, *HE* 5.23.2.

5. Eusebius, *HE* 5.23.3–4. Eusebius had his faults as a historian, but where he collects and preserves earlier sources he is extremely valuable.

6. Quoted by Eusebius, *HE* 5.16.10.

7. Tertullian, *On Fasting* 13.

8. Cyprian, *Letters* 57[53], 64[58], 67, 71[69], 72[71]; cf. *Judgment of Eighty-seven Bishops*.

9. The letter is quoted by Socrates, *Ecclesiastical History* (= *HE*) 1.8, and Theodoret, *Ecclesiastical History* (= *HE*) 1.11–12.

10. There were about 220 signatories to the creed, but the orthodox convinced themselves that there were 318 bishops present, based on number symbolism derived from Gen. 14:14.

11. Georges Florovsky, "The Authority of the Ancient Councils and the Tradition of the Fathers: An Introduction," in *Glaube, Geist, Geschichte: Festschrift für Ernst Benz* (ed. G. Müller and W. Zeller; Leiden: E. J. Brill, 1967), 177–88, reprinted in E. Ferguson, ed., *Church, Ministry, and Organization in the Early Church Era*, Studies in Early Christianity, vol. 13 (New York: Garland [Taylor & Francis], 1993), 211–22, makes the case that councils did not have authority over the church but were representations of the church. Hermann Josef Sieben, *Die Konzilsidee der Alten Kirche* (Paderborn: Schönigh, 1979), 306–43, discusses the difference of Western and Eastern views on councils and their reception.

12. Florovsky, 179.

13. Quoted by Eusebius, *HE* 4.23.11.

14. Cf. Hermas, *Vis.* 2.4.3 (= 8.3), for Clement whose task was to correspond with other cities.

15. Note the address to the church in Ignatius, *Letter to Polycarp* 6.

16. Eusebius, *HE* 5.1.3.

17. Eusebius, *HE* 4.23.1–13.

18. Persecution often left churches without a bishop for a period of time, for example, in Rome for over a year in 250 to early 251.

19. E.g., Cyprian, *Letters* 59[54].5–6; 67.3–5; Gregory of Nyssa, *Life of Gregory Thaumaturgus* 62–72 (*Patrologia Graeca* 46:933B–940B = *Gregorii Nysseni Opera* X.1.36,3–41,15). Origen knew other methods of selection in addition to election in the third century (*Hom.* 13 *in Num.* 4)—see Everett Ferguson, "Origen and the Election of Bishops," *Church History* 43 (1974): 26–33.

20. *Didascalia* 9.

21. Cyprian, *Letter* 38[33].1f.

22. Arles, can. 20; Nicaea, can. 4; *Apostolic Constitutions* 3.20.

23. For some instances in the fourth century of selection of a bishop by other bishops, see Theodoret, *HE* 2.28 at Antioch; 5.19.14 at Constantinople.

24. *Liber I ad Constantium* 1.1–4 (Hilary of Poitiers, in *Corpus Scriptorum Ecclesiasticorum Latinorum* 65:181–87); see R. P. C. Hanson, *The Search for the Christian Doctrine of God: The Arian Controversy, 318–381* (Edinburgh: T. & T. Clark, 1988), 853.

25. Paulinus, *Life of Ambrose* 3.6.

26. See my paper, which was disturbing to champions of a conventional episcopal understanding of the organization of the early church, "Attitudes to Schism at the Council of Nicaea," in *Schism, Heresy, and Religious Protest* (ed. Derek Baker; Studies in Church History, vol. 9; Cambridge: Cambridge University Press, 1972), 57–63.

27. On the Melitians, the letter of the Council of Nicaea to the Egyptian churches preserved in Socrates, *HE* 1.9, and Theodoret, *HE* 1.9.7ff.; on the Novatians and Paulianists, canons 8 and 19 of Nicaea.

28. Letter of Irenaeus of Lyons to Victor of Rome, quoted in Eusebius, *HE* 5.24.t7.

29. "The episcopate is one, each part of which is held by each one for the whole" (Cyprian, *On the Unity of the Church* 5).

30. Developments affecting this principle are surveyed in Bernard Callebat, "Origines et fondements du droit de la stabilité des ministres ordonnés dans l'Église d'Orient (Ier-Ve siècles)," *Bulletin de Littérature Ecclésiastique* 98 (1997): 211–33.

31. Not everyone, of course, agreed with the prohibition. The historian Socrates Scholasticus cited many instances when "bishops have been transferred from one city to another to meet the exigences of peculiar cases" (*HE* 7.35–36, 40).

32. Sardica, can. 11 and 16, placed a limit of three weeks for a bishop, presbyter or deacon to be away from his home church.

33. A singular extension of this idea comes in the charge that someone translated from one church to another was guilty of spiritual bigamy or adultery (Athanasius, *Defense against the Arians* 6; cf. Jerome, *Letter* 69.5).

34. Canon 17 had called for the excommunication of someone ordained as a bishop for a given church who would not accept the ministry. The council of Ancyra (314), can. 18, had already had to deal with the problem of bishops "not received by the parish to which they were designated."

35. Jerome, *On Isaiah* 16.58.

36. Everett Ferguson, "The Laying on of Hands: Its Significance in Ordination," *Journal of Theological Studies,* n.s., 26 (1975): 1–12; reprinted in Ferguson, *Church, Ministry, and Organization in the Early Church Era,* 147–58.

37. Augustine, *On Baptism against the Donatists* 1.1.2.

38. Dom Julian Stead, *The Church, the Liturgy, and the Soul of Man: The Mystagogia of St. Maximus the Confessor* (Still River, MA; St. Bede's Publications, 1982), 16.

39. John D. Zizioulas, *Being as Communion: Studies in Personhood and the Church* (London: Darton, Longman and Todd, 1985), 157. A patristic statement of the principle that "each eucharistic assembly is the church" is found in Cyril of Alexandria, *De adoratione* 3 (PG 68.640D).

9

Article Review of Dan Williams's *Retrieving the Tradition and Renewing Evangelicalism: A Primer for Suspicious Protestants*[1]

Abstract

Dan Williams challenges the "historylessness" of much contemporary evangelicalism and pleads for a recovery of the great Tradition as a way of "renewing evangelicalism." I agree with the need to pay attention to history but am not so optimistic about its resulting in renewal and find problems in the statement of the case that require further exploration. To follow Tradition is to affirm the authority of scripture. The Rule of Faith itself was a summary of the teaching found in scripture. Theological programs other than the "Bible alone" have not been notably successful in overcoming division. The early creeds and councils may be accepted as confessions of faith but not as tests of fellowship.

Distinguishing between Tradition (capital T) and tradition(s) (lowercase t), Dan Williams calls on evangelical and free churches to rediscover the patristic period of church history, the church's Great Tradition, as part of their heritage. He then traces the doctrinal history of the early church:

the formation of the Christian Tradition (relation to the Old Testament, teachings delivered by Jesus and Paul, confessions, and the *kerygma*); defining and defending the Tradition (apostolicity, catechism, the Rule of Faith, and scripture); the "corruption" of the church (refuting the paradigm of a "fall" of the church and offering another approach); and the preservation of the Tradition through councils and creeds (bishops, emperors, councils, the Nicene Creed, and their relation to Scripture). He concludes with a discussion of "Scripture and Tradition in the Reformation" (correcting misunderstandings of the Reformers' attitude toward the post-apostolic church), an epilogue on defining Christian faithfulness, and two appendices ("Why All Christians Are Catholics" and "*Sola Scriptura* in the Early Church").

Dan Williams delivers a forthright challenge to the "historylessness" of much contemporary evangelicalism. Where there is some consciousness of history among evangelicals, especially those in the free churches, there is something perhaps more problematic, and that is an artificial construction of history. Evangelicals and free churches are not the only religious people who may be charged with having an artificial history. Roman Catholics and Eastern Orthodox, who affirm and depend on a loyalty to history, often have their own artificial history. That is, they have sometimes affirmed a seamlessness in their history that will not stand up to scrutiny. Among the Orthodox in particular this approach becomes its own form of "historylessness."

I agree with the overall thrust of Williams's book. We need to pay attention to the early history (and to the intervening history) and to the early Tradition. We will be enriched by "retrieving the Tradition." Whether this will result in "renewing evangelicalism" may claim more than we can be certain about. Perhaps expressing my preferred way of saying some of the things Williams talks about will contribute to the clarification and sharpening of some issues.

Roman Catholic and Eastern Orthodox churches, for all their abuse of the idea of tradition, have preserved a sense that this is a part of Christian identity and reality that many Protestants have lost. Scripture was a part of Tradition (capital *T*), not opposed to it, and Tradition (capital *T*) witnessed to Scripture as the norm. Hence, to follow Tradition is to affirm the authority of scripture. All traditions stand under the judgment of Scripture and must always be tested by it (as in Jesus' criticism of the oral law, to which reference is made on 49–50).

With regard to the Rule of Faith, Williams agrees with Irenaeus that it was necessary to find "a reference outside of" scripture in order to interpret it (38). Clement of Alexandria too said that the Scriptures were to be explained according to the "canon of the truth" (*Miscellanies* 6.15), but he also insisted that the canon of truth must be derived from the Scriptures (7.16). The Rule was preserved outside of Scripture, but we need to remember that its content was a summary of the preaching that is found in Scripture, as Williams also says (96). As a caution against too much confidence in the Rule as the "interpretative guide" (98ff.) to Scripture and Tradition (capital T), we note that, although helpful to the Catholics of the second and third centuries in defending their position, it did not prevent multiple interpretations at the time. When one says "Scripture and something else," the same problems and others arise as when one says "Scripture only."

For instance, Williams says that the "Bible only" is no defense against sects (202), but I fail to see that other theological options have been either. One may disguise division within an institutional unity by bringing divergent communities under the umbrella of loyalty to a papacy (here I think of the rival religious orders in Roman Catholicism) or within the artificial unity of a World Council of Churches; but the unity for which Jesus prayed is surely a unity in the Spirit.

Division among Christians is an old objection. Clement of Alexandria replied to those who said they ought not to believe because of the different sects among Christians (*Miscellanies* 7.15). He points to the sects among the Jews and among Greek philosophers. One does not reject, he argues, philosophy because of the different philosophical schools, nor medicine because there are different schools of thought on the practice of medicine. He quotes Paul that indeed it is necessary for heresies to exist (1 Cor. 11:19), and so "we are bound in no way to transgress the canon of the church." Believers have failed miserably in making spiritual unity a visible unity, but those who work from other platforms than "Bible only" have few notable achievements toward the goal of unity.

With Williams, I would want to stress continuity in church history (83). Even the recipients of Paul's letters, whether innocently or deliberately, misunderstood him (1 Cor. 5:9–10; 2 Thess. 2:1–3), so the next generations could have misunderstood too. But where there was a broad agreement at many localities on matters of faith and practice, misunderstanding was less likely. Therefore, with reference to page 130, I too find the Tradition (capital *T*) helpful rather than an impediment to Scripture. That is, it is helpful if one means, as Williams does, the teaching found in the Tradition and not necessarily including all the institutional developments of the time. [My cautions about Williams's book stems from his attention to theological developments and my attention to institutional history.] Of course, the Christian perspective and Christian spirituality could be maintained in a less-than-desirable institution. And free churches also have created their less-than-desirable institutions. The affirmations on page 130 are correct about "the vitality and continuity of the "worshipping" and confessing church throughout the patristic era" and about the "complex and durable" continuity between the post-apostolic period and the fourth and fifth centuries.

Historians understandably focus on change, and there was change in the early centuries, as in subsequent centuries of Christian history. Not all changes were innocent in their consequences, whatever the intentions (or lack of consciousness) by the participants. "Fall," however, may be too strong a word for the changes that occurred during and after Constantine's reign. Proponents of the interpretation of the history as a "fall" have overstated the situation. There was continuity, but changes also were occurring. Where does one draw the line, or does one, with respect to the growing "web of tradition" (163)? The increasing prominence and even veneration of Mary is a case in point, affecting both faith and the practices of piety, during the time of the formulation of the doctrines of the Trinity and Christology in the fourth and fifth centuries. This development is a reminder of the need to be called back to the apostolic norm. To paraphrase the Reformers according to the language of the free church restitutionists, *ecclesia restituta, semper restituenda*, "the church restored, always being restored." It is not ours to judge when or if a "fall" occurred, for churches as well as individuals stand or fall before their Lord (Rom. 14:4). But changes occurred—institutionally, organizationally, liturgically, in piety, and doctrinally—that justify a "reform" or a "restoration." Roman Catholics themselves, since Vatican II, are reforming their church.

Some believers' church historians have claimed a succession for their churches or their ideas outside the Roman Catholic and Eastern Orthodox churches (see Williams, ch. 4). This succession was sought in order to counter Roman Catholic claims. The evidence for such a succession is slender, but there may have been more believers outside the institutional churches than is usually allowed for. And one should not judge too quickly that silence equates to nonexistence or too quickly despair of the Lord's raising up true believers in unlikely places. However, most of the efforts to establish a succession of free churches usually involve stretching the idea of a true church or a believers' church to include such heretical bodies that one might understandably prefer instead a Roman Catholic or Orthodox succession.

Although I agree with the approach of giving voice to the early church fathers in the interpretation of the Bible and have spent much time and effort in doing so, there is a question we must all face. Can we, this side of the Enlightenment and biblical criticism, read the Bible the way the church fathers did? If we allow for modern criticism and the modern historical approach to Scripture, what does this do to the Fathers' interpretations shaped in a quite different mentality?

Williams is right to point out the paradox of accepting the Nicene Trinity and Chalcedonian Christology and rejecting the church and tradition of the fourth and fifth centuries that formulated these doctrines. But the basic question is why a person accepts one doctrine and rejects another. In view of the political and other factors at work, it may be surprising that the Nicene Creed and Chalcedonian Definition came out as well as they did. That may be a testimony to the continuity of faith and devotion that Williams contends for. I consider that what was new about the Nicene Creed was not so much that it was a creed drawn up by a council. Confessions of faith were older, but it is notable that now it was not catechumens who needed a confession of faith but bishops! Nor was it entirely new to apply confessions as tests of faith—Williams points to the case of Paul of Samosata in 268 and the Council of Antioch in 325 (169, n. 66). What was new was attaching anathemas concerning rejected viewpoints to the positive affirmations of faith.

Hence, I would like to offer another perspective on the early councils and creeds. It is similar to a viewpoint expressed to me by a theologian from India, Paulos Gregorios, who is a member of the Syrian Orthodox Church, one of the so-called Monophysite churches that rejects the authority of Chalcedon (I say "so-called," because "Monophysite" is a label the members of these churches emphatically reject). He said that he was respectful of the early councils but did not feel bound by their wording. I would adopt a similar attitude. Given the philosophical context and the language in which the issues were formulated, I judge Nicaea and (unlike this Indian theologian) Chalcedon to be correct. I agree with the outcome in terms of the time and way the issues were phrased. But I do not feel bound by their wording, nor do I think we should bind their terminology on other times and other conceptual worlds. In other words, they may be accepted as confessions of faith but not imposed as tests of fellowship.

There is a question that needs to be explored more than Williams does. Would not the principle that says we should listen to the Tradition (capital *T*) and be guided by the doctrinal conclusions and theological reflections of the classical fathers of the church extend to later centuries also? How can the fourth and fifth centuries be privileged over later centuries? I think Williams has an answer here, but it needs to be spelled out more explicitly.

Some minor points may be noted: (1) On page 109, number 19, I presume the *Decree of Gratian* is the *Decretum*, but Anglicizing the title may cause misunderstanding; (2) Donatus is said to be a "third-century schismatic" (113)—is this the mistake of the Hutterite *Chronicle* or a slip by Williams or by an editor? (3) the source for Eusebius's letter to his church in Caesarea should be given for the benefit of the uninitiated (113, n. 32)—Socrates, *Ecclesiastical History* 1.8; Theodoret, *Ecclesiastical History* 1.12.

In summary, I welcome Dan's book and want to be his ally on the basic approach, but I am not so optimistic that this approach is going to be as much of a solution as is hoped for. There are some issues on which more discussion is needed in order to convince those who need to be convinced.

Chapter 9 Endnote

1. Grand Rapids: William B. Eerdmans, 1999. Review originally printed in *Scottish Journal of Theology* 55 (2002): 100–104.

10

Women in the Post-Apostolic Church

Women wrote very little of early Christian literature; and not much more was written about them. In these respects, early church history reflects the circumstances of the time. Consequently, women are known mainly as types and not often as individuals in the second and third centuries. Only in the fuller light of the fourth century are many known as individuals. Enough is recorded, however, to provide a glimpse of the significant place women had in the success of early Christianity.[1]

1. Women as Mothers and Wives

The place of women as wives and mothers was taken for granted and hence called forth less comment than their appearance in other roles. Two early non-canonical writings contain instructions about duties of various classes of persons comparable to the "household codes" in the New Testament. *First Clement,* in commending the "good past" of the Corinthians, includes the following praiseworthy conduct:

> And to the women you gave instruction that they should do all things with a blameless and seemly and pure conscience, yielding a dutiful affection to their husbands. And you taught them to remain in the rule of obedience and to manage their households with seemliness, in all circumstances. (1.3)[2]

This statement reflects the Hellenistic ideal of the wife as obedient to her husband and working at home, conducting its affairs under his instructions.

Polycarp's letter "on Righteousness" to the Philippians combines duties of members of the household with duties of leaders of the church. Concerning women, he says: "Next teach our wives to remain in the faith given to them, and in love and purity, tenderly loving their husbands in all truth, and loving all others equally in all chastity, and to educate their children in the fear of God" (4.2).[3] Here the role of the wife is extended to her responsibility to educate (train and discipline) the children.

Clement of Alexandria (late second century) and Tertullian (early third century) were quite different in personality and in approach to the relation of Christianity to pagan culture, yet they exhibit a remarkable similarity in their views on social morality. Both take the same positions on, among other things, the role of women, what constitutes modesty, and the understanding of marriage.[4] The usually irascible Tertullian, who could use some very negative words about women,[5] writes *To His Wife* (between 198 and 203), a sensitive and very appealing picture of Christian marriage:

> How beautiful, then, the marriage of two Christians, two who are one in hope, one in desire, one in the way of life they follow, one in the religion they practice. They are as brother and sister, both servants of the same Master. Nothing divides them, either in flesh or in spirit. They are, in very truth, two in one flesh; and where there is but one flesh there is also but one spirit. They pray together, they fast together; instructing one another, encouraging one another, strengthening one another. Side by side they visit God's church and partake of God's banquet; side by side they face difficulties and persecution, share their consolations. They have no secrets from one another; they never shun each

other's company; they never bring sorrow to each other's hearts. Unembarrassed they visit the sick and assist the needy. They give alms without anxiety; they attend the sacrifice without difficulty; they perform their daily exercises of piety without hindrance.... Psalms and hymns they sing to one another.... Hearing and seeing this, Christ rejoices. To such as these he gives peace: *Where there are two together,* there also he is present; and where he is, there evil is not. (2.8)[6]

From the fourth century, we know the names and something of the character of some outstanding mothers—Nonna, the mother of Gregory of Nazianzus; Anthusa, the mother of John Chrysostom; and Emmelia, the mother of Macrina the Younger, Basil the Great, and Gregory of Nyssa. I select the last for comment here, as less well-known but not less worthy.[7] The measure of Emmelia as a mother was her children. She had ten in all, and they included three bishops and a woman who was a model of ascetic piety. Gregory of Nazianzus, in the eulogy on his friend Basil, her eldest son, paid her this tribute:

> The union of [Basil's] parents, cemented as it was by a community of virtue, no less than by cohabitation, was notable for many reasons, especially for generosity to the poor, for hospitality, for purity of soul as the result of self-discipline.... [I]n my opinion, however, their greatest claim to distinction is the excellence of their children. For the attainment of distinction by one or two of their offspring might be ascribed to their nature; but when all are eminent, the honor is clearly due to those who brought them up. This is proved by the blessed roll of priests and virgins, and of those who, when married, have allowed nothing in their union to hinder them from attaining an equal repute. [After describing her husband, Basil the elder, Gregory continues:] Who has not known Emmelia, whose name [harmoniousness, gracefulness] was a forecast of what she became, or else whose life was an exemplification of her name? For she had a right to the name which implies gracefulness, and occupied, to speak

> concisely, the same place among women, as her husband among men. (*Oration* 43.9–10)[8]

Few women had such distinguished children, and not all Christian women possessed Emmelia's virtues, but descriptions of mothers like her and others show what qualities were admired in Christian motherhood.

Women as wives and mothers gave the Christian home the strength that made it such a powerful influence in the spread of Christianity in the Roman world.

2. Women as Martyrs

Justin Martyr tells of a wife converted from a wanton life to the teachings of Christ.[9] Her husband did not approve of her efforts to reform him and continued in his immoralities. Feeling that maintaining the marriage made her a partaker in her husband's vices, she divorced him. The husband then brought charges before the authorities against her and her teacher, Ptolemy, as being Christians. Imperial intervention delayed proceedings against the woman, but Ptolemy and two other Christians were executed (*2 Apol.* 2). Justin has not given us the name of the woman, nor the outcome of her case. The experience of one spouse converted and the other not was probably common, so this case was unusual only for its extremes; it is a reminder that domestic differences in matters of religion were often a factor in persecution.

Persecution was an equal opportunity experience shared by women and men. Some of the most famous martyrs of the early church were women. I select two of the heroic figures from the days of persecution for consideration. Unlike Justin's matron in Rome, their names are known: the slave Blandina and the noble woman Perpetua.[10]

In 177, a severe persecution against Christians broke out in Lyons and Vienne in the Rhone River valley of Gaul. When the persecution subsided, the survivors wrote to their fellow believers in Asia and Phrygia a letter preserved in Eusebius, *Church History* 5.1–5. Although a woman, a slave, and supposedly weak physically, Blandina's courage and endurance made her the heroine of the account. I quote from the sections of the letter devoted to her.

[The wrath of the mob fell, among others, on] Blandina, through whom Christ showed that the things that to men appear mean and deformed and contemptible, are with God deemed worthy of great glory, on account of love to him.... For while we were all afraid, and especially her mistress in the flesh, who was herself one of the combatants among witnesses, that she would not be able to make a bold confession on account of the weakness of her body, Blandina was filled with such power, that those who tortured her one after the other in every way from morning till evening were wearied and tired, confessing that they had been baffled, for they had no other torture they could apply to her; and they were astonished at Blandina bearing her testimony, for one kind of torture was sufficient to have killed her. But the blessed woman, like a noble athlete, recovered her strength in the midst of the confession; and her declaration, "I am a Christian, and there is no evil done amongst us," brought her refreshment, and rest, and insensibility to all the sufferings afflicted on her.... [Later she was exposed to the wild beasts.] Blandina was hung up fastened to a stake, and exposed, as food to the wild beasts that were let loose against her; and through her presenting the spectacle of one suspended on something like a cross, and through her earnest prayers, she inspired the combatants with great eagerness: for in the combat they saw, by means of their sister, with their bodily eyes, him who was crucified for them.... When none of the wild beasts at that time touched her, she was taken down from the stake and conveyed back to prison. She was thus reserved for another contest.... For though she was an insignificant, weak, and despised woman, yet she was clothed with the great and invincible athlete Christ. On many occasions she had overpowered the adversary, and in the course of the contest had woven for herself the crown of incorruption.... On the last day of the gladiatorial shows, Blandina was again brought in.... [The] blessed Blandina, last of all, after having like a noble mother encouraged her children and sent them on before her victorious to the King, trod

> the same path of conflict which her children had trod, hastening on to them with joy and exultation at her departure, not as one thrown to the wild beasts, but as one invited to a marriage supper. And after she had been scourged and exposed to the wild beasts, and roasted in the iron chair, she was at last enclosed in a net and cast before a bull. And after having been well tossed by the bull, though without having any feeling of what was happening to her, through her hope and firm hold of what had been entrusted to her and her converse with Christ, she also was sacrificed, the heathen themselves acknowledging that never among them did woman endure so many and such fearful tortures.[11]

A French writer remarked with Gallic flair, "It was not Spartacus who eliminated slavery; it was rather Blandina."[12] The element of truth in that exaggeration is that martyrdom created a new spiritual aristocracy. Christ was present with the martyrs and was seen in their sufferings, so there was a close identification of the martyr with the Lord. The heroic performance of women believers brought them a status equal to and higher than that of men, as devotion to the martyrs led to the cult of the saints.

Twenty-five years later (AD 203), a young woman about twenty-two years old, walked, singing a psalm, into a Roman arena in Carthage in North Africa to face a martyr's death. Her name was Vibia Perpetua and the contemporary account of her martyrdom describes her as "respectably born, well educated, a married matron, having a father and mother and two brothers, one of whom, like herself, a catechumen, and an infant son at the breast" (1.1).[13] She left a diary giving an account of her ordeal up to the day of her martyrdom; another person completed the story of that last day. Thus we not only know Perpetua's name but also have one of the rare documents from the early church written by a woman and one of our earliest documents of Latin Christianity.[14]

Perpetua was marked out for punishment along with other catechumens, including two slaves, one of whom, Felicitas, later gave birth prematurely in prison. The catechumens received baptism before being led away to prison. On four separate occasions, while she awaited martyrdom, Perpetua's father pled with her to reject her faith and offer sacrifice to the gods, giving demonstration of Jesus' words that "One's foes will be those of his [her] own household"; but she insisted, "I cannot call myself anything else than what I am, a Christian" (1.2). Much of Perpetua's diary is occupied with accounts of visions she had while in prison. In one of these she saw her approaching martyrdom in terms of a gladiatorial contest with an Egyptian (the devil). She was stripped and rubbed with oil, "as is the custom before a contest," "and I became a man" (3.2).[15]

The compiler's account of the martyrdom relates how the new Christians "proceeded from the prison into the amphitheatre, as if into an assembly, joyous and of brilliant countenance" (6.1).

> Perpetua . . . was tossed [by a very fierce cow], and fell on her loins; and when she saw her tunic torn from her side, she drew it over her as a veil for her thigh rather mindful of her modesty than her suffering. . . . [W]hen she saw Felicitas crushed, she approached and gave her her hand, and lifted her up. And both of them stood together. . . . (6.3)

The Christians were then individually dispatched by the sword.

> Perpetua, that she might taste more pain, being pierced between the ribs, cried out loudly, and she herself placed the wavering right hand of the youthful gladiator to her throat. Possibly such a woman could not have been slain unless she herself had willed it, because she was feared by the impure spirit. (6.4)

The "trembling hand of the young gladiator" (Mursurillo) speaks eloquently of the moral dilemma the persecution of Christians posed.

In martyrdom, women equaled or excelled men in the "manly" virtues of courage and endurance. The blood of female martyrs was part of the seed from which Christians multiplied (Tertullian, *Apol.* 50), and so women contributed to the victory of Christianity over paganism.

3. Women as Monastics/Ascetics

Asceticism had deep roots in second- and third-century Christianity. It became institutionalized in the monasticism of the fourth century. When martyrdom ceased with the triumph of Christianity in the fourth century, those who chose the interior martyrdom of ascetic self-denial were exalted as the spiritual heroes and heroines of the church, the "real" Christians. Women often gained recognition in the early Christian texts for breaking with tradition and adopting a celibate lifestyle. Celibacy gave women a freedom from a male-dominated world of family and home and, in accord with ancient ideas, provided a closer communication with the divine. Asceticism may be seen as the path to women's liberation in the early church.[16]

Second-century apologists,[17] in contrasting Christian sexual morality with paganism, took note of the number of Christians, male and female, who chose to live continent lives. The phenomenon was noted by the pagan Galen.[18] Even writers defending marriage against its rejection by heretics saw continence as superior.[19] Although virgins may have been identified as a separate group already by Ignatius in the early second century,[20] the earliest asceticism seems to have been practiced individually and privately. There is no evidence of virgins living together in separate communities before the third century, but small group living arrangements earlier are not to be ruled out. Communities of celibate women did apparently precede those of men.[21] Organized monastic communities of women in the fourth century gave women opportunities for leadership and administration not often available in the larger society.

A special kind of living arrangement spawned by the ascetic impulse in the early church was "spiritual marriage," in which a man and woman (unmarried) lived in the same house as brother and sister.[22] The practice gave the woman the protection of a man in the house and was designed to provide mutual support and encouragement to the spiritual life. We know about the practice from those who warned of its dangers, even where there were the best of intentions. Cyprian, bishop of Carthage in the mid-third century, knew of couples that slept in the same bed and yet the woman claimed to be a virgin; he instructed that such be separated.[23] A few years later, the bishop of Antioch, Paul of Samosata (condemned for faulty Christology by synods in 264 and 268), left himself open to suspicion and gossip by keeping spiritual sisters in his household.[24] The fullest invective against the threat to celibacy and the danger of scandal to outsiders from "spiritual marriage" comes in two treatises by John Chrysostom (late fourth century), one directed against the men and one against the women.[25]

In the second century, the strongest advocacy within the Christian movement of a life of asceticism comes from the apocryphal Acts. As in the Hellenistic novels, similar in literary genre to the apocryphal Acts, the women are sexually attractive and inflame the desires of men, must experience great trials to protect chastity, and are delivered by a divine power through a man who does not treat them as a sex object. The reader of the *Acts of Paul, Acts of John, Acts of Thomas,* and others gains the impression that the gospel invitation was, "Repent and separate from your spouse and you will be saved." The conversion stories follow a consistent literary pattern. Names are given of women, usually wealthy and prominent, who, under the influence of the teaching of the apostles, refused to marry their betrothed or refused further sexual relations with their husbands and experienced persecution for their rejection of traditional female sociosexual roles. Although we cannot now verify the historicity of these persons, undeniable is the appeal to sexual continence as implicit within the Christian message. The life of chastity becomes a means for women to be freed from social structures based on their sexuality.[26] Women are so prominent in the apocryphal Acts, not only as ascetics but also as devoted followers of the apostles, as teachers, and as miracle workers, that some have thought that these works were written by and/or for women, even specifying the setting as groups of widows.[27]

Tertullian indicated that among the "heretics" women took a more prominent role than in the mainstream churches: "For they are bold enough to teach, to dispute, to enact exorcisms, to undertake cures—it may be even to baptize."[28] Gnostics are his probable target, and Gnostic influence is suspected in some of the apocryphal Acts. The publication of the Gnostic writings from Nag Hammadi in Egypt[29] has stimulated interest in women in Gnosticism.[30] There is an ambivalence about the feminine in these writings. Female figures are prominent in the Gnostic mythology, but a strain of antifemininity also runs through the texts,[31] and "even when the feminine is highly valued, it is often done so at the expense of real sexuality."[32] Women may have had a prominent role in Gnosticism, but it is difficult to go from these mythological texts to a sociological description of Gnostic sects. Although there were libertine

Gnostics,[33] the Nag Hammadi texts represent the ascetic alternative, and the observations on the significance of asceticism for women in other texts would apparently apply to women in ascetic Gnostic circles as well.

Literature on virginity began to appear in the third century,[34] and became a flood in the fourth.[35] Moreover, collections of stories about hermits and ascetics of the fourth and fifth centuries and collections of their sayings put us on firmer historical ground about the names and the actual attitudes and the teachings of the champions of Christian asceticism in its classical period. The sayings of three women (Theodora, Sarah, and Syncletica) are included in the *Sayings of the Desert Fathers,* and nineteen of the sixty-eight histories of hermits and monks in *The Lauisiac History of Palladius* concern women. Some of the greatest examples of female asceticism are known from the correspondence of John Chrysostom and Jerome with admired and admiring female associates in their work: Olympius (John Chrysostom), Eustochium, and others (mentioned below—Jerome).

An early ascetic discipline in which women took a lead was pilgrimage. The conversion of Constantine and the travels of his mother, Helena, to identify the historical sites of the faith opened the way for a steady stream of pilgrims to the Holy Land. The most famous of these pilgrims, and author of the most informative account, was Egeria, an ascetic woman from southern Gaul or northern Spain who made a journey to Sinai and Palestine at the turn of the fourth to the fifth century.

4. Women as Missionaries

Missionary work is pilgrimage in reverse and often involves suffering and an ascetic discipline. Clement of Alexandria (*Miscellanies* 3.6.53) refers to wives of apostles assisting in missionary work as the means through which the gospel reached the women's quarters of households. Representative of early female missionaries is a woman from the apocryphal Acts—Thecla, who could as well be treated as representative of asceticism or martyrdom.

According to the *Acts of Paul and Thecla* (part of the larger *Acts of Paul*), Thecla was converted to Paul's message, "You must fear one single God only, and live chastely" (9).[36] Thamyris, an important man in Iconium to whom she was engaged, brought charges before the governor against Paul. Paul was released after a scourging, but the governor condemned Thecla to be burned for refusing to marry Thamyris. A thunderstorm quenched the fire, however, and Thecla was saved. She said to Paul, "I will cut my hair short and follow thee wherever thou goest" (25). At Antioch a certain Alexander tried to force his attentions on Thecla, and when she refused, for a second time she was brought before a governor and condemned to death, this time, by fighting wild beasts. There was a pit full of water in the arena, and Thecla jumped in and baptized herself "in the name of Jesus Christ" (34). The beasts would not touch her, and eventually the governor released her.

Paul commissioned Thecla, "Go and teach the word of God!" (41). This section of the *Acts* concludes, "after enlightening many with the word of God she slept with a noble sleep" (43).

The most successful woman missionary of the ancient Church was Nino, "the apostle of Georgia."[37] She was a slave from Cappadocia whose miraculous healing abilities brought her to the attention of the queen of Georgia. Nino healed her in the name of Christ. Eventually the king was converted and built a church. Nino's influence brought about the conversion of the country of Georgia to Orthodox Christianity from the top down.

5. Women as Ministers

Women performed many serving functions in the early church. Organization was given to their work through the orders of widows and deaconesses. Many references to widows in early Christian literature are to women who had lost their husbands and were in need of charity. Some early passages may reflect the existence of a special order of widows.[38] Such may be implied by Ignatius's words about "virgins who are called widows."[39] Hermas refers to a woman named Grapte whose task was to instruct the widows and orphans (*Visions* 2.4.3). The association of widows and orphans here and in some other texts may be due not to the fact that these were the principal classes of needy persons but to the practice of the church in supporting widows to care for orphan children.[40] We are on firmer ground with the *Apostolic Tradition* of Hippolytus, who says about ordination of church offices:

> When a widow is appointed she is not ordained but she shall be chosen by name. . . . Let the widow be instituted by word only

and (then) let her be reckoned among the (enrolled) widows. But she shall not be ordained, because she does not offer the oblation nor has she a (liturgical) ministry. But ordination is for the clergy on account of their (liturgical) ministry. But the widow is appointed for prayer, and this is (a function) of all (Christians). (11)[41]

Hippolytus gives separate treatment to the Virgins: "(The Virgin is not appointed but voluntarily separated and named.) A Virgin does not have an imposition of hands, for personal choice alone is that which makes a Virgin" (13). From the mid-third century, the Pseudo-Clementines have Peter, when he established a church, not only ordaining a bishop, presbyters, and deacons, but also instituting the order of widows (*Recog.* 6.15; *Hom.* 11.36).

The fullest discussion of the order of widows in the Ante-Nicene literature occurs in chapters 14 and 15 of the *Didascalia*, from Syria in the third century.[42] The description, qualifications, duties, and warnings closely follow 1 Timothy 5, except that the minimum age is set at fifty. The appointed widows' responsibility was primarily to pray, but they were also to engage in benevolence and to fast, pray for, lay hands upon, and visit the sick. They were forbidden to teach and to preside at baptisms, a prohibition applying to all women, although as explained below deaconesses did assist at baptisms of women.[43]

Somewhat later the *Apostolic Church Order* distinguishes two types of work for widows:

> Three widows shall be appointed, two to persevere in prayer for all those who are in temptation, and for the reception of revelations where such are necessary, but one to assist the women visited with sickness, she must be ready for service, discreet, communicating what is necessary to the presbyters, not avaricious, not given to much love of wine, so that she may be sober and capable of performing the night services, and other loving service if she will. (5)[44]

The widows who are not able to go out and be actively involved are to stay home and spend their time in prayer; a widow able still to be active visits the sick and cares for the needy. This document seems to reject female deacons (8).

Deaconesses[45] appear to have succeeded the order of widows, at least in the eastern church.[46] "Women servants" (*ministrae*) among the Christians are referred to by Pliny the Younger in the early second century (*Epistle* 10.96.8). At the end of the century, Clement of Alexandria understood the "women" of 1 Timothy 3:11 as "women deacons."[47] Only later was the word deaconess (*diakonissa*) coined for the special order of female servants of the church.

The first description we have of deaconesses occurs in the *Didascalia* 16, where they are discussed with deacons, separately from widows but less extensively. The bishop is instructed to choose and appoint helpers, "a man for the performance of most things that are required, but a woman for the ministry of women." The deaconess could enter the women's quarters, where a man could not go, "to visit those who are sick, and to minister to them that of which they have need, and to bathe those who have begun to recover from sickness." Also, the pre-baptismal anointing (according to the Syrian rite) of the body of women was to be done by the deaconess, the bishop only anointing the head. A man pronounced the invocation of the divine names while the baptizand stood in the water. "[W]hen she who is being baptized has come up from the water, let the deaconess receive her, and teach and instruct her how the seal of baptism ought to be (kept) unbroken in purity and holiness." The fact that the Lord was ministered to by women justified the appointment of women deacons to perform things "needful and important."

Although women were denied public preaching and liturgical functions, including baptism, there were many opportunities for women to serve, e.g., private teaching.

6. Women as Mentors

Women in their capacities as wives, mothers, ascetics, missionaries, and ministers have already been observed teaching in various home and private settings, in spite of a feeling by many that women could not be trusted to teach.

There had been many places where women functioned as teachers and prophets in New Testament times, and the attempted revival of prophecy in the second-century Montanist movement gave women once more a prominent speaking ministry. Although the presence of Priscilla and Maximilla in the company of Montanus caused some raised eyebrows, the church's objections against the Montanists were not to its having female as well as male prophets but to their manner of prophesying (in ecstasy) and to the content of their messages.[48] The setting in which they did their prophesying is not clear. Even in Montanism there was no regular practice of women speaking in church. Tertullian relates that a woman who had visions during the assembly reported their contents privately after the dismissal.[49]

The most noteworthy examples of learned women who served as mentors of others come from the fourth century.[50] I select for comment here from the Greek east Gorgonia, sister of Gregory of Nazianzus, and from the Latin west Paula, close associate of Jerome.

Gregory of Nazianzus celebrated the virtues of Gorgonia in his oration for her funeral (*Oration* 8). She was married, the mother of three daughters, and won her husband, her children, and her grandchildren for the Lord. In addition to modeling the virtues of modesty, hospitality, self-denial, and charity, her intellect made her a mentor of others, even outside her family.

> What could be keener than the intellect of her who was recognized as a common advisor not only by those of her family . . . but even by all men round about, who treated her counsels and advice as a law not to be broken? What more sagacious than her words? What more prudent than her silence? . . . Who had a fuller knowledge of the things of God, both from the Divine oracles, and from her own understanding? But who was less ready to speak, confining herself within the due limits of women? [She surpassed] not only women, but the most devoted of men, by her intelligent chanting of the psalter, her converse with and unfolding and apposite recollection of the divine oracles, her bending of her knees which had grown hard and almost taken root in the ground. . . . (11, 13)[51]

Thus, in Gregory's words, she demonstrated "that the distinction between male and female is one of body and not of soul" (14).

Paula came from a noble and wealthy family in Rome, tracing her ancestry to the Gracchi and Scipios, while her husband was of the Julian family. She bore five children, one of whom, Eustochium, shared her combination of learning and asceticism and succeeded her in the direction of her monastery at Bethlehem. On her husband's death, Paula adopted a life of chastity and service to the Lord. Jerome praised her as a model of ascetic piety, commending her humility, self-restraint, patience, and perseverance.[52] Especially noteworthy was her liberality to a fault, so that she died leaving her daughter with a debt. She gave generously to the poor and built twin monasteries at Bethlehem, one for men and one for women, where she settled after a pilgrimage to the east. Jerome commended her administration of the monastery, where she was a mentor of the women under her charge, giving instruction, correction, and encouragement. She financed Jerome's studies and writings, but she was more than a patron of the learning of others. Already knowing Greek as well as her native Latin, she learned Hebrew, succeeding so well that she could chant the Psalms in Hebrew and speak the language without a trace of Latin pronunciation. She studied with Jerome to the point that she was able publicly to refute heresy.

Conclusion

Except in some heretical and schismatic groups, the churches in the early patristic period, as in the New Testament, evidence prohibitions on women speaking in the assembly and serving in leadership positions of bishop/presbyter or presiding at liturgical functions. On the other hand, in ministering functions women were actively involved and exercised leadership responsibilities in a variety of other ways.

Although the quantity of information from the early church about women is not as great as we would like, there is much that can be learned. The interest in women's studies in recent years has brought to the surface much more than previously was generally recognized. A story can be presented, if still in rough draft. This brief survey will indicate something of the scope and direction the available material provides. Women in no way played only insignificant roles in the unfolding drama of early Christianity.

*Originally printed in Carroll D. Osburn, ed., *Essays on Women in Earliest Christianity* (Joplin: College Press, 1993), 493–513.

Chapter 10 Endnotes

1. Adolf Harnack, *The Expansion of Christianity in the First Three Centuries* (New York: G. P. Putnam's Sons, 1905), 2. See 217–39 on the spread of Christianity among women.

2. Translation by K. Lake, *Apostolic Fathers* (LCL; Cambridge: Harvard University Press, 1952), 11.

3. Ibid., 287–89.

4. See Clement of Alexandria, *Miscellanies* 4.20; *Instructor* 3.11; Tertullian, *Against Marcion* 1.29; *On the Veiling of Virgins* 9.

5. *On the Apparel of Women* 1.1.

6. Translation by W.P. Le Saint, *Tertullian: Treatises on Marriage and Remarriage* (ACW 13; Westminster, MD: Newman, 1951), 35–36.

7. On Nonna and Anthusa, see Everett Ferguson, *Early Christians Speak,* Vol. 2 (Abilene: ACU Press, 2002), 267–69.

8. Translation by C. G Browne and J. E. Swallow in NPNF, Second Series (ed. P. Schaff and H. Wace; Grand Rapids: Eerdmans, 1955 reprint): 7.398. Gregory refers to Emmelia also in his *Epistle* 5 (a "great supporter of the poor") and he wrote her epitaph.

9. Robert M. Grant has studied the episode and ascribed the name of "Flora" to the woman—"A Woman of Rome: The Matron in Justin, *2 Apology* 2:1–9," CH 54 (1985): 461–72.

10. They are studied by W. H. C. Frend, "Blandina and Perpetua: Two Early Christian Martyrs," *Les Martyrs de Lyon* (177) (Paris: Centre National de la Recherche Scientifique, 1987), 167–72. For women martyrs in general, see Francine Cardman, "Acts of Women Martyrs," ATR 70 (1988): 144–50.

11. Translations by B. P. Pratten (but at one place adopting his alternative in a footnote) in ANF, 8.779–83.

12. Quoted in ibid., 784.

13. The translations from this work follow, with slight modification, R. E. Wallis in ANF, 3. In the Mursurillo edition, the reference is section 2, and other references also differ.

14. Rosemary Rader, "*The Martyrdom of Perpetua:* A Protest Account of Third Century Christianity," *A Lost Tradition: Women Writers of the Early Church* (ed. Patricia Wilson-Kastner, et al.; Washington: University Press of America, 1981), 1–32; Alvyn Peterson, "Perpetua—Prisoner of Conscience," VC 41 (1987): 139–53; J. E. Salisbury, *Perpetua's Passion: The Death and Memory of a Young Roman Woman* (New York: Routledge, 1997).

15. See David M. Scholer, "'And I Was A Man': The Power and Problem of Perpetua," *Daughters of Sarah* 15.5 (1989): 10–14. The philosophical background and

early Christian development are explored by Kerstin Aspegren and Rene Kieffer, *The Male Woman: A Feminine Ideal in the Early Church* (Uppsala, Almqvist & Wiksell, 1990): 133–39.

16. Elizabeth A. Clark, "Ascetic Renunciation and Feminine Advancement: A Paradox of Late Ancient Christianity," ATR 63 (1981): 240–57 (reprinted in the next-cited work, 175–208). She takes note of this while also sketching the ambivalence of the Church Fathers about the female sex (cursed as the source of temptation and sin yet honored as models of celibate dedication to God) in "Devil's Gateway and Bride of Christ: Women in the Early Christian World," *Ascetic Piety and Women's Faith: Essays on the Late Ancient Christianity* (Lewiston: Edwin Mellen, 1986): 23–60, esp. 25–29, 42–52. See also the introduction to her collection of texts on *Women in the Early Church* (Wilmington: Michael Glazier, 1983): 15–25. Most of these texts are from the fourth century. For a discussion of the earlier period, see Jo Ann McNamara, *A New Song: Celibate Women in the First Three Christian Centuries* (New York: Institute for Research in History, 1983); on the general theme, see *idem*, "Sexual Equality and the Cult of Virginity in Early Christian Thought," *Feminist Studies* 3 (1967): 145–58. Cf. a different view in T. K. Seim, "Ascetic Autonomy? New Perspectives on Single Women in the Early Church," ST 43 (1989): 125–40.

17. Justin, *1 Apology* 15, 29; Athenagoras, *Plea* 33.

18. Richard Walzer, *Galen on Jews and Christians* (London: Oxford University, 1949), 15.

19. Especially as applied to second marriages (Tertullian, *Exhortation to Chastity*; *On Monogamy; On Modesty*). See Origen's evaluation of virginity as the foremost sacrifice one could offer to God (*Commentary on Romans* 9). Clement of Alexandria has the most favorable comments about marriage among early Christian authors, placing it and celibacy on the same level as pertains to salvation (*Miscellanies* 3).

20. *Smyrn.* 13, but included in the order of widows, for which see below; see Polycarp, *Phil.* 5.

21. Athanasius, *Life of Antony* 3.

22. The practice has not received much study in recent literature, but see Rosemary Rader, *Breaking Boundaries: Male/Female Friendship in the Early Christian Communities* (New York: Paulist, 1983): 62–71, and Elizabeth A. Clark, "John Chrysostom and the Subintroductae," CH 46 (1977): 171–85; Blake Leyerle, *Theatrical Shows and Ascetic Lives: John Chrysostom's Attack on Spiritual Marriage* (Berkeley: University of California Press, 2001).

23. *Epistle* 4; see Pseudo-Cyprian, *De singularitate clericorum*; Psuedo-Clement, *Two Epistles on Virginity* 1.10–13; 2.1–5; *Epistle of Titus*.

24. Eusebius, *Church History* 7.30.12–14.

25. See Elizabth A. Clark, *Jerome, Chrysostom, and Friends: Essays and Translations* (New York: Edwin Mellon, 1979): 158–348.

26. For this paragraph, see Ross S. Kraemer, "The Conversion of Women to Ascetic Forms of Christianity," *Signs* 6 (1980): 298–307; see also V. Burrus, *Chastity as Autonomy: Women in the Stories of the Apocryphal Acts* (Lewiston: Edwin Mellen, 1987).

27. Stevan L. Davies, *The Revolt of the Widows: The Social World of the Apocryphal Acts* (Carbondale: Southern Illinois University, 1980); Dennis MacDonald, ed., *The Apocryphal Acts of the Apostles, Semeia* 38 (1986), esp. 43–52 on the composition of the *Acts of Thecla* and 101–35 on women in the apocryphal Acts.

28. *On Prescription Against Heretics* 41; trans. by Peter Holmes in ANF, 3.263.

29. English translation in James Robinson, ed., *The Nag Hammadi Library* (rev. ed.; San Francisco: Harper, 1988).

30. Karen King, ed., *Images of the Feminine in Gnosticism* (Philadelphia: Fortress, 1988).

31. Frederik Wisse, "Flee Femininity: Antifemininity in the Gnostic Texts and the Question of Social Milieu," ibid., 297–307.

32. King, ibid., xvii.

33. James E. Goehring, "Libertine or Liberated: Women in the So-called Libertine Gnostic Communities," ibid., 329–44.

34. Cyprian, *On the Dress of Virgins;* Pseudo-Clement, *Two Epistles on Virginity.*

35. See Clark, *Women in the Early Church,* esp. ch. 3, and Rader, *Breaking Boundaries,* 72–110. Notable is Methodius, *Symposium* (ca. 300) because it presents the speeches in favor of virginity as spoken by women.

36. The translation is from E. Hennecke and W. Schneemelcher, *New Testament Apocrypha* (rev. ed.; trans. R. McL. Wilson; Louisville: Westminster, 1992): 2.240. On Thecla, see Aspegren, *The Male Woman,* 99–114, 158–64.

37. The subject of the inaugural address at the Ninth International Conference of Patristic Studies at Oxford, 1983, by Fairy von Lillienfeld was "St. Nino, Apostle and Illuminator of Georgia." I have not seen the articles (in English) about her in the *Journal of the Moscow Patriarchate* 2 (1985): 77–82 and 3 (1986): 49–56.

38. See 1 Tim. 5:3ff. C. H. Turner, "Ministries of Women in the Primitive Church: Widow, Deaconess and Virgin in the First Four Christian Centuries," *Catholic and Apostolic* (ed. H. N. Bate; London: Mowbray, 1931): 316–51; B. B. Thurston, *The Widows—A Women's Ministry in the Early Church* (Minneapolis: Fortress, 1989).

39. *Smyrn.* 13. J. B. Lightfoot understands this as referring to widows who by purity of life were really virgins rather than to virgins incorporated into the order of widows—*Apostolic Fathers* 2.2 (London: Macmillan, 1885): 323–24. On the other hand, Tertullian, *On the Veiling of Virgins* 9, knows "that in a certain place a virgin of less than twenty years of age has been placed in the order of widows." This may be a clue as to how the order of widows in the New Testament became Virgins later, viz., the widows had to remain unmarried and soon those who had not married took the same vow.

40. See Lucian, *The Passing of Peregrinus* 12.

41. I follow the translation of Gregory Dix, *The Apostolic Tradition of St. Hippolytus* (London: SPCK, 1968), 20–21.

42. R. H. Connolly, *Didascalia Apostolorum* (Oxford: Clarendon, 1929).

43. Tertullian concurred in objecting to women baptizing (*On Baptism* 17; *On the Veiling of Virgins* 9), but there are reports of women among the Montanists baptizing (Cyprian, *Epistle* 74.10).

44. A. Harnack, *Sources of the Apostolic Canons* (London: Black, 1895), 19–21.

45. A. G. Martimort, *Deaconesses: An Historical Study* (San Francisco: Ignatius, 1986).

46. *Canons of Basil* 24, "A widow put into the catalogue of widows, that is, a deaconess."

47. *Miscellanies* 3.6.53; or does he mean the widows of 1 Timothy 5:9–11?

48. Eusebius, *Church History* 5.16–18; Epiphanius, *Panarion* 48. See all the relevant texts now conveniently classified in Ronald E. Heine, *The Montanist Oracles and Testimonia* (Macon: Mercer University Press, 1989); William Tabbernee, *Montanist Inscriptions and Testimonia* (Macon, GA: Mercer University Press, 1997).

49. *On the Soul* 9. For celebrating the Eucharist and baptizing, see Cyprian, *Epistle* 71.10; Didymus the Blind, *Trinity* 3.41.3; Epiphanius, *Panarion* 49.2.

50. I discussed Macrina the Younger (Gregory of Nyssa, *Life of Macrina*), whom Gregory calls "teacher" (*On the Soul and the Resurrection*), and Marcella (Jerome, *Letter* 127), with whom Jerome discussed scholarly questions, *in Early Christians Speak*, 2.270–72, 275–77.

51. Translation by C. G. Browne and J. E. Swallow in NPNF, Second Series, VII: 241–42.

52. Jerome, *Letter* 108.

Part II

Baptism and Initiation

11

Baptismal Motifs in the Ancient Church

The design of this paper will be to lay out some of the important doctrinal conceptions associated with baptism in the early centuries of the church. An examination will be made to determine which motifs can be traced back to the New Testament. We are thus presented with an opportunity to test the validity of using the practices and teaching at the early church as a tool in the interpretation of New Testament texts. Then, how the doctrinal conceptions found expression in the baptismal ceremony will be shown. Our grouping of the motifs is largely arbitrary, but in general they relate to the preparation, performance, and effects of baptism.

Motifs of Conversion: Faith and Repentance

The catechetical instruction given candidates for baptism was an essential part of the preparation for the rite.[1] Justin states that baptism is for "as many as are persuaded and believe that what we teach and say is true, and undertake to be able to live accordingly."[2]

Faith was the essential subjective condition of pardon. Regeneration according to Justin was through "water, faith, and wood."[3] Gregory of Nyssa writing *On the Holy Spirit* states concerning baptism that "belief in our Lord must precede." Baptism as an act of faith is seen in the accompanying verbal confession: "When we have entered the water, we make profession of the Christian faith in the words of its rule."[4] "You were led to the holy pool of divine baptism . . . and each of you was asked, whether he believed in the name of the Father and of the Son and of the Holy Spirit, and you made that saving confession."[5]

The close connection of faith and baptism in the New Testament is apparent in Galatians 3:26f. and Colossians 2:12. In Hebrews 10:19–22 we have the same grouping of faith, water, and the blood (of the cross) as in Justin. The confession with the mouth of the faith in the heart is expressed in Romans 10:9f. This profession of faith may be the "word" which accompanies the water in Ephesians 5:19.[6] "Calling upon the name of the Lord" (as in Acts 22:16) may be a reference to the baptismal confession and the basis for speaking of baptism as "in the name of Christ."

Baptism was also viewed as an act of repentance. Justin describes the one being baptized as him who "chooses to be reborn and repents of his sins."[7] Thus Hermas speaks of the "repentance . . . which takes place when we descended into the water."[8] Benoit has developed the relationship of repentance and baptism in the apostolic fathers—Hermas, *Barnabas*, *1* and *2 Clement*.[9] The last three of these writers view the Christian life as a life of penitence, so that baptism is not only a result of repentance but an act committing one to a penitent life. Even as baptism is an act of repentance, so the life it inaugurates is one of faith and repentance.[10] Later, Cyril of Jerusalem can speak of believing in the "one baptism of repentance."[11] The same writer applies the terminology of putting off the old and putting on the new to baptismal repentance:

> You had a penitence of forty (days); you had full time to put off, and to wash yourself, to put on, and to enter in. But if you abide in your evil purpose . . . you must not look for grace: for though the water shall receive you, the Spirit will not accept you.[12]

> At the holy laver of regeneration God has wiped away every tear from off all faces. For you shall no more mourn, now that you have put off the old man; you shall keep holy-day, clothed in the garment of salvation, even Jesus Christ.[13]

In the New Testament John's baptism was a "baptism of repentance" (Mark 1:4), and the command of Peter was "repent and be baptized" (Acts 2:38). The "putting off and putting on" of Colossians 2 and 3 continues the baptismal imagery of 2:12 and may be considered an elucidation of performing "deeds worthy of repentance" (Acts 26:20; cf. the white robes of the redeemed in Hermas, *Sim.* 8.2).

The repentance, as a renunciation of the devil, and the profession of faith, as an adherence to Christ, were viewed as a pledge of allegiance, a promise, a contract. Justin describes baptism as "the manner in which we dedicated ourselves to God" (*1 Apol.* 61). Tertullian, *De Baptismo* 18, indicates that the confession of faith was a promise.[14] But Theodore of Mopsuestia's *Sermons on the Lord's Prayer and the Sacraments* 2 and 3 give the fullest discussion of the baptismal ceremony as a contract with God to live in harmony with his commands.[15] This understanding of the baptismal rite, and especially of the profession of faith, as marking a new loyalty may provide the proper explanation of the "answer of a good conscience" in 1 Peter 3:21. Bo Reicke has shown that *eperōtēma* often means an "agreement," "undertaking," or "contract," and so would translate "an agreement about," or "an undertaking to" a good conscience (genitive of content).[16]

Thus the profession of faith marks a new allegiance, a change of relationship, and so is the counterpart, on the human side of the triadic formula by which the divine "name is called upon"[17] the one being baptized. From the earliest post-apostolic times in *Didache* 7,[18] the consistent testimony is to baptism administered "in the name of the Father, Son, and Holy Spirit."[19] By baptism, believers are brought under the authority or control of God; by imposing his name upon the person, God lays a claim to his life.[20] The formula expressed God's ownership.[21] One now wore Christ's name. "May you then enjoy the fragrant waters which bear Christ: may you then receive Christ's name and the efficacious power of divine things."[22]

The origin of triple immersion is obscure, but its widespread practice from at least the end of the second century is a good illustration of how the doctrine of baptism was made explicit in the ritual. To the verbal confession was added the bodily confession, each immersion expressing the faith in one divine person. Our fullest early account reads as follows:

> Let him who baptizes lay hand on him saying thus:
> Do you believe in God the Father Almighty?
> And he who is being baptized shall say:
> I believe.
> Let him forthwith baptize him once. . . .
> And after this let him say:
> Do you believe in Christ Jesus, the Son of God. . . ?
> And when he says: I believe, let him baptize him the second time.
> And again let him say:
> Do you believe in the Holy Spirit. . . ?
> And he who is being baptized shall say: I believe.
> And so let him baptize him the third time.[23]

Tertullian states, "And indeed it is not once only but three times that we are baptized at each separate name into each separate person."[24] Ambrose brings the baptizing into close relation with the confession: "You were baptized in the name of the Trinity, you confessed the Father—remember what you did—you confessed the Son, you confessed the Holy Spirit."[25]

Preceding the baptismal confession of faith there was a verbal renunciation of the devil.[26] The wording varies, but "I renounce you, Satan, and all your service and all your works"[27] is typical. This was followed by "I adhere to you, O Christ" in some rites.[28] One faced west for the renunciation and turned east for the adherence and so enacted repentance.[29] The renunciation was connected with the removal of the clothing for baptism. "You put off your garment; and this was an image of putting off the old man with his deeds."[30]

Motif of Cleansing: Washing

Water was prominent in the ceremonial cleansings of the Old Testament and in the purification ceremonies of pagan antiquity.[31] And the early church spoke of baptism as a washing.[32] Justin explains, "For in the name of God, the Father and Lord of the universe, and of our Saviour Jesus Christ, and of the Holy Spirit, they then receive the washing with water."[33]

Christians made clear that their cleansing was not external. Tertullian puts the idea succinctly, "The flesh indeed is washed, in order that the soul may be cleansed."[34] The favorite way of describing the moral value of baptism was in terms of a remission or forgiveness of sins.[35] Irenaeus states, "The faith above all teaches us that we have received baptism for the forgiveness of sins."[36] The phrase "baptism for (unto) the remission of sins" is fairly common.[37] *Barnabas* expressly contrasts this feature with the deficiency of the Jewish washings.[38]

The cleansing, purifying effect of baptism is attributed, not to the water, but to the Holy Spirit. Cyprian declares, "For water alone is not able to cleanse away sins, and to sanctify a man, unless he has also the Holy Spirit."[39] Gregory of Nyssa asks the following:

> Is that life-giving power in the water itself...? Or is it not rather clear to every one that this element...of itself contributes nothing towards the sanctification unless it be first transformed itself by the sanctification and that what gives life to the baptized is the Spirit.[40]

Tertullian describes pagan cleansings as "widowed waters."[41] Also common is the attributing of the efficacy of the water to the invocation of the triune name.[42]

The New Testament often employs the cleansing motif. In Ephesians 5:26, the church is saved "by the washing of water," and in Titus 3:5, salvation is the "washing of regeneration." "Our bodies washed with pure water" of Hebrews 10:22, is phrased on the model of Old Testament washings. "Not the putting away of the filth of the flesh" in 1 Peter 3:21, contrasts the bodily purification with the purpose of Christian baptism. The Holy Spirit as the active agent in baptism is implied in several passages (John 3:5; Titus 3:5; 1 Cor. 12:13).

The act of baptism itself, of course, suggested the ideas of bathing, cleansing, and purifying. In the later ritual, the idea of cleansing was reinforced by the clothing of the newly baptized in white garments for their entrance into the assembly.[43]

The Christian Victory: Death and the Devil

The strongest expression for conversion, the turning from evil, is in the figure of dying. This was a favorite conception with the compiler of the *Apostolic Constitutions*:

> This baptism therefore is given into the death of Jesus: the water is instead of the burial . . . the descent into the water the dying together with Christ; the ascent out of the water the rising again with him.[44]

> Look down from heaven and sanctify this water and give it grace and power, so that he that is baptized according to the command of your Christ, may be crucified with him, and may die with him, and may be buried with him and may rise with him to the adoption which is in him, that he may be dead to sin and live to righteousness.[45]

This figure of dying with Christ and being raised with him, obviously drawn from Romans 6:3f., was noticeably absent from second-century literature.[46]

There is more to the conception than a symbolism of individual psychological experience. A real community with Christ is established, for Christ is present and his death is actualized in baptism.[47] One of the favorite descriptions of the benefits of baptism (as we have seen) was pardon or the forgiveness of sins.[48] This was also the achievement of the cross.[49] *Barnabas* is our earliest post-apostolic writer to bring the two ideas into rapport: baptism as the subjective appropriation of the remission of sins objectively accomplished by the death on the cross. "Let us further inquire whether the Lord took any care to foreshadow the water and the cross. . . . Blessed are those who, placing their trust in the cross, have gone down into the water."[50] Justin, as pointed out above—in agreement with Hebrews 10—connects baptism on one side with the blood of Christ as the divine work of purification and on the other with faith, which concerns the manner by which man is prepared to receive it.[51] A later writer states, "Giving thanks that he undertook to die for all men by the cross, the type of which he has appointed to be the baptism of regeneration."[52] Baptism therefore was regarded as more than one's dying to sin in repentance—it brought one into saving contact with the death on the cross.

In the New Testament, baptism is "for the remission of sins" (Acts 2:38) as also is the shedding of Christ's blood (Matt. 26:28). Baptism and the death of Christ are in close relation also in 1 John 5:6–8; Ephesians 5:25f.; and Hebrews 10:19–22. The designation of baptism as a "death" may be based on the very words of Jesus about his own death—Mark 10:38; Luke 12:50.[53]

Underlying this identification of death and baptism was yet another conception. In ancient mythology the sea was the kingdom of the dead and to die was to go down into the waters of death.[54] Thus the connection between the baptism of Jesus and his death on the cross was a natural one. Recent scholars have called attention to the baptism of Jesus as an announcement of the Passion.[55] And the convert's immersion was a passing through the realm of death.

But death is especially the domain of the devil. In the early church, Christ's death and resurrection were a victory over the demonic forces of evil. Serapion's statement, "By which cross Satan and every opposing power was routed and triumphed over" (*Prayer* 16), is in a baptismal context.[56] Colossians 2:15 (once more a baptismal context—v. 12), is the classic New Testament text for this idea. Christ's baptism too was thought of as a victory over the demonic forces dwelling in the water (the symbol of death).[57] Even so, in the Christian's baptism "liberty is restored" from the "evil one who had brought them into the slavery" of sin.[58] In *Barnabas* 16.8, the soul is a house of demons until the forgiveness of sins makes one a new creature. The baptismal formula of the divine name was considered efficacious in dispelling demons.[59]

A New Testament reflection of this type of thinking may be found in 1 Peter 3:18ff. According to this viewpoint there would be no digression, but a logical progression, in Peter's moving from a descent of Christ into a description of Christian baptism, the symbolism of the waters of death providing the transition.[60] It is not hard to find baptismal allusions in Luke 11:24–26, and the passage becomes very meaningful in the framework of ideas we have been considering. Baptism as a death required no special elaboration in the ceremony, for the action of immersion amply suggested the idea.[61]

Baptism as a deliverance from the power of Satan may be seen in two ceremonies. An elaborate series of exorcisms preceded the baptism itself.[62] And the power of God was evoked in blessing and purifying the water in which the baptism was to take place.[63] These rites supplanted mention of baptism itself expelling demons in most texts. Nevertheless, the prominence, frequency of notice, and importance given to these rites show how real was the fear of demons and how closely their power was associated with water in the early days of the church. The victory won by Christ in their own element gave a basis for the Christian hope of life through water.

Motifs of the New Life: Resurrection and Rebirth

The concept of newness, a new beginning, is quite prominent in early Christianity. Completing the imagery of baptism as a death was the baptismal resurrection. The earlier cited passages are applicable here, to which we may add Narsai's statement that in baptism the resurrection is preached.[64]

Much more frequent, indeed one of the favorite baptismal conceptions, is the idea of the new birth. John 3:5 was the favorite text on baptism in the second century,[65] and Benoit states that it is the best commentary on Irenaeus's baptismal theology.[66] *The History of John Son of Zebedee* speaks of the one baptized as a "firstling" and later as one who has "become a youth." Cyril describes him as "true born," as receiving the "life giving baptism," in the "laver of regeneration," and receiving the new name "Christian" at the new birth.[57] In the *Apostolic Constitutions* VII.45, the newly baptized signifies his new sonship by reciting the "Our Father." Theodore of Mopsuestia speaks of the "water of second birth" and calls the water a "womb."[68] These are but some of the more striking statements which show the unanimous understanding of the ancient church about John 3:5. And this verse is but another bringing together of the ideas of sonship and the gift of the Holy Spirit with baptism also to be seen in the baptism of Jesus (Matt. 3:16ff.).[69]

The word for "regeneration" in Titus 3:5 is not related to the new birth concept, but to the idea of a new creation; it is baptism that brings one into the new age.[70]

Once more the symbolism of the resurrection was implicit in the act and required no additional ceremonial expression. The new birth motif may be found in certain other actions. The removal of the clothes was identified with the stripping off of sin (as seen above), but proceeding from the water unclothed could suggest a birth. Narsai, who also employs the penitence motif, says, "As a babe from the midst of the womb he looks forth from the water; and instead of garments the priest receives him and embraces him."[71] The practice of giving milk and honey (the food of infants) to the newly baptized at their first Eucharist may also be seen as carrying out the new birth motif. Tertullian explains, "When we are taken up as newborn children, we taste first of all a mixture of milk and honey."[72] The milk and honey also remind one of entering the land of promise (*Barnabas* 6.13), and that may be the idea behind this liturgical practice.[73]

Motifs Associated with the Holy Spirit: The Seal and Illumination

If baptism is the driving out of the evil spirits of demons, something positive must be put into the life. Moreover, the Holy Spirit is the power of renewal in the motifs of the new life. Many writers connect the bestowing of the Holy Spirit with baptism.[74] The phrase "baptism of the Holy Spirit" is used for water baptism at which time the Holy Spirit is conferred.[75] The Holy Spirit is the distinctive gift of Christian baptism distinguishing it from other washings.[76] The Holy Spirit as the gift of baptism (Acts 2:38) or as the agent of the renewing power of baptism (John 3:5; Titus 3:5) is clearly the New Testament teaching also.

Especially related to the gift of the Holy Spirit in baptism is the terminology of the "seal." "The seal then is the water" in Hermas, *Similitude* 9.16.4, is perhaps the first allusion to this concept.[77] But it is especially in *2 Clement* that *sphragis* ("seal") is synonymous with baptism.[78] Benoit concludes that by "seal," *2 Clement* simply means baptism in all of its implications, not one notion such as the Holy Spirit alone.[79] But more often the baptismal "seal" refers to the gift of the Holy Spirit.[80]

After Tertullian identified the bestowal of the Holy Spirit with the post-baptismal imposition of hands[81] rather than with the baptism itself, the seal became especially the word for the signing with oil.[82] From this separation of baptism from the gift of the Holy Spirit came the separate sacrament of confirmation.

In the New Testament, the "seal" is the Holy Spirit (Eph. 4:30; 1:13f; 2 Cor. 1:22); but, since the Holy Spirit was given in baptism, there was a close connection accounting for the application of the term later to the baptismal ceremony. The association with the Holy Spirit seems to have been fairly constant. As long as the gift of the Holy Spirit was still connected with baptism, that rite was called the "seal," and, when the gift of the Spirit was separated from baptism, the anointing became the "seal."

The seal and illumination are united in the phrase from the *Epistle of the Apostles,* "the light of the seal."[83] Whereas the "seal" was popular with the common people, the terminology of "illumination" is found mainly in more educated circles.[84]

Illumination, or enlightenment, is especially the work of the Holy Spirit. On the basis of association of ideas Benoit finds the motif of illumination in *1 Clement, 2 Clement,* and Hermas.[85] The knowledge of God by faith and eternal life are prominent in the complex of ideas dominated by "light." However, it is in Justin that we meet for the first time *phōtismos* ("illumination") as a designation for baptism.[86] But he uses it as a traditional term equivalent to baptism. Justin explains it as a rational, intellectual illumination. According to this explanation the illumination would seem to be produced by the catechumenate and would be applied to baptism as that which summarizes, confirms, and manifests what has taken place in the catechumenate. A second possibility (and the two ideas are not mutually exclusive) is the gift of the Spirit. The vision of God is a grace made possible by the illumination of the Holy Spirit.[87] The concept of spiritual illumination prevails over that of intellectual illumination. Tertullian says that the soul is "enlightened by the Holy Spirit."[88] Thus I see in this terminology the light of God which now fills one's life and prepares for the eschatological vision of God.

The normal reference of illumination to baptism makes probable a similar reference in Hebrews 10:32 and 6:4f. It is to be noted that the grouping of spiritual blessings in 6:4, 5 are benefits of the Holy Spirit. The enlightenment motif may also be present in the healing of the blind man in John 9, a story otherwise full of baptismal allusions and a favorite in the symbolism of baptism in early Christian art.[89]

The conception of the giving of the Holy Spirit was made concrete in the ceremony of anointing with oil, a traditional symbol of the Holy Spirit even in biblical times. "The oil instead of the Holy Spirit"[90] is one writer's description of the outward action for the spiritual reality.

Not only was the term "sealing" applied to the anointing or signing with oil,[91] but it was also used of the invocation of the triune name at baptism.[92] Since the "seal" was a mark of ownership[93] and the baptismal formula signified the same thing, there was a mingling of motifs, a phenomenon not at all unusual.

The illumination was made vivid in the ceremony by leading the newly baptized out of the darkened baptismal chamber into a room filled with lights.[94]

Conclusion

The most frequent conceptions of the earlier second century—remission of sins and the bestowal of the Holy Spirit[95]—may fairly be considered the main themes of the New Testament in connection with baptismal blessings.[96] In time, the new birth and the dying and rising with Christ assume the largest roles—perhaps because of a superficial similarity with the pagan mysteries. Remission of sins became explained in reference to original sin after the spread of infant baptism.[97] This practice also relegated the ideas of faith and repentance to a purely formal connection with baptism. The victory over Satan became attached to the pre-baptismal exorcisms and the bestowal of the Holy Spirit was attached to the post-baptismal rites of confirmation. Of the less common motifs, the "seal" found its future in the sacrament of confirmation and other signings with oil, and "illumination" had its future as a theme in Christian mysticism.[98]

The use of early church literature in interpreting New Testament teaching has the danger of reading later concepts back into the New Testament. There is often the possibility that a writer is quoting a passage to support a later interpretation or practice without preserving the original meaning or framework or thought. Nonetheless, when used with discretion and critical skill, the literature of the early church offers a valuable aid in New Testament interpretation and gives perspective to its total teaching. At the same time the New Testament balance may show the shifting emphases of later times and thus alert believers to the necessity of maintaining not only scriptural conceptions but also the scriptural relationships and proportions in regard to these conceptions.

It is seldom clear which came first—ritual action (which came to be connected with a doctrine) or the doctrine (which was taught through the ceremony). Tertullian's embarrassment over the multiplication of rites in connection with baptism seems to be behind his separating the bestowal of the Holy Spirit from the remission of sins so as to give a doctrinal explanation to the existing rites of anointing and imposition of hands. An anointing was part of the regular bathing procedure. Also, the taking off and putting on of clothes may be regarded as necessary parts of the rite to which doctrinal explanation was given. On the other hand, the giving of milk and honey may have been added to carry out a theme. Exorcism and blessing the water were extensions of ideas connected with the efficacy of baptism. The general course of religious history is that actions precede doctrines, and it may just be lack of information that prevents our seeing this sequence in each instance. Yet it is not unknown that ritual prescriptions were adopted as teaching devices; indeed much the same thinking is involved in giving doctrinal content to previously existing or necessary actions.

*Originally printed in *Restoration Quarterly* 7 (1963): 202–16. The substance of this paper was read at the Biblical Forum at Abilene Christian College, February 1964.

Since the first draft of this paper was prepared, I have received and read J. Ysebaert, *Greek Baptismal Terminology* (Nijmegen: Dekker & Van de Vegt, 1962). This work will now be a standard reference work in its field. Compare this writer's review in *Restoration Quarterly* 7 (1963): 253–57. In general his linguistic analysis supports conclusions I have reached from a motif approach—for a notable example the separation of *palingenesia* from the rebirth concept (130ff.). I would register a strong dissent to his separation of the "gift of the Holy Spirit" from baptism (252ff.). Some account of Ysebaert's notable contributions will be taken in the footnotes.

For a fuller discussion of the motifs of baptism see the author's *Baptism in the Early Church: History, Theology, and Liturgy in the First Five Centuries* (Grand Rapids: Eerdmans, 2009), where the subject index will identify major discussions.

Chapter 11 Endnotes

1. *Did.* 1–6 may represent a model for pre-baptismal catechesis. A clear description is found in the *Apostolic Tradition* 16–19 and documents dependent upon it such as the *Canons of Hippolytus* and the *Apostolic Constitutions*. The catechetical lectures of Cyril of Jerusalem (or, in part, his successor John), John Chrysostom, and Augustine, among others, have come down to us. The earliest catechetical instruction appears to have been moral in content; the lectures of the later men are more doctrinal.

2. *1 Apol.* 61.

3. *Dialogue* 138.

4. Tertullian, *De Spectaculis* 4. Joseph Crehan, *Early Christian Baptism and the Creed* (London: Burns, Oates and Washbourne, 1950) for fuller evidence on the confession of faith.

5. Cyril Jerus., *Mystagogical Catechesis* ii.4. When infant baptism was practiced, sponsors made the confession on behalf of the child, for example in the *Barberini Euchologion* of the Byzantine Rite, written c. 790, translated by E. C. Whitaker, *Documents of the Baptismal Liturgy* (SPCK: London, 1960; 3rd edition by Maxwell Johnson, Collegeville, MN: Liturgical, 2003), 68. Cf. Tertullian, *De Baptismo* 18.

6. Cf. B. F. Westcott, *St. Paul's Epistle to the Ephesians* (Grand Rapids: Wm.B. Eerdmans, 1952), in loc. for this interpretation. This view brings the passage into relation with other passages where the value of baptism is connected with the moral response of the convert—Acts 2:38; Gal. 3:26f.; Col. 2:12; 1 Pet. 3:21. The other interpretation for which there is support in the baptismal ceremony of the early church, that the "word" is the formula, finds no support in the New Testament. It would be consistent with other New Testament passages to refer this "word" to the preached gospel, but this finds little support in patristic exegesis; see Cyril Jerus., *Cat. Lect.* iii 5.

7. Justin, *1 Apol.* 61.

8. Hermas, *Mand.* IV.3.

9. André Benoit, *Le Baptême Chrétien au Second Siècle* (Paris: Presses Universitaires de France, 1953).

10. In Hermas and, as Benoit argues, in some passages in Justin and Irenaeus a different view of repentance is taken—an act rather than an attitude, a temporary rather than an enduring state. Here baptism commits you not to a life of penitence but to a life without sin. "This notion certainly differs from that of the Synoptics where *metanoia* is a dynamic notion, an attitude, which has its origin in a precise act but characterizes the whole life of believing"—Benoit, 156. The thought of Hermas was the starting point for the sacrament of penance, a second "baptism" bringing forgiveness of post-baptismal sins. The view that repentance inaugurates a life offers a different solution to the problem of sins committed after baptism: the continuing effects of baptism, as of the death of Christ, means that one appropriates the pardon continually by the same things that give baptism its initial value, namely, faith and repentance.

11. Cyril Jerus., *Mys. Cat.* i.9.

12. *Procatechesis* 4.

13. *Mys. Cat.* i.10.

14. In *Ad Martyras* 3 Tertullian compares the profession of faith to the taking of an oath as a soldier does on entering military service. For baptism as a contract see *De Bapt.* 6.

15. See Crehan, *Early Christian Baptism*, ch. 5. Chrysostom, *Cat. Bapt.* II.17, 21, 22 speaks of the renunciation and adherence as an "agreement." In the Byzantine rite they are called a "contract" (Whitaker, ibid., 62). May Pliny's description (*Ep.* X.96) that "it was their habit on a fixed day to assemble before daylight and recite by turns a form of words to Christ as a god; and that they bound themselves with an oath . . . ." refer to a baptismal instead of a communion service? So, Crehan, 176f.; contra, R. P. Martin, "The Bithynian Christians' Carmen Christo," *Studia Patristica* 8 (1966): 159-165. Cf. Origen, *Exhortation to Martyrdom* 17 for baptism as an "agreement."

16. Bo Reicke, *The Disobedient Spirits and Christian Baptism* (Copenhagen,1946), 182ff.

17. Justin, *1 Apol.* 61.

18. Benoit, *op. cit.,* 7ff., says the triadic expression here is the baptismal formula, whereas "name of the Lord" in 9.5 is a summary statement of the character of the baptism (Christian baptism in contrast to other kinds). This is a distinction which would seem to hold true generally.

19. Matthew 28:19 is the only verbal formula attested for use at baptism in the earliest literature— Irenaeus, *Demonstration* 3; the baptisms in the *Acts of Judas Thomas; History of John Son of Zebedee; Acts of Xanthippe and Polyxena* 2 and 21; *Didascalia* 16; *Apos. Const.* VII.44.1; *Can. Hipp.* 133, to mention but a few of the references. For other references, see Crehan, 78ff. and F. H. Ely, "The Lord's Command to Baptize (St. Matthew xxviii 19)," *Journal of Theological Studies* 8 (1907): 161–84 (patristic texts on "to baptize into name" meaning "to baptize into" quoted on 173–76).

20. Cullen I. K. Story, "Justin's Apology I.62–64: Its Importance for the Author's Treatment of Christian Baptism," *Vigiliae Christianae* XVI (1962), 172–78. The author calls attention to Justin's triple repetition of *onoma;* the name of each divine person is imposed upon the baptizand.

21. Cf. J. H. Moulton and George Milligan, *The Vocabulary of the Greek Testament* (London: Hodder and Stoughton, 1930), 451. Ysebaert, *op. cit.,* 48–51 treats *eis to onoma* and *en to onoma*, as both telic, "with a view to." He notes the rabbinic phrase used in such a way that one now has the name of that "into the name of which" he was baptized.

22. Cyril, *Procat.* 15. On the other hand, in the *Mys. Cat.* iii.1 disciples are said properly to be called "Christs" because they are anointed with oil. The name "Christian" is also derived from the practice of anointing in *Apos. Const.* III.16. Cf.

Tert., *De Bapt.* 7. Since anointings preceded baptism, the name "Christians" came to be applied to the catechumens awaiting baptism—Augustine, *Tract. in St. Jn.* 44.2.

23. *Apos. Trad.* 21.

24. *Adv. Praxean* 26. In *De Corona* 3 Tertullian writes, "We are thrice immersed, replying somewhat more fully than the Lord has appointed in the Gospel." Does Tertullian mean the triple immersion (Matt. 28:19) or the triple confession (Matt. 10:32) is fuller than the gospel requires?

25. Ambrose, *De Mysteriis* 21. Cf. 28 and *De Sacramentis* II.20. It should be noted that some writers refer the trine immersion to the three days burial of Christ—Cyril, *Mys. Cat.* ii.4; Narsai, *Hom.* 21; Gregory Nyssa, *On the Baptism of Christ.* Crehan, 107.

26. *Apos. Trad.* 21.9; Tert., *De Spec.* 4; *De Cor.* 3; Cyril, *Mys. Cat.* 1.2–8; Serapion, *Prayer* 9; Ambrose, *De Sac.* I.4f.; *De Mys.* 5.7.

27. *Apos. Trad.* 21.9.

28. *Apos. Const.* VII.40f.; Chrysostom, *Cat. Bapt.* 11.18, 20.

29. Cyril, *Mys. Cat.* i.9; Narsai, *Hom.* 22.

30. Cyril, *Mys. Cat.* ii.2.

31. For a survey of the terminology, Ysebaert, *op. cit.*, 12–39.

32. Ambrose, *De Sac.* I.9 and *De Mys.* 21; Serapion, *Prayer* 10 and 15; *Acts of Xanthippe and Polyxena* 2.21; the "Baptism of the Priests of Artemis" in *History of John Son of Zebedee.*

33. *1 Apol.* 61; cf. ch. 65.

34. *De R. Carn.* 8.

35. For example, Hermas, *Mand.* IV.3; Justin, *1 Apol.* 61; Theophilus, *Ad Autolycum* II.16; Tert., *De Bapt.* 18; *Apos. Trad.* 22.1; Cyril, *Procat.* 9, 15 ; Narsai, *Hom.* 21.

36. *Dem.* 3; cf. also ch. 41.

37. *Clem. Hom.* XI.27; Clem. Alex., *Paed.* I.vi (note in the same chapter, the "washing by which we cleanse away our sins"). Other references in Ysebaert, *op. cit.*, 69.

38. *Barn.* 11.

39. *Ep.* 73.5; cf. Iren., *Adv. Haer.* III.17.2. See further the references in footnote 63.

40. *On the Holy Spirit.* For the sanctification of the waters by the invocation of the Holy Spirit, see endnotes 45 and 63.

41. *De Bapt.* 5.

42. Narsai, *Hom.* 21, "The defilement of men he cleanses with water; yet not by water, but by the power of the Name of the Divinity.... The names give forgiveness of iniquity." Note the claim in the rebaptism controversy of the third century that the baptismal formula gave baptism its efficacy—Cyp., *Epp.* 72–74.

43. *History of John Son of Zebedee;* Theod. Mops., *Serm.* 4 *On the Lord's Prayer and the Sacraments*; Ambrose, *De Mys.* 34.

44. III.17

45. VII.43.5

46. Benoit, *op. cit.*, 227. Was this the avoidance of a common pagan conception?

47. Per Lundberg, *La Typologie Baptismale dans l'Ancienne Église* (Uppsala: Lorentz, 1942), 209–15.

48. See the references in note 35. Benoit suggests that "to receive remission of sins" may be a technical term for baptism—Acts 10:43; *Barnabas* 16.8; Hermas, *Mand.* III.3.1; Justin, *Dial.* 111.4; 141.2—*op. cit.*, 148ff.

49. Justin, *Dial.* 54.1; *1 Clem.* 7.4.

50. *Barnabas* 11.1, 8. For the connection of the passion of Christ with water, note Ignatius, *Eph.* 18 and Justin, *Dial.* 86.

51. Benoit, *op. cit.*, 153, with reference to *Dial.* 13–14 and 138 ("water, faith and wood"). Gregory Nyssa, *Vita Moysis* (Migne, XLIV, 361 D) on the crossing of the Red Sea develops the same grouping with the addition of the Holy Spirit; "The water, by virtue of the rod of faith and of the luminous cloud, became the vivifying principle for those who sought there a refuge." The rod of Moses is a type of the cross and the cloud of the Holy Spirit. The grouping of water, blood and the Spirit in patristic thought is well brought out in A. A. Maguire's monograph *Blood and Water: The Wounded Side of Christ in Early Christian Literature* (Washington: Catholic University of America Press, 1958), esp. 2, 11, and 24f.

52. *Apos. Const.* VII.43.3.

53. Ysebaert calls attention to the connotation of "perishing" which *baptizō* had in the classical profane usage, a feature which he thinks led the apologists writing for non-Christians to avoid the use of this word and to adopt substitutes wherever possible (*op. cit.*, 13, 66ff.). This connotation of perishing may have aided the identification of the motif of death with baptism.

54. Lundberg, *op. cit.*, 64–72.

55. E.g., Oscar Cullmann, *Baptism in the New Testament* (London: SCM Press, 1950), 13–22.

56. Cf. also Cyril, *Mys. Cat.* ii.2.

57. Cyril, *Cat.* III.10, "Since, therefore, it was necessary to break the heads of the dragon in pieces, He went down and bound the strong one in the waters, that we might receive power to tread upon serpents and scorpions."

58. Narsai, *Hom.* 22; cf. also the *Excerpta ex Theodoto* 76.2; Iren., *Adv. Haer.* III.8.2.

59. Narsai, *Hom.* 21 and 22; Armenian baptismal rite (Whitaker, *op. cit.*, 54).

60. Reicke, *op. cit.*, 245–47.

61. Cf. Cyril, *Mys. Cat.* ii.4; Ambrose, *De Sac.* II.20; III.1.

62. *Apos. Trad.* 20.8, "And laying his hand on them he shall exorcise every evil spirit to flee away from them and never return." 21.7ff., "And he shall take other oil

and exorcise over it, and it is called the Oil of Exorcism.... And when he has said this (renunication of Satan) let him anoint him with the Oil of Exorcism, saying 'Let all evil spirits depart far from you.'" *Can Hipp.* 108, 120; Cyril, *Procat.* 9; *Mys. Cat.* ii.3; Theodore Mops., *Sermons* 2 and 3 *On the Lord's Prayer and the Sacraments*; Ambrose, *De Sac.* I.2f.

63. Tert., *De Bapt.* 4; *Apos. Trad.* 21.1; *Apos. Const.* VII.43; Theodore Mops., *Sermon On the Lord's Prayer and the Sacraments*; Ambrose, *De Sac.* I.18; II.14. Serapion, *Prayer* 7 is typical: "Look down now from heaven and behold these waters and fill them with the Holy Spirit. Let your ineffable Word come to be productive.... And as your only begotten Word coming down upon the waters of the Jordan rendered them holy, so now also may he descend on these and make them holy and spiritual." See J. D. C. Fisher, "The Consecration of Water in the Early Rite of Baptism," *Studia Patristica* (Berlin, 1958): Vol. II, 41–46.

64. *Hom.* 21.

65. E.g., Justin, *1 Apol.* 61; Irenaeus, *Adv. Haer.* III.17.1f.; Theophilus, *Ad Autolycum* II.16; Tertullian, *De Bapt.* 13; Clem. Alex., *Strom.* IV.25. Cf. Ysebaert, *op. cit.*, 149–152. Cf. *Barnabas* 16.8. Hermas uses "Kingdom" only in relation to baptism—*Sim.* 9, 12–16, 20, 29.

66. *Op. cit.*, 222.

67. *Mys. Cat.* i.1, 10; iii.5.

68. *Sermon 4 On the Lord's Prayer and the Sacraments*. This motif may offer the explanation for the baptizand ordinarily being represented as child-sized in early Christian art. Cf. C. F. Rogers, "Baptism and Christian Archaeology," *Studia Biblica, et Ecclesiastica,* Vol. V (1903), 244f.; Robin Jensen, *Understanding Early Christian Art* (London: Routledge, 2000), 176–77.

69. Cf. Ysebaert, *op. cit.,* 151, for passages connecting the Holy Spirit with the rebirth.

70. On the basis of the common association of *palingenesia* with the theme of the new creation, I had been led to question the usual identification of it with the rebirth concept (as in Benoit, *op. cit.,* 40, and passim). Now Ysebaert has given linguistic confirmation for a distinction (*op. cit.*, pp. 130ff.). He finds in the Latin translation *regeneratio* for *palingenesia* the basis for the confusion (134, 148).

71. *Hom.* 22 for the penitence motif; the quotation is from *Hom.* 21.

72. *De Corona* 3.

73. The *Barnabas* passage, however, goes on to mention milk and honey as the food of infants. Similarly, *Can. Hipp.* 144 says that the milk and honey remind the new converts that they are little children, but 148 regards the custom as a symbol of the future life in the promised land. See Crehan, 171ff. for the varied symbolism. For the suggestion that a pagan practice has been borrowed, see W. R. Halliday, *The Pagan Background of Early Christianity* (New York: Cooper Square Publishers, 1925), ch. X; Franz Cumont, *After Life in Roman Paganism* (New Haven: Yale University Press,

1922), 52, for milk and honey as food of the gods, which when the dead receive it makes them immortal.

74. Irenaeus, *Dem* 3; 7; 42; Novatian, *De Trinitate* 29; Cyprian, *Ep.* 62.8; Athanasius, *Ad Serapion* I.4; Jerome, *Dial. c. Lucif.* 6; 9. Hippolytus, *Fragment* 18 on Song of Solomon 4:4 refers to "the power of the Holy Spirit which we experience through holy baptism in faith."

75. Justin, *Dial.* 29.1; Iren., *Dem.* 42.

76. Cyril, *Mys. Cat.* ii.6.

77. Benoit, *op. cit.*, 131. *Barnabas* 4.8 is a probable allusion to baptism. Hermas, *Sim.* 9.17, makes the reception of the seal follow upon the hearing and believing in the name of the Son of God. See A. Hamman, "La signification de *sphragis* dans le Pasteur d' Hermas," *Studia Patristica* IV (1961), 286ff.

78. Cf. 6.9 with 7.6 and 8.6. Other passages using "seal" of baptism include the *Acts of Paul* 25; Iren., *Dem.* 3; 63; 100 (of circumcision in 24); Tert., *Repent.* 6; Clem. Alex., *Quis Dives* 42; Origen, *Jer.* 2, 3; *Life of Polycarp* 19. Clement's conception of baptism as a seal has received special study in Harry A. Echle's *The Terminology of the Sacrament of Regeneration According to Clement of Alexandria* (Catholic University of America, Studies in Sacred Theology; Washington: Catholic University of America Press,1949).

79. *Op. cit.,* 97–100. F. J. Dölger has found the following different acceptations in the usage of *sphragis:* (1) Seal of the preaching (1 Cor. 9:2; Hermas, *Sim.* 9.16.5) or of faith (Tert., *Repent.* 6) and so of the baptismal confession or oath; (2) distinctive mark on a slave or beast, so a mark imprinted by God marking his property and a sign identifying Christians; (3) God's protection given to his property; (4) the baptismal formula which invokes the name of the divine person on the baptized and signifies the entrance into the souls of the neophyte of a new principle of life; (5) Christ himself who is imprinted as a new impression on a person at the moment of baptism; and (6) a seal authenticates a document, and in religious language the seal authenticates eternal life, hence the expression "seal of life eternal." *Sphragis: Eine altchristliche Taufbezeichung* (Studien zur Geschichte und Kultur des Altertums V:3/4; Paderborn, 1911). Ysebaert, *op, cit.*, 374–421, should also be consulted.

80. Cf. Serapion, *Prayer* 16; Ambrose, *De Mys.* 42.

81. *De Bapt.* 6, 7. Cf. Cyril, *Mys. Cat.* iii.1ff.

82. *Apos.Trad.* 22; Theod. Mops., *Sermons* 3 and 4 *On the Lord's Prayer and the Sacraments*; cf. Ambrose, *De Sac.* III.8 and *De Mys.* 41f.

83. Ch. 41. Cf. Clem. Alex., *Strom.* VI.12, "gleaming seal of righteousness."

84. Ysebaert, *op. cit.*, 176 and 395.

85. With reference to *1 Clem.* 35, 36; *2 Clem.* opening chapters; Hermas, *Sim.* 9.18.1; 16.3.

86. *1 Apol.* 61, 65.

87. Benoit, *op. cit.*, 165–67.

88. *De R. Carn.* 8. For baptism as an illumination see also *Acts of Judas Thomas* "Baptism of Siphor" (Greek version); Cyril, *Procat.* 1; Clem. Alex. *Paed.* I.25 (and often, for this is his favorite term).

89. Oscar Cullmann, *Early Christian Worship* (London: SCM Press, 1953), 102–5. F. van der Meer and C. Mohrmann, *Atlas of the Early Christian World* (London: Nelson, 1958), 127.

90. *Apos. Const.* III.17. For this as the explanation of the name "Christian" see footnote 22. Ysebaert, *op. cit.*, 340–67, has a large number of references, not all of which do I think are correctly interpreted.

91. See note 81.

92. Perhaps in Ign., *Mag.* 5; Iren., *Dem.* 100; and Clem. Alex., *Strom.* V.12; more explicitly in Epiphanius, *Haer.* 76.20.12 and Tert., *De Bapt.* 6. Cf. Ysebaert, *op. cit.*, 379ff. Revelation 14:1 and 22:4 compared with 7:2 may afford a New Testament indication of the "naming" at baptism as a "seal." Cf. E. Stauffer, *New Testament Theology* (London: SCM, 1955), 148, for the name of Jesus as the seal; A. Hamman, "La signification de σφραγίς dans le Pasteur d'Hermas," *Studia Patristica* 4 (1961): 286–90 for the idea of calling a name upon someone as a seal (286).

93. Ysebaert, *op. cit.*, 390–421.

94. Perhaps the first indication of this practice is in the baptism of Gundaphorus in the *Acts of Judas Thomas*.

95. Benoit, *op. cit.*, 223f.

96. Cf. Acts 2:38. This negative and positive treatment of conversion may also be seen as underlying the discussion in Romans and Colossians.

97. J. N. D. Kelly, *Early Christian Doctrines* (London: Adam and Charles Black, 1960), 430.

98. Jean Daniélou, *Platonisme et Théologie Mystique* (2nd Edition; Paris, 1953), 23–35. From the illumination motif the episode of the Burning Bush became a baptismal text.

12

Baptism in the Patristic Period

Every Christian group has some form of a rite they call baptism. This rite serves as an initiation into the group. Its initiatory significance is indicated by the word used in some churches that practice infant baptism for that ceremony—"christening," literally "to make a Christian." Only secondarily has christening come to mean, "to give a name to," and this as a consequence of the practice at earlier times (and some places now) in adult conversion of taking a new name on becoming a Christian. Different denominations may have different ceremonies, different ways of administering baptism, differences about to whom baptism is administered, and differences in the interpretation of the significance of the rite. But all have something they call baptism.

This being the case, it is of interest to study how baptism was done in the early formative centuries of Christian history. For this presentation, I am going to focus on the fourth century, the center of the Patristic period, but with some reference to earlier centuries, and primarily on Greek authors. A single, general presentation will have a somewhat synthetic result. I will try to be sensitive to major differences between various geographical locations and changes over time, but if I tried to make careful nuances between authors, this chapter would outlast the patience of the reader.

There are two major kinds of literary evidence from the fourth century for our subject:

(1) Exhortations to baptism. One can tell much about the concerns of an age by its hortatory literature. In the third century, most of the exhortations were to martyrdom; in the twelfth and thirteenth centuries, to come to communion. In the fourth century, the exhortations were to baptism. In the church's newfound favor with the imperial government, many wanted to be identified with the church but were not ready to assume full obligations of Christian living. Therefore, many enrolled as catechumens and postponed baptism until they approached death, as did the emperor Constantine. Serious-minded preachers tried to get these half-converts to take the step of full commitment.

(2) Catechetical lectures. These were given by presbyters or bishops, usually immediately after the baptism in order to explain to the newly baptized the significance of what they had experienced. Pre-baptismal instruction had mainly to do with the creed and to a lesser extent the obligations of a Christian. Because so many people postponed their baptism, church leaders sought to make baptism and first communion a very special privilege, so they did not allow the non-baptized to be present at these ceremonies or to hear descriptions of them and their significance. The non-baptized could be present for the scripture readings and sermons in church but were dismissed before the Eucharist, and they were not present to observe baptisms. Hence, most of the instruction about baptism and Eucharist and their meaning was reserved until after the baptism.

Ceremony

I begin with some discussion of the ceremony involved in the administration of baptism. At the beginning of the calendar year a candidate turned in his or her name to be enrolled for baptism at the coming paschal season (Basil, *Exhortation to Baptism* 7; Gregory of Nyssa, *To Those Who Defer Baptism* [46.417B]). This enrollment began the immediate preparation for baptism.

The third-century *Apostolic Tradition* (17.2) had prescribed that admission to enrollment for baptism be preceded by a three-year period as hearers of the word, and this provision is repeated in the fourth-century *Apostolic Constitutions* (8.32.16), but both documents qualify the requirement with the statement that it is not the time but the manner of life that is determinative of one's readiness for baptism. The long period of probation was likely a product of the time of persecution when the church wanted assurance of the commitment and readiness of new converts, for it had too much experience with those who fell away in the face of persecution.

During the forty days leading up to the Pasch, the candidates came several times a week to receive instruction from the bishop or a presbyter in the Scriptures and in the Christian faith. These teachings are well represented in the surviving catechetical lectures of Cyril of Jerusalem on the creed of the Jerusalem church, delivered about 350. The contents of such instruction was summarized in the *Apostolic Constitutions*:

> Let those who are to be taught the truth in regard to piety be instructed before baptism in the knowledge of the unbegotten God, in the understanding of his only begotten Son, in the assured acknowledgment of the Holy Spirit. Let them learn the order of the several parts of the creation, the series of providence, the different dispensations of the divine laws. Let them be instructed why the world was made, and why the human being was appointed to be a citizen therein; let them also know their own nature; let them be taught how God punished the wicked with water and fire and glorified the saints in every generation ... and how God took care of and did not reject humanity but called them from their error and vanity to the acknowledgment of the truth from eternal death to everlasting life. (7.39)

The instruction thus was to be in Christian doctrine and the main points of biblical history.

The elaboration of ceremonies surrounding administration of the baptism itself served to heighten the importance of the occasion, enhance the experience for the candidates, and ritualize the meaning of the act. The week preceding the baptism on Easter Sunday saw a concentration of activity. Details differed at different cities, but we shall note some common features.

When a person enrolled to receive baptism, witnesses attested the person's manner of life and readiness to become a full member of the church. These sponsors continued in close contact with the candidates as the time for the baptism approached.

Exorcisms were the part of the ritual that are most foreign to our religious experience today. Their frequency during the baptismal preparation varied from place to place, as did the person performing them, whether a member of the clergy or an individual Christian. Exorcism involved the calling on evil spirits to depart from a person by the authority of the name of Jesus. John Chrysostom spoke of "those frightening and horrible words" of the exorcist (*Baptismal Instructions* 10.16). Laying on of hands, making the sign of the cross, anointing with oil, and breathing or spitting on the person might accompany the invocation. The purpose of the baptismal exorcisms was to further the process of removing the candidate from the realm of evil and cleansing him or her in preparation for baptism. The exorcisms indicate that the candidates were not yet regarded as saved or in the church.

The entire Lenten season saw the observance of fasting, the duration and intensity of which depended on one's strength and health. The rigor of the fast increased in the days immediately preceding the baptism. Time spent in prayer and attendance at scripture readings and teaching also increased during the week prior to the baptism. The candidates were delivered the creed (*traditio symboli*) and taught to memorize it in anticipation of repeating it as part of the baptismal ceremonies themselves.

The climax of the preparation for baptism came on Saturday evening in the context of the paschal vigil. The waters of the baptismal pool were consecrated through prayer. By the fourth century, specially constructed baptismal fonts were common. When natural sources of water were no longer used, the symbolism of "living water," that is running or flowing water (*Didache* 7.1), was no longer evident, so the Holy Spirit was invoked to come on the water and impart to it life-giving power.

The candidates for baptism made a verbalized repentance by renouncing the pagan way of life. According to John Chrysostom's *Baptismal Instructions*

(2.20), the renunciation was made with these words: "I renounce you, Satan, your pomps, your service, and your works." The "pomps" referred to the religious processions of paganism, "service" to pagan worship, and "works" to the pagan lifestyle. The renunciation was made facing west; the candidate then turned to the east and declared an association with Christ; the wording used in Chrysostom's church was, "I enter into your service, O Christ" (2.21).

At some point the creed was recited individually (*redditio symboli*), and this was done in the presence of the entire congregation.

We read of both pre-baptismal and post-baptismal anointings. The anointings constitute one of the knottier problems in the history of liturgy and sacramental doctrine, one that I will not attempt to untie but will only present the major alternatives. Anointing for some *symbolized* the bestowal of the Holy Spirit; for others it was the *means* of the bestowal of the Spirit.

A major difference between Syrian and other baptismal rites was that the earliest sources for the Syrian liturgy know only a pre-baptismal anointing, and major significance was given to it. Ephraem the Syrian says of the pre-baptismal anointing:

> The oil is the dear friend of the Holy Spirit. . . . With it the Spirit signed priests and anointed kings: for with the oil the Holy Spirit imprints his mark on his sheep. Like a signet ring whose impression is left on wax, so the hidden seal of the Spirit is imprinted by oil on the bodies of those who are anointed in baptism; thus they are marked in the baptismal mystery. (*Hymns on Virginity* 6)

Nevertheless, in spite of this importance of the pre-baptismal anointing with oil, the Syrian tradition viewed the oil and the water as parts of one act in which the Spirit was active. In other churches the pre-baptismal anointing was more a preparatory act, and the post-baptismal anointing came to be associated with the bestowal of the Holy Spirit.

Tertullian of Carthage in the early third century was the starting point for what developed much later as the separate sacrament of confirmation in the western church. He affirmed, "Not that in the waters we obtain the Holy Spirit, but in the water . . . we are cleansed and prepared for the Holy Spirit"

(*On Baptism* 6). He associated the post-baptismal anointing with entering the priesthood (7) and the laying on of a hand and prayer with the coming of the Holy Spirit (8). He elsewhere analyzed the actions in the initiation by associating the washing with cleansing, the anointing with consecration, the signing (with the cross) with strengthening the soul, and the imposition of hands with the illumination by the Holy Spirit (*On the Resurrection of the Flesh* 8). In the Greek church, although anointing represented the Holy Spirit, some (most?) identified the actual imparting of the Spirit with baptism. This is true for Chrysostom, who says that you go down into the sacred waters, bury the old person, raise up the new person, and "is at this moment that, through the words and the hand of the priest, the Holy Spirit descends upon you" (*Baptismal Instructions* 2.26; cf. *Homilies on Matthew* 12.4).

After the baptism it was by now early Sunday morning and the newly baptized person was led into the church to share in the Eucharist, his or her "first communion." In addition to the usual bread and cup of wine for the redemptive body and blood of Jesus, there might also be a cup of water to represent the saving baptism and a cup of milk and honey, the traditional food of the newborn infant and symbolizing further the entrance into the promised land characterized as flowing with milk and honey. What of the central act, the baptism itself? That brings us to the second division of our study.

Action

The usual practice was a triple immersion. The earliest explicit attestation of a triune immersion comes at the beginning of the third century from Tertullian, who mentions this among other traditional practices that had no express scriptural warrant and describes it as "making a somewhat ampler pledge than the Lord has appointed in the Gospel" (*On the Crown* 3). If we may accept Tertullian's evidence that the practice was already traditional in his time but lacked express apostolic authorization, we may inquire of reasons for its origin. Possible influences on adoption of the practice are the triune formula in Matthew 28:19, "baptizing them in the name of the Father, of the Son, and of the Holy Spirit," or an effort to contrast Christian baptism with Jewish proselyte baptism, or the trinitarian controversies of the second century. If the trinitarian formula was not the occasion for triune immersion, there was certainly a close association between the practice of triple immersion and the trinitarian confession. In the *Apostolic Tradition* (21.12–18), each immersion is preceded by a confession, in turn of God the Father, Christ Jesus the Son of God, and the Holy Spirit—the confession of the Holy Spirit was joined with the holy church and the resurrection. Another association, although not a causal factor but a result of the practice, was seeing in the triple immersion a symbol of Jesus' three days in the tomb before his resurrection (e.g., Cyril, *Cathechetical Lectures* 20.4; Gregory of Nyssa, *Catechetical Oration* 35).

Numerous express written statements attest that the practice was full immersion. Gregory of Nyssa, in preaching *On the Baptism of Christ,* declares baptism to be an imitation of the burial of Christ. "We in receiving baptism, in imitation of our Lord ... are not indeed buried in the earth ... but coming to the element akin to earth, to water, we conceal ourselves in that as the Savior did in the earth" (46.585B). Gregory makes the same comparison in his *Catechetical Oration* 35, where he speaks of being "laid and hidden" in the earth, to which the water is parallel. However, he proceeds twice to speak of the baptizand being "poured over with water three times" (35). I understand these two passages as saying that just as in burial the body is lowered into the grave and earth "poured" over it, so in baptism the person is lowered into the water, which comes over the body. Therefore, the pouring does not refer to what the administrator does with the water but to what the water does when the administrator plunges the body into the water. Whatever the exact meaning, the result was that the body was covered with water in imitation of a dead body buried in the earth. The interpretation of this passage is relevant to the contention of some Greek Orthodox theologians that there is a difference between submersion (putting the body under the water) and immersion (the body being covered with water however it comes to be applied); hence the usual practice in modern Greek Orthodox churches of holding the baby in the water up to the shoulders and scooping water over the head three times. The same approach is applied to the interpretation of some early artistic evidence, namely that water was channeled to flow over the person standing in a pool or font. Whether such a distinction between submersion and immersion is valid, the result would seem to be the same—the body was covered with water.

John Chrysostom, on the other hand, if we are to make a distinction between immersion and submersion, is explicit about a submersion, "[The priest] puts your head down into the water three times and three times he lifts it up again" (*Baptismal Instructions* 2.26). Many more literary sources could be cited. Moreover, the early baptismal fonts were clearly designed for something more than a sprinkling or pouring.

In early Christian art, the hand of the baptizer uniformly rests on the head of the baptizand. Thus it was in position to guide the head under the water as the person stood in the font. The gesture had more than a functional significance, however. According to the *Apostolic Tradition* (21.12–18), it was with his hand on the candidate's head that the administrator asked for the confession of faith in each of the three divine persons. The art in depicting the baptizer in this way is alluding to the confession of faith made in baptism. Accordingly, Chrysostom explains that the eye of flesh sees water, but the eye of faith sees the Spirit. Bodily eyes see the priest lay his right hand on the person's head; spiritual eyes see the heavenly High Priest touch the head with his invisible hand. Hence, the priest does not say, "I baptize so and so," but "so and so is baptized," because the three divine names that are invoked actually do the baptizing (*Baptismal Instructions* 11.11, 14; also 2.10 and 26).

Just prior to entering the water the candidates removed their clothes, for the baptism was received nude. This surprises moderns, for we wonder about modesty. This may be a consideration in the instructions of the *Apostolic Tradition* (21.4–5) to baptize the small children first, the grown men next, and finally the women. In order to observe decency, women deacons assisted at the baptism of women according to the third-century *Didascalia* (16), repeated in the fourth-century *Apostolic Constitutions* (3.15–16). In the baptism of a woman, the male presbyter anointed the forehead, pronounced the formula, and dipped the head, but the female deacon anointed the body and received the woman as she came out of the water. Some baptisteries may have had curtains. Another factor is that the ancient world seems to have had a more relaxed attitude toward nudity. The nudity expressed the idea of new birth—hence in art the baptizand is shown not only nude, but also smaller than the baptizer. This manner of representation is not an indication of infant or child baptism but follows artistic convention. The newly baptized person put on a white garment, symbolizing purity.

Ancient sources provide two circumstances when alternatives to immersion were allowed. One exception to the rule is included in the present form of the text of our earliest noncanonical description of baptism. The *Didache* (7) allows, in the absence of sufficient water for an immersion, the pouring of water three times over the head of a person. There are some internal grammatical and stylistic indications that this passage is a later insertion in the original document, in which case we cannot date the exception. The description of baptismal water is either passed over as outdated in the fourth-century rewriting of the *Didache* in *Apostolic Constitutions* 7, or perhaps it was absent from the compiler's copy.

The other exception is a circumstance that drew a great deal more comment: sickbed or clinical baptism. In this case the illness or weakness confined the person to bed, and proximity to death prevented the usual baptismal ceremony. One of the earliest pieces of evidence for the practice and a defense of it comes from Cyprian of Carthage in the mid-third century. He responds to an inquiry as to whether persons who have received sickbed baptism are to be considered legitimate Christians because instead of being washed they had water poured or sprinkled on them (*Epistle* 75 [69].12). Cyprian defended such "divine abridgements" or "accommodations" (his words) in cases of necessity when done in the context of sound faith by both the giver and the receiver.

Misgivings continued to be expressed about clinical baptism, as much or more because of the circumstance of waiting this long to receive baptism as because of the method of applying water to the recipient. The three great Cappadocians of the fourth century—Basil of Caesarea, Gregory of Nyssa, and Gregory of Nazianzus—all spoke negatively of the practice but without an outright denial of its validity. Their negative words occur in their exhortations to get catechumens to enroll for baptism and so are shaped in part by the hortatory purpose, but imply doubts about sickbed baptism (Basil, *Exhortation to Baptism* 5, 7; Gregory of Nyssa, *To Those Who Defer Baptism* [46.425A]; Gregory of Nazianzus, *Oration* 40.11–12). They warn against the delay of baptism because of the "tumult and confusion" (the words of John

Chrysostom, *Baptismal Instructions* 9.8) attending the person's last hours. They do not say anything about the manner of the baptism, but something other than an ordinary immersion seems implicit in their description of the surrounding circumstances. What I find notable is their indication of what they considered essential to the efficacy of the rite. All the statements emphasize the importance of the candidate being able to speak the confession of faith. Basil speaks of the danger of an ill person not being able "to utter the saving words" (*Exhortation to Baptism* 5; cf. Gregory of Nyssa, *To Those Who Defer Baptism* [PG 46.425A]; Gregory of Nazianzus, *Oration* 11). John Chrysostom in a similar manner seems to consider the renunciation of Satan and the covenant with Christ essential even in clinical cases; he asks, "When a person cannot make the responses [is this the baptismal confession?], what benefit does he get from his initiation" (*Baptismal Instructions* 9.9–10)?

This emphasis on a verbal confession of faith raises a question about infant baptism. In the case of clinical baptism, even if the person was now unable to speak, that person was a catechumen or otherwise could be presumed to believe and to desire baptism although having failed to submit to it as yet. What about small children? That brings us to the topic of the subjects of baptism.

Subjects

The early accounts of baptism all have to do with persons who "believed that the things taught by [Christians] are true and promised to live accordingly" (Justin, *1 Apology* 61). This emphasis on faith and repentance continued consistently in the early literature relevant to the practice of baptism. The liturgies for baptism were clearly designed for people able to speak and act for themselves, and this remained the liturgical norm, not infant baptism. Given the inherent conservatism of liturgical language and practice, not surprisingly a liturgy presupposing those of accountable age continued until long after infant baptism became normal. Baptismal fonts too were for a long time designed for persons of some years. However, accommodation began early, while continuing to follow the same liturgy, by providing for parents or other family members to speak for those too young to speak for themselves (*Apostolic Tradition* 21.4).

Our earliest unambiguous evidence for infant baptism once more comes from Tertullian (*On Baptism* 18). Unlike his treatment of triple immersion, however, he does not defend it as a traditional practice but opposes it and seems to imply it was a relatively recent development in North Africa. He responds to the justification for infant baptism that was made by appealing to the words of Jesus in Matthew 19:14, "Do not forbid [the children] to come to me," by saying: "Let them 'come' while they are growing up, while they are learning, while they are instructed why they are coming. Let them become Christians when they are able to know Christ. In what respect does the innocent period of life hasten to the remission of sins?"

Tertullian's passage refers to cases of "necessity." I have elsewhere argued on the basis of inscriptions that mention the time of baptism and the time of one's death that infant baptism had its origin in emergency situations where death was imminent and a family, convinced of the necessity of baptism for salvation, did not want their child to die without baptism ("Inscriptions and the Origin of Infant Baptism," *Journal of Theological Studies*, n.s. 30 [1979]: 37–46). Emergency situations have a way of giving rise to routine practices (we may compare the new security measures in the wake of the terrorist attacks of 9/11), and that, I think, is what happened in the development of infant baptism. An emergency practice tended to become a normal practice, in view of the uncertainties of life.

Infant baptism spread during the third century and became fairly common in the fourth, but not as rapidly or as widely as is often assumed. It is striking that nearly all the prominent church leaders of the fourth century, including those from strong church families, the date of whose baptism we know, were baptized as adults (David F. Wright, "At What Ages Were People Baptized in the Early Centuries?" *Studia Patristica* 30 [1997]: 389–94). This is true of the three Cappadocian fathers on whom I am relying to a great extent. The brothers Basil and Gregory of Nyssa came from one of the prominent Christian families, whose Christianity went back to the conversion of the region a century earlier by Gregory the Wonderworker and included martyrs in their ancestry, and Gregory of Nazianzus was son of a bishop.

The Cappadocians themselves, however, did not oppose infant baptism. Gregory of Nazianzus said any age is suitable for baptism and if one has an infant child, let the child "be sanctified . . . and consecrated by the Spirit from the very tenderest age" (*Oration* 40.17). He offers some support for my argument for the origins of infant baptism in emergency situations when in answer to a question about baptizing children, he responds: "Certainly, if any danger presses, for it is better that they should be unconsciously sanctified than that they should depart unsealed and uninitiated." He proceeds, then, to consider other children who are not in danger, and he recommends three years of age as suitable, "when they are able to listen and to answer something about the mystery," for "at that time they begin to be responsible for their lives, when reason is matured" (40.28). Gregory was more optimistic than I would be about the maturity of reason in a three-year old, and we do not know that his recommendation had any following in his own time. His proposal was something of a compromise between the urge to baptize early because of the "sudden dangers that befall us" and his own convictions about a person being able to verbalize answers to the baptismal interrogations.

The practice of infant baptism became an important argument for Augustine on behalf of original sin in his controversy with Pelagius. Pelagius accepted the church's practice of infant baptism, so Augustine could reason that since baptism was for the remission of sins, and infants had no sins of their own, yet the church baptized infants, therefore the sin forgiven in baptism must be the sin inherited from Adam and Eve (*On the Merits and Forgiveness of Sins, and on the Baptism of Infants* 1.23, 28, 39; 3.2, 7). The connection of infant baptism with original sin is a result of Augustine's influence. It was not originally a feature of the eastern church fathers' reasoning.

Gregory of Nazianzus in the passage from which quotation was made (40.28) acknowledged that infants had no sins of their own and were not conscious of loss nor of need for grace, so he spoke of the benefit of baptism in terms of sanctification and being "fortified by the font." John Chrysostom, too, defended infant baptism without resort to an argument from forgiveness of sin. He said that although many think the only gift conferred in baptism is remission of sins, he could count ten gifts. Hence, baptism is appropriate for infants, although they have no sins. He proceeded to list six items in addition to remission of sins: sanctification, righteousness, filial adoption, inheritance, brothers and sisters and members of Christ, and a dwelling place of the Spirit (*Baptismal Instructions* 3.5–10; cf. *Homilies on Matthew* 11 that includes these and adds pardon and redemption).

Purpose

From the earliest Christian writers accounted as orthodox, there was an association between baptism and the forgiveness of sins. This continued to be true in the fourth century. Even those Greek authors who supported infant baptism did not deny that baptism brought forgiveness of sins; they rather chose to emphasize baptism's other benefits in reference to infants. Representative of fourth-century church leaders is Cyril of Jerusalem, speaking with reference to Acts 2:37–38, "What can be a greater sin than to crucify Christ? Yet even of this, baptism can purify" (*Catechetical Lectures* 3.15). Commenting on John 3:5, he says, "The one baptized with water but not found worthy of the Spirit [because of lack of faith and repentance—3.2] does not receive the grace in perfection; nor if a person be virtuous in deeds but does not receive the seal by water shall he enter into the kingdom of heaven" (3.4). Hence, Cyril can declare, "If anyone receives not baptism, that person does not have salvation" (3.10).

The necessity of baptism for salvation, if not always stated so plainly, was a uniform view. Yet there was one exception or qualification, and Cyril himself makes it in the remainder of the sentence just quoted, "If anyone receives not baptism, that person does not have salvation; except only martyrs, who even without the water receive the kingdom." Those who live in times of peace are baptized in water, but in times of persecution in their own blood, he says (3.10). Persecution often caught catechumens in its net before they had received baptism. It obviously did not make any sense to tell such who were preparing for baptism to deny Christ before the authorities so that they could go get baptized and then wait for the authorities to come again. The martyr's confession was considered equivalent to the baptismal confession (13.21). Hence, the assurance was offered that martyrdom, a "baptism of blood," was equivalent to water baptism and brought forgiveness of sins; it also brought a forgiveness of post-baptismal sins for those who had been baptized (Origen, *On Martyrdom* 30).

In addition to the forgiveness of sins, the two predominant images for the meaning of baptism were drawn from the Gospel of John 3:5—rebirth—and from Romans 6:1–11—death and resurrection. Gregory of Nyssa's treatment of baptism in his *Catechetical Oration* may be taken as representative. He takes up in turn three motifs connected with baptism. The first is new birth: here he parallels the effects of baptism with the incarnation of Christ. He draws an analogy between physical birth and spiritual birth. One cannot perceive a connection between the moist seed (the sperm) and the resulting human person endowed with reason, yet if divine power can change that visible underlying matter into a human being, it is nothing marvelous for the divine power to use water to bring about a "new birth through this sacramental dispensation" (33; cf. *On the Baptism of Christ* [46.584 B–D]). The second motif is death and resurrection. In this regard, the effectiveness of baptism derives from its imitation of the death and resurrection of Christ. The Pioneer of our salvation experienced death for three days and then came to life again. In a similar manner one is plunged under the water three times and raised in imitation of the grace of the resurrection (35; cf. *Against Apollinaris* [GNO 3.1.227, 4–9]). This connection of baptism with the resurrection makes baptism necessary for salvation: "It is not possible apart from the rebirth in the bath for a person to be in the resurrection" (35). The third motif Gregory introduces is that of cleansing, that is forgiveness. "It is impossible for one not thoroughly cleansed of every evil spot to enter the divine presence" and "this salvation becomes effective through the cleansing in water," he says (36).

In extolling baptism, patristic authors often give lists of its benefits. Cyril called baptism "a ransom to captives, a remission of offenses, a death of sin, a new birth of the soul, a garment of light, a holy indissoluble seal, a chariot to heaven, the delight of paradise, a welcome into the kingdom, the gift of adoption" (*Procatechesis* 10; repeated by Basil, *Exhortation to Baptism* 5). Gregory of Nyssa says that at the paschal baptism we "call strangers to adoption, those in need to participation in grace, those filthy in transgressions to the cleansing of sins" (*To Those Who Defer Baptism* [46.416C]). Gregory of Nazianzus outdoes John Chrysostom, doubling his total of ten benefits:

> Illumination [the baptismal ceremony] is the splendor of souls, the conversion of the life, the pledge of a good conscience to God. It is the aid to our weakness, the renunciation of the flesh, the

following of the Spirit, the fellowship of the Word, the improvement of the creature, the overwhelming of sin, the participation of light, the dissolution of darkness. It is the chariot to God, the dying with Christ, the bulwark of faith, the perfecting of the mind, the key of the kingdom of heaven, the exchange of life, the removal of slavery, the loosing of chains, the remodelling of the whole person ... the greatest and most mangificent of the gifts of God. (*Oration* 40.3)

The significance of baptism was further emphasized by the names given to it. Gregory of Nazianzus follows his listing of baptism's benefits with a list of its names: "We call it gift, grace, baptism, illumination, anointing, clothing of immortality, bath of regeneration, seal, and everything that is honorable" (*Oration* 40.4). Favorite terms with him were illumination, grace, gift, and seal. Gregory of Nyssa in the *Catechetical Oration* preferred the term bath or washing (*loutron*), taken from Titus 3:5, "the bath of regeneration." In his sermon *On the Baptism of Christ* he preferred regeneration (*palingenesia*) and new birth (*anagenesis*), terms which he seems to have used interchangeably, the former derived from Titus 3:5 and the latter from John 3:5 and 1 Peter 1:23.

With all their emphasis on baptism and its necessity, the patristic authors include something as its corollary often neglected in the history of the church for its connection with baptism. That is, the moral consequences of baptism. Perhaps historians of Christian thought perpetuated the disjuncture by putting sacraments and ethics in separate categories. The very catechetical practices in which the fourth-century preachers were involved may have unintentionally contributed to a failure in the intended moral regeneration. There was a place in the catechetical curriculum for doctrinal instruction, for teaching about the sacraments and liturgy, and to some extent for the contents of scripture. But there was no set place or set content for moral instruction. All the preachers included moral teaching, but it tended to be lost on the hearers by not having a separate place or set text to be followed.

However, let us see how some bishops drew the moral consequences of their baptismal instruction. Gregory of Nazianzus devotes a long section toward the close of his sermon to an exhortation that the whole self is to be sanctified (*Oration* 40.38–41). Basil of Caesarea offers a description of the "Gospel way of life": "vigilance of eyes, control of tongue, enslavement of body, humble thinking, purity of thought, extinction of wrath; being pressed into service, do more; being defrauded, do not go to court; being hated, love; being persecuted, forbear; being blasphemed, comfort" (*Exhortation to Baptism* 7). Gregory of Nyssa in his sermon *To Those Who Defer Baptism* begins and ends with the phrase "life according to the Gospel" (46.421A–B; 429B; 432A). He concluded his *Catechetical Oration* by pointing out that his instruction was not complete if it did not result in a changed life by his hearers. If the one baptized is the same after as before baptism and there is no change in the one who was washed, then "what you have not become, you are not" (40). According to Gregory, salvation is given in the water but does not come from the water, for it is not automatically assured unless accompanied by genuine faith and repentance.

The Roman Catholic Church adopted a revised liturgy for baptism that takes seriously the faith and practice of the early church as the norm for the administration of baptism. Other denominations would do well to do likewise.

*Originally published in *Australian E-Journal of Theology* 1 (2003), a lecture delivered at Australian Catholic University, Brisbane, Queensland, March 28, 2003.

Part III

Demonology

13

The Demons According to Justin Martyr

Justin Martyr, who was active in the mid-second century, is the earliest Christian author whose writings contain a rather comprehensive doctrine of demons. Demons, moreover, were central to Justin's understanding of reality and to his exposition of his faith.[1] In his two *Apologies,* addressed to a pagan audience, he regularly uses the term *daimon,* but since this was a neutral word to the Greeks for superhuman activity, he usually qualifies it by the adjective "wicked." In his *Dialogue* with the Jew Trypho he normally uses the form *daimonion,* the usual word in the New Testament. Justin probably reflects word usage of his audience and appears not to make a distinction in meaning.

Origin of Demons

One Greek explanation of demons was that they were disembodied souls that inhabited the regions around the earth and sometimes gained control of a person.[2] Justin Martyr alludes to this belief when he refers to "those whom all call demoniacs and insane" as "possessed and driven about by the souls of the deceased."[3] This was part of his proof from pagan beliefs that even after death souls are in a state of sensation and thus subject to punishment for sin and to a return to bodies in the resurrection. Justin's own idea on the origin of demons follows the Jewish view, developed in intertestamental literature,[4] that evil spirits resulted from the union of angels ("sons of God") and women ("daughters of men") in Genesis 6:1–4. He says, "Angels transgressed their appointed place and were captivated by love of women; they begat children who are those called demons."[5] The prince of the wicked demons is called "the serpent, and Satan, and the devil."[6]

Methods of Working

The wicked demons subdued the human race to themselves by deception. They worked through magical arts, appearances in dreams and apparitions, punishments, and playing upon the fears of people.[7] They are the cause of all evil in the world, "sowing among men murders, wars, adulteries, licentiousness, and all wickedness."[8]

The demons accomplish their ends by working through human weakness. They "take as their ally the desire which by nature is in each person for every different kind of evil."[9] They "subdue all who do not struggle against them on behalf of their own salvation."[10] Justin is throughout a champion of free will,[11] so he does not allow that the demons overpower human beings; rather human beings cooperate with the demons as they yield to evil desires and are deceived by the working of demons.

Pagan Religion

Demonic activity in deceiving mankind was especially evidenced in pagan religion. The demons invented the myths on which pagan (Greek) religion rested.[12] As Hellenistic philosophers, who found a contradiction between their conception of deity and the deeds of the gods in mythology, had said in their criticism of the traditional religion,[13] Justin declares that wicked demons perpetrated the immoral things attributed to the pagan gods.[14] The poets and mythologists ascribed to a god what the fallen angels and demons had done.[15] Men "not knowing that these were demons, called them gods, and gave to each the name which each of the demons chose for himself."[16] Justin had an Old Testament proof text for his identification of the pagan gods with demons: Psalm 96:5, which in the Greek translation says, "For all the gods of the nations are demons." Although he could quote the passage correctly,[17] he regularly expanded it to say "idols of demons."[18] The images worshipped in paganism had the names and forms of those wicked demons that had appeared to human beings.[19]

The demons demanded sacrifice and service.[20] Justin once more attached his thought to the contemporary philosophical criticism of traditional religion[21] in saying that the demons had need of "sacrifices, incense, and libations."[22]

Not only were the demons responsible for the mythology, images, and sacrifices of paganism, they influenced the Jews to adopt pagan religious practices. This was chiefly done in sacrificing children to demons.[23] According to Deuteronomy 32:16–23 and Isaiah 65:9–12 the Jews at other times had worshipped demons instead of the true God,[24] and false prophets among the people had glorified the spirits and demons of error.[25]

The divine Word, however, was not without witness among the Greeks, for Socrates had taught men to reject wicked demons.[26] Justin developed a parallel between Socrates and Christ/Christians who suffered for the truth. The demons had caused the death of Socrates,[27] and they cause all good persons to be hated.[28]

Opposition to Christianity

Justin considered the chief manifestation of the working of demons in his own day to be the opposition to Christianity. The demons had caused the Jews to inflict suffering on Jesus.[29] The opponents of Christianity were "impelled by evil demons,"[30] but they were still accountable, for they "yielded to the instigation of evil demons," who displayed a similar activity in regard to Christians as they had in regard to Socrates.[31] "Punishments even to death have been inflicted on us by the demons and the host of the devil through the aid given to them by you (Jews)."[32] That the demons caused the persecution of Christians, usually in combination with wicked men, is frequently stated.[33] The wicked demons "scattered many false and godless accusations" against

Christians.³⁴ The demons hated Christians and kept the judges subject to themselves and incited them to put Christians to death.³⁵

The characteristic activity of the demons was deception. The emperors whom Justin was addressing must be careful lest the demons should deceive them and divert them from understanding what he said.³⁶ The demons were responsible for laws that kept men from learning the truth.³⁷ They tried to turn men aside from joining the Christians by misrepresenting Christian teachings.³⁸ Even as the demons deceived and led astray the human race by the myths of the poets, so on hearing the prophets, they had invented imitations so men would think Christian teaching was in the same category with the pagan myths.³⁹ Among those biblical teachings for which there were demonic imitations in paganism, Justin mentions a virgin birth of the son of God,⁴⁰ baptism,⁴¹ Lord's Supper,⁴² Moses removing his sandals,⁴³ and the Spirit moving upon the water at creation.⁴⁴ Never imitated, however, was the crucifixion.⁴⁵

The efforts at imitation preceded the coming of Christ; after he came, the demons raised up heretics in order to deceive people. Justin names Simon Magus, Menander, and Marcion as put forward by the demons and deceiving many persons.⁴⁶ This agrees with their consistent activity: "Those called demons strive for no other goal than to lead men away from the creator God and the Christ his firstborn." They keep those concerned with earthly things attached to the earth and those contemplating divine things they try to hinder.⁴⁷

Victory of Christ

The preceding description has emphasized the power and influence of demons; it serves to highlight all the more the significance of Christ for Justin's thought. His understanding of redemption, even as his understanding of the source of evil and the character of life in this world, is structured in terms of the demonic and is described as a victory over these malignant powers.⁴⁸

The victory of Christ is sometimes associated with his incarnation, most frequently with the crucifixion, sometimes with the second coming. Isaiah 8:4, with Samaria and Damascus understood symbolically, "foretold that the power of the evil demon that dwelled in Damascus should be overcome by

Christ as soon as he was born."[49] The magi were formerly in the power of that demon, and their coming to worship Christ demonstrated their change of allegiance. "The hidden power of God," however, was revealed primarily "in the crucified Christ, before whom the demons and all rulers and powers of the earth tremble."[50] It was through Jesus who was crucified that the demons were destroyed; and the victory of Joshua (Jesus in Greek) foretold that the demons would be defeated and would dread his name, that all rulers and kingdoms would fear him, and that there would be believers in Christ out of all nations.[51]

Nevertheless, there is a tension of the "now and not yet" maintained in Justin's thought.[52] The victory is not yet complete; the demons attempt to escape from the power of Christ.[53] After the resurrection, Christ remains in heaven "until he has smitten the demons, who are his enemies."[54] Even in reference to the second coming there is a certain lack of consistency (or clarity) in Justin's statements. He can say that at the destruction of the world "wicked angels, demons, and men will no longer exist,"[55] but then immediately speaks of "just punishment and penalty in eternal fire,"[56] to which he elsewhere expressly consigns the demons.[57] Thus the statement about no longer existing seems to mean no longer in a position to work their evil.

The message and cross of Christ were the means by which many had left the dominion of demons and been converted to the service of God. "His mighty word has persuaded many to abandon the demons whom they formerly served and through it to believe on the almighty God."[58] "Out of all the nations some through the power of this mystery (of the cross) . . . have turned from vain idols and demons to serve God."[59] Nevertheless, it is necessary for those converted to continue to pray to God by Jesus Christ to be kept from the deceitful demons in order to remain blameless.[60]

The practical demonstration of Christ's power over demons, still evident in Justin's day, was the effectiveness of Jesus' name in driving away demons. Indeed the most frequent references to demons in his writings are in the context of exorcisms. The power of Jesus' name to drive out demons was an important argument in Justin's apologetic arsenal. Christ became incarnate, Justin declares, "for the sake of believers and for the destruction of demons." The proof of this is the number of demoniacs who could not be cured by other means who were exorcised "in the name of Jesus Christ, who was crucified under Pontius Pilate."[61] The way in which Justin regularly adds the phrase about "crucified under Pontius Pilate" to his statements about exorcism in the name of Jesus indicates that this was a regular formula in exorcism[62] and also testifies to the significance of the crucifixion for the understanding of Christ's victory over the demons. The name of Jesus Christ is now sufficient for the overthrow of demons.[63] The name of the Son of God (and here Justin expands a full confessional statement: "who is the Firstborn of all creation, was born through a virgin, became a man who suffered, was crucified under Pontius Pilate, died, and arose from the dead and ascended to heaven") subdues every demon, in contrast to Jewish exorcisms ("in the name of the God of Abraham, Isaac, and Jacob"—perhaps effective, he concedes) and pagan magic.[64] Since the demons are subject to Christ, so also are they to Christians. With reference to Luke 10:19 and Matthew 7:22 Justin says: "And now we who believe on our Lord Jesus who was crucified under Pontius Pilate exorcise all demons and evil spirits and have them subject to us."[65]

If Christ has won the victory, and the demons are now subject to him and his followers, why are Christians still put to death in the persecutions instigated by the demons? Justin's reply to such an objection is perhaps one of his weaker points, and yet it fits the total framework of his thought in which there is warfare between the demons and God wherein a decisive victory has been won by Christ but wherein the struggle still continues so that sin must take its toll. "Neither would we be put to death, nor would wicked men and demons be more powerful than we, were not death a debt due by every man that is born."[66]

Certainly Justin never weakens in his conviction that because of Christ the demons are subjected to Christians. The emphasis that "the demons are subdued to his name and to the dispensation which came by his suffering"[67] has significance beyond the apologetic value of exorcisms. The Christian is delivered from demonic power and can live in confidence in a world otherwise hostile and threatening.

> If he so shone forth and was so mighty in his first advent (which was without honor and comeliness and very contemptible), that

in no nation is he unknown and everywhere men have repented of the old wickedness in each nation's way of living so that even demons were subject to his name more than they feared all the dead, shall he not on his glorious advent destroy by all means all those who hated him and who unrighteously departed from him but give rest to his own, rewarding them with all they have looked for?[68]

*Originally printed in Wil C. Goodheer, ed., *The Man of the Messianic Reign and Other Essays: A Festschrift in Honor of Dr. Elza Huffard* (Wichita Falls, TX: Western Christian Foundation, 1980), 102–12.

Chapter 13 Endnotes

1. For books in English on Justin's theology in general with references to their treatment of his demonology see E. R. Goodenough, *The Theology of Justin Martyr* (Jena, 1923), 196–205; L. W. Barnard, *Justin Martyr: His Life and Thought* (Cambridge, 1967), 106–10; E. F. Osborn, *Justin Martyr* (Tübingen, 1975), 55–65, who gives the most evidence of appreciation of the importance of demons in Justin's thought.

For recent treatments, A. Y. Reed, "The Trickery of the Fallen Angels and the Demonic Mimesis of the Divine: Aetiology, Demonology, and Polemics in the Writings of Justin Martyr," *JECS* 12 (2004): 141–71; T. Korteweg, "Justin and a Demon Ridden Universe," *Demons and the Devil in Ancient and Medieval Christianity*, eds. N. Vos and W. Otten (Leiden: Brill, 2011), 145–58.

2. E.g., Hesiod, *Works and Days* 122; Plutarch, *Dion* 2, 1–3; *Obsolescence of Oracles* 38–39; Lucian, *On Funerals* 24; Pausanias, *Description of Greece* VI. 6.8.

3. *1 Apology* 18.

4. *1 Enoch* 6–10; 15.

5. *2 Apology* 5.

6. *1 Apology* 28. Cf. quotation from Justin in Irenaeus, *Against Heresies* V.26.2, that Satan apostatized of his free will and is doomed to eternal fire.

7. *2 Apology* 5; *1 Apology* 5; 14.

8. *2 Apology* 5.

9. *1 Apology* 10.

10. *1 Apology* 14.

11. *1 Apology* 43; *Dialogue* 102; 141.

12. *1 Apology* 25.

13. Cf. Plutarch, *Obsolescence of Oracles* 13–15; *Isis and Osiris* 25.

14. *1 Apology* 21.

15. *2 Apology* 6.

16. *1 Apology* 5.

17. *Dialogue* 73; 79; 83. For the passage in the LXX, see W. A. L. Emslie, *The Mishnah on Idolatry* (Cambridge, 1911), 42f.

18. *Dialogue* 53; 73; *1 Apol.* 41. Cf. 1 Cor. 10:19–21 for identification of demons with idols.

19. *1 Apology* 9.

20. *1 Apology* 12.

21. Celsus in Origen, *Against Celsus* VIII, 60–63; Porphyry, *Abstinence* 2.42; Plutarch, *Obsolescence of Oracles,* 13–14.

22. *2 Apology* 5.
23. *Dialogue* 19; 27; 73; 133.
24. *Dialogue* 119; 135.
25. *Dialogue* 7.
26. *2 Apology* 10.
27. *1 Apology* 6; *2 Apology* 7.
28. *2 Apology* 8.
29. *1 Apology* 63.
30. *2 Apology* 7.
31. *1 Apology* 5.
32. *Dialogue* 131.
33. *1 Apology* 57; *2 Apology* 8; 12; *Dialogue* 18.
34. *1 Apology* 10.
35. *2 Apology* 1.
36. *1 Apology* 14.
37. *1 Apology* 44.
38. *2 Apology* 13.
39. *1 Apology* 54.
40. *1 Apology* 23; cf. 56.

41. *1 Apology* 62. See Cullen I. K. Story, "Justin's *Apology I*. 62–64: Its Importance for the Author's Treatment of Christian Baptism," *Vigiliae Christianae* 16 (1962): 172–78.

42. *1 Apology* 66.
43. *1 Apology* 62.
44. *1 Apology* 64.
45. *1 Apology* 55.
46. *1 Apology* 26; 56; 58.
47. *1 Apology* 58.

48. For Justin's doctrine of redemption see the works cited in note 1: Goodenough, 252–61 (who recognizes the importance of the demons in Justin's interpretation but is reluctant to take at face value Justin's statements about the crucifixion); Barnard, 122–125 (very brief); Osborn, 62–63. For the redemptive work of Christ as a victory over demons according to early Christian thought, see H. E. W. Turner, *The Patristic Doctrine of Redemption* (London, 1962), 47–69, with occasional reference to Justin.

49. *Dialogue* 78; cf. 45 and 125 on the incarnation.
50. *Dialogue* 49.
51. *Dialogue* 131.

52. L. W. Barnard, "Justin Martyr's Eschatology," *Vigiliae Christianae* 19 (1965): 87f.

53. *1 Apology* 40; cf. *Dialogue* 121.

54. *1 Apology* 45; cf. *Dialogue* 36 on the Ascension.

55. *2 Apology* 7.

56. *2 Apology* 8.

57. *1 Apology* 52.

58. *Dialogue* 83; cf. *1 Apol.* 14, "After being persuaded by the Word, we keep away from demons."

59. *Dialogue* 91.

60. *Dialogue* 30.

61. *2 Apology* 6.

62. *Dialogue* 30; 76; 85; *2 Apol.* 6. Does Justin refer to a formal, ritual exorcism such as we know later preceded baptism? (Hippolytus, *Apostolic Tradition* 20.)

63. *2 Apology* 8.

64. *Dialogue* 85.

65. *Dialogue* 76.

66. *2 Apology* 11.

67. *Dialogue* 30.

68. *Dialogue* 121.

14

Origen's Demonology

Frank Pack's dissertation, "Methodology of Origen as a Textual Critic in Arriving at the Text of the New Testament," expressed two of his lifelong interests—the Gospel of John and textual criticism. The present paper submitted in his honor takes up the other element in his dissertation: Origen. The purpose will be to survey Origen's response to demonology, which was an important aspect of the worldview of Greeks, Romans, and Jews.[1]

Second-century Christian apologetics had accepted the views shared by the common people and philosophers alike that the demons were objective beings intermediary between the divine and the human. Justin Martyr, for instance, blamed on them all that was opposed to Christianity—pagan religion with its mythology, magic, and sacrificial rituals; moral evils such as murder, war, adultery, and wickedness; persecution; and heresy.[2] Origen, as is shown below, continued this apologetic argument.

There were other strands of thought in Origen's background. Greek physicians had identified demon possession with mental illness.[3] The association of the word demon with madness or being out of one's mind characterized the usage of the Gospel of John (7:20; 8:48f., 52; 10:20ff.). Another interiorization of demons occurred in some Jewish sources (followed by Christians), which attributed to evil spirits the sinful impulses within a person.[4] Clement, Origen's predecessor at Alexandria, said the demons cause sin and testified to the Gnostic appropriation of the idea.[5] Because of sins, spiritual powers rule over human beings.[6] The trend toward psychologizing the demons was carried further by Origen and became almost the exclusive use of demons in monastic literature, as exemplified by another Alexandrian, Athanasius, in his *Life of Antony*.

This brief attempt to situate Origen in relation to both the objective and the subjective strands of thought about demons will introduce a more detailed description of his comments.

Origen repeated the Jewish view,[7] which Christians also adopted, that the heathen gods were demons. "It is then not the idols but the demons living in the idols who are called 'gods,'" he says.[8] An extended discussion in *Contra Celsum* brings out the viewpoint, one which is basic to Origen's demonology:

> It is not only we who say that there are evil daemons, but almost all people who hold that daemons exist.... However, in the view of the majority of people who hold that daemons exist, it is only evil daemons who do not keep the law of God but transgress it. But in our opinion all daemons have fallen from the way of goodness, and previously they were not daemons; for the category of daemons is one of those classes of beings which have fallen away from God. That is why no one who worships God ought to worship daemons.
>
> The worship of the supposed gods is also a worship of daemons. For "all the gods of the heathen are daemons" (Ps. 95:5, LXX).... That is the reason why we have decided to avoid the worship of daemons like a plague. And we maintain that all the supposed worship of gods among the Greeks with altars and images and temples is a worship offered to daemons.[9]

Origen adopted the criticisms directed by certain philosophers against the popular religion. This criticism attributed the grosser features of paganism, and indeed all activities which brought the divine into direct contact with human beings (something which philosophers, particularly those influenced by Platonism, deemed unworthy of spiritual being), to the working of demons.[10] These criticisms against the popular religion had already been turned by Christian apologists against paganism as a whole.[11]

For instance, Origen frequently refers to the idea that the demons fed on the sacrifices and so delighted in these because they were dependent on them.[12] Particularly pointed are his remarks in *Exhortation to Martyrdom* 45:

> Some do not consider the truth concerning daemons, namely that if they are to remain in this gross air near the earth they need food from sacrifices and so keep where there is always smoke and blood and incense. . . . Indeed, I think that because of the misdeeds committed by the daemons who work against mankind those who feed them with sacrifices are no less responsible than the daemons who commit wicked deeds. For both the daemons and those who keep them on earth have injured men in like degree, since without the smoke and sacrifices and the food thought to be suited to their bodies the daemons would not be able to subsist.[13]

The demons were said to have given the oracles,[14] and Origen's cynical comment was that "the daemons seem to perform the petitions of those who bring requests to them more because of the sacrifices they offer than because of their virtuous actions."[15] The demons, as immaterial beings having some perception of the future, entered into animals and made possible divination through them.[16]

Origen seems especially concerned to attribute magic to the demons.

> The truth about daemons is also made clear by those who invoke daemons for what are called love-philtres and spells for producing hatred, or for the prevention of actions, or for the countless other such causes. This is done by people who have learnt to invoke daemons by charms and incantations and to induce them to do what they wish. On this account the worship of daemons is foreign to us who worship the supreme God.[17]

Celsus had charged that Christians did miracles by calling on daemons[18] and argued that Jesus performed his miracles by sorcery, not by divine power. Origen did not deny the possibility of demon-worked miracles; his approach rather was to appeal to the moral character of those performing the wonders and the moral effects of their works in order to determine which were from God and which from demonic powers:

> What is accomplished by God's power is nothing like what is done by sorcery....
>
> If we once agree that it is a corollary from the existence of magic and sorcery, wrought by evil daemons who are enchanted by elaborate spells and obey men who are sorcerers, that wonders done by divine power must also exist among men, then why should we not also examine carefully people who profess to do miracles, and see whether their lives and moral characters, and the results of their miracles, harm men or effect moral reformation? We should know in this way who serves daemons and causes such effects by means of certain spells and enchantments, and who has been on pure and holy ground....[19]

Although Origen accepted the reality of magical power, Christians, according to him, were not subject to its influence:

> We affirm that we know by experience that those who worship the supreme God through Jesus according to the way of Christianity and live according to his gospel, and who use the appointed prayers continually and in the proper way day and night, are not caught either by magic or by daemons.[20]

It might go without saying, but Origen makes it explicit, that, whereas on the Greek view demons might be either good or bad beings,[21] Christians never used "demon" in a good sense. This was necessary to say because it was an important difference in terminology between Origen and Celsus.

> Celsus fails to notice that the name of daemons is not morally neutral like that of men, among whom some are good and some

> bad; nor is it good like the name of gods, which is not to be applied to evil daemons or to images or to animals, but by those who know the things of God to beings truly divine and blessed. The name of daemons is always applied to evil powers without the grosser body, and they lead men astray and distract them, and drag them down from God and the world beyond the heavens to earthly things.[22]

In accord with this negative view of demons, Origen shared with early Christian thought in attributing various evils to demons. The demons did not give food, drink, and air to human beings, as Celsus asserted, but brought natural disasters on the earth.

> [The daemons] are responsible for famines, barren vines and fruit trees, and droughts, and also for the pollution of the air, causing damage to the fruits, and sometimes even the death of animals and plague among men. Of all these things daemons are the direct creators; like public executioners, they have received power by a divine appointment to bring about these catastrophes at certain times, either for the conversion of men when they drift towards the flood of evil, or with the object of training the race of rational beings.[23]

They led men astray by teaching false doctrine.[24] The activity most on the minds of early Christian apologists was persecution; this too was attributed to the working of demons.[25] Origen states that those who "condemn Christians and betray them, and delight in fighting against them are filled by evil daemons."[26] The demons "have stirred up the emperors, and the Senate, and the local governors everywhere, and even the populace . . . to oppose the Gospel and those who believe in it."[27] This charge was perhaps the more readily made because the demons ("the opposing powers") were generally identified with the "rulers of this world" who stood behind the existing political authorities.[28]

In spite of this malevolent activity of demons, Origen insists that "the word of God is mightier than them all . . . so that it has advanced and won over more souls."²⁹ Christians are not subject to the demons and are not hurt by them directly. Rather, they are guarded and protected by the angels of God.

> The Christian, the real Christian who has submitted himself to God alone and His Logos, would not suffer anything at the hands of daemons, since he is superior to them. . . . For even if daemons are slighted, they are able to do nothing to us who are devoted to the Person that is alone able to help all those who deserve it. He does no less than set His own angels over those whose lives are devoted to Him, that the opposing angels and the so-called ruler of this world who governs them may be unable to do anything against those who are dedicated to God.³⁰

Christians do not have to fear the demons because Christ has triumphed over them. At the birth of Jesus, "the demons lost their strength and became weak"; the coming of the magi to worship Jesus indicated their recognition that a superior power had appeared.³¹ After the coming and teaching of Jesus, souls of believers have freedom from demons.³² At Jesus' crucifixion in particular the evil powers were defeated.³³ The benefits of Jesus' victory were extended through the preaching of the gospel. "God, who sent Jesus, destroyed the whole conspiracy of daemons, and everywhere in the world in order that men might be converted and reformed He made the gospel of Jesus to be successful."³⁴ The Christian entered the sphere of safety at his baptism. As the waters of the Red Sea destroyed the army of Pharaoh, so the waters of baptism destroyed the demons:

> Paul calls that crossing accomplished by Moses in the cloud and the sea a baptism (1 Cor. 10:1–4) in order to bring home to you who were baptized in Christ, in water and the Holy Spirit, that the Egyptians are pursuing you, striving to subject you to them, I mean, the "rulers of this world" and the "spirits of this wickedness" to whom you gave your allegiance. They strive to follow you, but you go down into the water, where you are safe, and when you have been purified from all stain of sin, come forth a new man, to sing the new song.³⁵

The martyrs especially demonstrated Christ's victory over the evil powers and were themselves conquerors. "The powers of evil suffer defeat by the death of the holy martyrs," Origen affirmed.[36] The martyrs, by sharing in Christ's sufferings, shared in his triumph over the "principalities and powers."[37]

A special instance of the Christians' power over demons was the ability to cast them out of a person in whom they had come to dwell.[38] Origen attributed this power to "the name of Jesus,"[39] prayer, and words from the scriptures.[40] Origen knew that the Jews accomplished the same task by invoking "the God of Abraham, the God of Isaac, and the God of Jacob"[41] and that there were pagan accounts of exorcism.[42] In all cases, the potency was supposed to reside in the words or formulas recited.[43] Origen contrasted the simplicity of Christian practice with the elaborate incantations and magical procedures in paganism:

> ... the race of daemons which many Christians drive out of people who suffer from them, without any curious magical art or sorcerer's device, but with prayer alone and very simple adjurations and formulas such as the simplest person could use. For generally speaking it is uneducated people who do this kind of work.
>
> The power of the word of Christ shows the worthlessness and weakness of the daemons; for it is not necessary to have a wise man who is competent in the rational proofs of the faith in order that they should be defeated and yield to expulsion from the soul and body of a man.[44]

Elsewhere Origen said that Christians did not use adjuration, invocations, or direct address to the impure spirit but only prayer and fasting.[45]

Thus far the material covered may be regarded as standard Christian thought in the first centuries of our era. For the most part, Origen's arguments in *Contra Celsum* stand in the mainstream of earlier Christian apologetics; but even here some of his more distinctive emphases stand out. Origen had his own views on some subjects about which early Christians differed, e.g., the origin of demons. He rejected the view of *1 Enoch* that demons were the souls of the giants produced by the union of angels with women, pointing out that *1 Enoch* was "not generally held to be divine by the churches."[46] He preferred to interpret Genesis 6:1–4 about the "sons of God" marrying the "daughters of men" as referring to souls afflicted with a desire of bodily life.[47]

Origen emphasized that demons were not created evil but became that way through transgression. The thought of a fall of good spiritual beings was certainly not original with Origen,[48] but he integrates it with ideas which serve to introduce his more distinctive approach. Here the key factor was free will, a central element in Origen's thought.[49] He began his discussion of spiritual beings (angels, demons, principalities, powers) in *De principiis* I.5.3 by raising the question whether some were made incapable of evil, some capable of both virtue and evil, and some incapable of virtue. He laid it down that goodness and wickedness were not part of the essence of the rational powers, for that would mean that God created some things intrinsically evil.

> We conclude then, that the position of every created being is the result of his own work and his motives, and that the powers above mentioned which appear as holding sway or exercising authority or dominion over others, have gained this superiority and eminence over those whom they are said to govern or on whom they exercise their authority, not by some privilege of creation but as the reward of merit.[50]

As a corollary the evil powers departed from good of their own free will. The "opposing powers" were at one time "stainless" and dwelt among those who have remained pure, but they became "fugitives."[51] Origen interpreted the "prince of Tyre" in Ezekiel 28 and "Lucifer" in Isaiah 14 as Satan, who had once been among the pure angels, an interpretation which has had a long history in Christianity.[52] The demons were not God's servants anymore, but they were "servants of the evil one, the prince of this world, who tries to persuade any whom he can win over to forsake God."[53] Satan is himself called an "evil daemon."[54] The demons, like the devil whom they serve, have fallen away from goodness. Previously they were not demons, "for the category of daemons is one of those classes of beings which have fallen away from God."[55] Nevertheless, they remained under God's ultimate providential rule; they "have received power by a divine appointment to bring about" evil.[56]

They served as "public executioners" to punish the wicked.⁵⁷ Even their worst actions were finally subject to God's government of the world.

The demons, as one of their evil works, tempt to sin.⁵⁸ "According to the scriptures, the opposing powers and the devil himself are engaged in a struggle with the human race, provoking and inciting men to sin."⁵⁹ To commit sin is to be initiated into the cult of demons,⁶⁰ and no sin is committed without their collaboration.⁶¹ The victory of Christ on the cross was a foreshadowing of what will be consummated at the second coming;⁶² in the meantime the Christian is engaged in a continual combat against the "spiritual hosts of wickedness in heavenly places" (Eph. 6:12, often cited by Origen in his homilies). The moral application of the Old Testament in Origen's homilies frequently employs the motif of fighting against the evil powers.⁶³ "There is a diabolical race of opposing powers against whom we fight and struggle with great effort during this life."⁶⁴ The Christian must slay the demons within himself.⁶⁵ He can overcome them by following Jesus and thus will come to dwell in their heavenly realm.⁶⁶ The struggle against the demonic forces actually serves a useful purpose:

> If the demons were deprived of free will, the athletes of Christ would have no adversaries; without adversaries they would have no contest; and without a contest they would have neither reward nor victory.⁶⁷

Although Origen attributes the cause of sin to demons, he seems more especially to point out that the demons find their occasion and opportunity in the natural drives and desires of human beings. "We derive the beginnings and what we may call the seeds of sin from those desires which are given to us naturally for our use."⁶⁸ So the demons are not the only cause of sin, but they gain their hold on human life because no resistance is offered to them.

> The daemons have been allowed to occupy a place in their minds, a place which intemperance has first laid open, and have then taken complete possession of their intelligence, especially as no thought of the glory of virtue aroused them to resistance.⁶⁹

Human beings in their free will yield to demonic influence.

> It is possible for us, when an evil power has begun to urge us on to a deed of evil, to cast away the wicked suggestions and to resist the low enticements and to do absolutely nothing worthy of blame; and it is possible on the other hand when a divine power has urged us on to better things not to follow its guidance since our faculty of free will is preserved to us in either case.[70]

God provides help to resist temptation.[71] A good angel fights on behalf of the person,[72] and without divine help one could not overcome the opposing powers. But this divine assistance by itself does not guarantee victory. "This strength, therefore, which is given to us in order that we may be able to conquer, we by the exercise of our free will either use diligently and conquer or feebly and suffer defeat."[73] The purpose of Jesus is to conquer the kingdom of sin in mankind.[74]

Origen moved toward a psychological explanation of the working of demons in the following passage:

> The soul of man, while in the body, can admit different energies, that is, controlling influences, of spirits either good or bad. Now the bad spirits work in two ways; that is, they either take whole and entire possession of the mind, so that they allow those in their power neither to understand nor to think as is the case, for example, with those who are popularly called "possessed" whom we see to be demented and insane, such as the men who are related in the Gospel to have been healed by the Saviour; or they deprave the soul, while it still thinks and understands, through harmful suggestion by means of different kinds of thoughts and evil inducements, as for example Judas was incited to the crime of the betrayal. . . .
>
> On the other hand a man admits the energy and control of a good spirit when he is moved and incited to what is good and inspired to strive towards things heavenly and divine. . . . From this we learn to discern clearly when the soul is moved by the presence of a spirit of the better kind, namely, when it suffers no mental disturbance or aberration whatsoever as a result of

the immediate inspiration and does not lose the free judgment of the will.[75]

There is, according to Origen, for every sin a particular demon. He can speak of the "spirit of fornication . . . the spirit of anger and wrath, the demon of avarice," etc.[76] There is only one spirit for each of the vices, but each has innumerable servants under him to invade different persons.[77]

Some features of Origen's teachings about demons go beyond concurrence with his characteristic emphases and become part of his peculiar teachings. This is notably the case with his view that God's love and disciplinary judgments will persuade even the rebellious spiritual powers to submit to him. In commenting on 1 Corinthians 15:28, Origen says as follows:

> If therefore that subjection by which the Son is said to be subjected to the Father is taken to be good and salutary, it is a sure and logical consequence that the subjection of his enemies which is said to happen to the Son of God should also be understood to be salutary and useful; so that, just as when the Son is said to be subjected to the Father the perfect restoration of the entire creation is announced, so when his enemies are said to be subjected to the Son of God we are to understand this to involve the salvation of those that have been lost.
>
> But this subjection will be accomplished through certain means and courses of discipline and periods of time; that is, the whole world will not become subject to God by the pressure of some necessity that compels it into subjection, nor by the use of force, but by word, by reason, by teaching, by the exhortation to better things, by the best methods of education.[78]

Much of what Origen says about the demons in an apologetic context can be paralleled from the second-century apologists. Origen seems to be the first, however, to develop the view that the decline of demonic influence in the world is associated with the spread of the gospel. The standpoint seems quite modern, almost rationalist. Whether the change be attributed to the preaching itself, some objective change in reality, the lack of belief any longer in the demons, or whatever factor, Origen points to the end of antiquity in seeing the advance of Christianity as continuing the victory won by the death and resurrection of Christ over the demonic powers. Their defeat was internalized in the moral triumphs of the individual believer, but this was more than a psychological experience, because the demons (although causing psychological experiences) were more than something psychological. The defeat of the demons also had a cosmic significance.

> If by living a chaste and modest life, for example, one has triumphed over a spirit of fornication, it is no more permitted to this spirit who has been conquered by the saint to attack another man.... Each spirit conquered by the saints is sent by Christ, the just judge who presides over the struggles of mortals in this life, "into the abyss" or "into the outer darkness" or some such place as it deserves. It follows, then, that since many demons have already suffered defeat, the nations may more readily come to the faith, something which would have been impossible if the legions of demons remained intact as they did formerly.[79]

Conversion from sin to God and a life of virtue is a punishment of the demons.[80]

This promise of victory over demonic power was no doubt an important part of the appeal of the Christian faith in the ancient world. We may concur with the judgment of Harnack that deliverance from demons "formed one very powerful method of [Christian] mission and propaganda."[81] And so Origen affirmed the confident stance which Christians took toward the demonic:

> We do not, then, deny that there are many demons upon the earth, but we maintain that they exist and exercise power among the wicked, as a punishment of their wickedness. But they have no power over those who "Put on the whole armour of God." (Eph. 6)[82]

*Originally printed in James E. Priest, ed., *Johannine Studies: Essays in Honor of Frank Pack* (Malibu, CA: Pepperdine University Press, 1989), 54–66.

Chapter 14 Endnotes

1. Everett Ferguson, *Demonology of the Early Christian World* (New York: Edwin Mellen Press, 1984). A fundamental collection of references is found in the article on "Geister (Dämonen)" in Th. Klauser, ed., *Reallexikon für Antike und Christentum* IX (Stuttgart, 1976). For Jewish demonology see K. Kohler, "Demonology," *The Jewish Encyclopedia* IV (New York, 1910), 514–20; and L. Strack and P. Billerbeck, *Kommentar zum Neuen Testament aus Talmud und Midrasch* IV (München, 1961), 501–535. For the Greek background see especially Guy Soury, *La démonologie de Plutarque* (Paris, 1942) with modification by F. E. Brenk, *In Mist Apparelled: Religious Themes in Plutarch's Moralia and Lives* (Leiden, 1977). An interpretation of Origen giving major attention to demons is S. Bettencourt, *Doctrina Ascetica Origenis seu quid docuerit de ratione animae humanae cum daemonibus, Studia Anselmiana* 16 (Rome, 1945). For the spirit world in general according to Origen see Cécile Blanc, "L'angélologie d'Origène," *Studia Patristica* XIV (T.U. 117; Berlin, 1976): 79–109, and for the devil and demons, H. Crouzel, "Diable et démons dans les homélies d'Origène," *Bulletin de Littérature Ecclésiastique* 95 (1994): 303–31.

2. Everett Ferguson, "The Demons According to Justin Martyr," in *The Man of the Messianic Reign and Other Essays: A Festschrift in Honor of Dr. Elza Huffard*, ed. Wil C. Goodheer (Wichita Falls: Western Christian Foundation, 1980), 103–12. For the apologists in general see H. Wey, *Die Funktionen der bösen Geister bei den griechischen Apologeten des zweiten Jahrhunderts nach Christus* (Winterthur, 1957). Specialized studies of demonology in early Christian authors include H. J. Schoeps, "Die Dämonologie der Pseudoklementinesen," *Aus frühchristlicher Zeit* (Tübingen, 1950), 38–81; E. Schneweis, *Angels and Demons According to Lactantius* (Washington, 1944); M. P. McHugh, "The Demonology of Saint Ambrose in Light of the Tradition," *Wiener Studien,* Neue Folge 12 (1978): 205–31; A. C. Baynes, "St. Anthony and the Demons," *Journal of Egyptian Archaeology* 10 (1954): 7–10.

3. Hippocrates, *The Sacred Disease* 1–3; cf. Plutarch, *Lives* 309.

4. *Testament of Reuben* 2; *Testament of Benjamin* 3.3f.; *Testament of Asher* 6.5; for the personification of vices cf. Hermas, *Mandates* 2.3; 5.2–7; 8.3–7;10.1; *Similitudes* 6.2; 9.22–23.

5. *Strom.* II.20.113

6. *Ecl. Proph.* 20.1; cf. *Exc. Theod.* 51–52.

7. Psalm 96:5 LXX; Deut. 32:17; *Jubilees* 1.11; 1 Cor. 10:19–21; Rev. 9:20.

8. *Hom. Num.* XXVII.8. Cf. *C. Cels.* VII.64 and Minucius Felix, *Octavius* 26f., for demons occupying images and temples.

9. *C. Cels.* VII.69. Quotations from Origen, *Contra Celsum* are taken from the translation by Henry Chadwick (Cambridge, 1953). Cf. VII.65, God, Christ, and angels "are different from all the gods of the heathen who are daemons"; also VIII.13.

10. Plato, *Symposium* 202E–203A; *Epinomis* 984D–985B; Diogenes Laertius VIII.32; Plutarch, *Moralia* 415A–418D; Apuleius, *De Deo Socratis*; cf. Celsus's own use of demons for gods in *C. Cels.* VIII.24ff.

11. For different standpoints see Wey, *op. cit.*, and J. Geffcken, *Zwei griechische Apologeten* (Leipzig, 1907). For the philosophical criticism see H. W. Attridge, "The Philosophical Critique of Religion under the Early Empire," *Aufsteig und Niedergang der römischen Welt.* Principat. II. 16.2 (Berlin, 1978), 45–78.

12. Cf. the satire in Lucian, *Juppiter tragoedus* 15, 22; *Icaromenippus* 26f.; Porphyry, *De abstinentia* 2.34 assigned the usual sacrifices to demons but spiritual sacrifice to the higher gods.

13. Translation by Henry Chadwick in *Alexandrian Christianity,* Library of Christian Classics II (London, 1954). Cf. *C. Cels.* III.28f., 37; IV.32; VII.5, 6, 35, 64; VIII.29f., 61–63; *De princ.* I.8.1 (Latin); *Comm. in Matt.* XIII.23. This was a prominent theme in earlier Christian apologetics: Cf. Justin, *2 Apol.* 5; *1 Apol.* 12; Athenagoras, *Leg.* 26f.

14. *C. Cels.* VII.3; IV.93; VIII.62.

15. *C. Cels.* VII.6.

16. *C. Cels.* IV.92. Origen suggested an affinity between the demons "who have fallen from heaven to roam about the grosser bodies on earth" and the wilder animals. See H. Crouzel, *Théologie de l'image de Dieu chez Origène* (Paris, 1955), 197–201, for Origen's allegorizing of wild animals in the Bible as demons who attack the inner man; the one who sins takes on the characteristics of these animals. For demons having some perception of the future which they use to lead men astray, cf. Tertullian, *Apol.* 22.

17. *C. Cels.* VII.69. Cf. VI.45. Other authors who attribute magic to demons include Minucius Felix, *Octavius* 26f.; Tertullian, *Apol.* 23; 35; *De idol.* 9; Hippolytus, *Ref. omn. haer.* IV.28; 35; Lactantius, *Div. inst.* II.17.

18. *C. Cels.* I.6.

19. *C. Cels.* II.51. Origen frequently appealed to this moral argument to rebut the charge of Celsus that Jesus was a sorcerer: *C. Cels.* I.67; 68; III.28; cf. VI.80; VIII.43. See Henry Chadwick, "The Evidences of Christianity in the Apologetic of Origen," *Studia Patristica* II (Berlin, 1957): 331–39. For demons working miracles see Rev. 16:14. For God working miracles and demons working magic cf. Lactantius, *Div. inst.* IV.15.

20. *C. Cels.* VI.41.

21. Origen reflects the Greek usage when he refers to "good-daemons" (*C. Cels.* III.37) which were associated with heroes (VII.7 and 9), alludes to the demon of Socrates (VI.8), and quotes Celsus on the genius of the emperor (VIII.65). Cf. Tertullian, *Apol.* 32.

22. *C. Cels.* V.5. Cf. VIII.31, "the entire race of whom is evil." VIII.39; VII.69; Clement of Alexandria, *Protrep.* II.40–41.

23. *C. Cels.* VIII.31f.; cf. I.31; Clement of Alexandria, *Strom.* VI.3. Tertullian had earlier compared the effects of demons upon a person to the way an unseen poison in the breeze can blight crops; he particularly attributed illnesses to the work of demons—*Apol.* 22.

24. *De princ.* III.3.2–3. Cf. Justin, *1 Apol.* 26; 56; 58; Hippolytus, *Ref. omn. haer.* VI.2 on demons introducing heresy.

25. From Justin Martyr alone note *1 Apol.* 5; 57; *2 Apol.*, 1; 7; 8; 12; *Dial.* 18; 131.

26. *C. Cels.* VIII.43. Cf. VIII.41; 39; and 69 for discussion of the problem of God not saving Christians from persecution.

27. *C. Cels.* IV.32; cf. *Hom. in Jesu Nave* IX.10.

28. *De princ.* III.3.2. See H. Schlier, *Principalities and Powers in the New Testament* (New York, 1961); G. B. Caird, *Principalities and Powers: A Study in Pauline Theology* (Oxford, 1956); G. H. C. MacGregor, "Principalities and Powers: The Cosmic Background of Paul's Thought," *New Testament Studies* I (1954): 17–28.

29. *C. Cels.* IV.32.

30. *C. Cels.* VIII.36; cf. VIII.27; 34; VI.41.

31. *C. Cels.* I.60. For the association of the victory over demons with the incarnation cf. Justin, *Dial.* 45; 78; *2 Apol.* 5; cf. Ignatius, *Eph.* 19.

32. *Hom. in Jesu Nave* XIV.1.

33. *Comm. in Matt.* XIII.18,40; *Hom. Ex.* VI.8; *Hom. Num.* III.4; XVII.5; *Hom. in Jesu Nave* VIII.3; XIII.4; XV.5. Colossians 2:15 is often cited by Origen in this connection. Cf. J. Daniélou, *Origène* (Paris, 1948), 265–67.

34. *C. Cels.* III.29.

35. *Hom. Ex.* V. 5. Cf. VI.3; Cyprian, *Ep.* 75.15. P. Lundberg, *La Typologie baptismale dans l'ancienne église* (Uppsala, 1942), ch. 7; J. Daniélou, *From Shadows to Reality* (Westminster, MD, 1960), 175–201.

36. *Comm. in Joh.* VI.54 (36). Cf. *C. Cels.* VIII.44; Tertullian, *Apol.* 27.

37. *Exh. ad mart.* 43. Cf. W. Völker, *Das Vollkommenheitsideal des Origenes* (Tübingen, 1931), 176f.

38. The earlier apologists had made much of the power of Christians to expel demons by the name of Jesus—Justin, *2 Apol.* 5; *Dial.* 76; Tertullian, *Apol.* 23.

39. *C. Cels.* VIII.58; I.6, "by the name of Jesus with the recital of the histories about him," with which cf. Justin, *Dial.* 30; 76; 85; *2 Apol.* 6; 8; " by the invocation of the name of God" in *Hom. in Jesu Nave* XXIV.1.

40. *C. Cels.* VII.67.

41. *C. Cels.* IV.33. Cf. the use of Jewish names for God in the magical papyri, e.g., *Paris Magical Papyrus* 11.3, 007–3, 085, which is studied by W. L. Knox as an example of "Jewish Liturgical Exorcism," in *Harvard Theological Review* 31 (1938): 191–293. For an account of Jewish exorcism see Josephus, *Ant.* VIII.46–49.

The Early Church and Today

42. Celsus in *C. Cels.* I.68; VI.39f.; cf. Philostratus, *Vita Apoll.* IV.20; Lucian, *Philopseudes* 16.

43. The name of Jesus was so potent that Origen claims it was effective when used by those who were not true disciples—*C. Cels.* II.49.

44. *C. Cels.* VII.4. Cf. I.46; *Hom. in Jesu Nave* XX.1; Ps. Clem., *De virg.* I. 12. For accounts of Christian exorcism see *Acta Pet.* 11; *Acta Thom.* 42–49; 73–81.

45. *Comm. in Matt.* XIII. 7; cf. Irenaeus, *Adv. Haer.* II.32.4. Cf. Bettencourt, *op. cit.* (n. 1), 44.

46. *C. Cels.* IV.54. The reference is to *I Enoch* 6 and 15; its interpretation was accepted, for example, by Justin, *2 Apol.* 5 and Athenagoras, *Leg.* 24f.

47. *C. Cels.* V.55.

48. Origen puts the thought that the devil "was formerly an angel, but became an apostate and persuaded as many angels as he could to fall away with him" among the opinions generally held among Christians—*De princ.* Pref. 6.

49. On the origin of evil and importance of free will in Origen's system see H. Koch, *Pronoia and Paideusis* (Berlin, 1932), 96–159. On free will in relation to sin see Georg Teichtweier, *Die Sündenlehre des Origenes* (Regensburg, 1958), 77–85. Cf. also Völker, *op. cit.* (n. 31), 25–44; E. de Faye, *Origène, se vie, son oeuvre, sa pensée* (Paris, 1928), vol. 3, 179–98; Daniélou, *op. cit.* (n. 33), 203–20, 279–81; B. D. Jackson, "Sources of Origen's Doctrine of Freedom," *Church History* 35 (1966): 13–23.

50. Translations from *De principiis* are taken from G. W. Butterworth, *Origen on First Principles* (London, 1936).

51. *De princ.* I.5.5.

52. *De princ.* I.5.4f. Cf. I.8.3; *Comm. in Joh.* II.7. Tertullian offers the same interpretation—*Adv. Marc.* II.10 and agrees with Origen in the emphasis on the fall occurring by free will—cf. *Apol.* 22. The classic English statement is John Milton's *Paradise Lost*, esp. I.34–39, 157–68, 249–63.

53. *C. Cels.* VIII. 13. Cf. *Hom. in Jesu Nave* XV.5 for a hierarchy of evil beings and *Comm. in Matt.* XI.1 for a diabolical counterpart to the Trinity.

54. *C. Cels.* VI.45.

55. *C. Cels.* VII.69. See note 9 for the context.

56. *C. Cels.* VIII.31. See note 23 for the context.

57. *C. Cels.* VII.70; cf. VIII.33; Blanc, *op. cit.* (n. 1), 107.

58. Teichtweier, *op. cit.* (n. 49), 102–11, 155–57.

59. *De princ.* III.2.1. Cf. *C. Cels.* V.5; *Comm. in Matt.* XIII.22f. For earlier Christian statements that the demons cause sin, see Tatian, *Or.* 14; Justin, *2 Apol.* 5.

60. *Hom. Num.* X.3.

61. *Hom. Num.* XXVII.8.

62. *Hom. in Jesu Nave* VIII.4.

63. *Hom. in Jesu Nave* I.7; VIII.2; XII. 1–2; XV.6; *Sel. in Ps.* 36, *Hom.* II.8. See Bettencourt, *op. cit.* (n.1), 62–86.

64. *Hom. in Jesu Nave* 1.6.

65. *Hom. in Jesu Nave* VIII.7. Völker, *op. cit.* (n. 31), 175f.

66. *Hom. Num.* VII.5.

67. *Hom. Num.* XIII.7.

68. *De princ.* III.2.2.

69. Ibid.

70. *De princ.* III.2.4.

71. *Hom. Luc.* 34.4. Although Origen questioned the interpretation of the robbers as demons, he transmitted this interpretation of the parable to his successors—G. J. M. Bartelink, "The démons comme brigands," *Vigiliae Christianae* 21 (1967): 12–24.

72. *De princ.* III.2.4–5. Origen refers in the passage to *Barnabas* 18 and Hermas, *Mand.* VI.2; *Hom. in Jesu Nave* XV.6 refers to *Testament of Reuben* 2–3 and *Testament of Judah* 16. M. Simonetti, "Due note sul' angelogia origeniana," *Rivista cultura classica e medioevala* 4 (1962): 165–208: Blanc, *op. cit.* (n. 1), 99, 103.

73. *De princ.* III.2.3. Cf. *C. Cels.* VIII.36 for one voluntarily in the power of the demons according to whether he chooses to obey them.

74. *Hom. in Jesu Nave* XV.4–5.

75. *De princ.* III.3.4. Cf. *Comm. Cant.* III.15 for demons using base thoughts to destroy virtue in the soul. On sin as a psychological event for Origen, cf. Völker, *op. cit.* (n. 37), 42. See notes 4 and 5 and cf. Clement of Alexandria, *Ecl. Proph.* 46, "The Passions of the soul are called spirits," but Clement adds, "not spirits of power, since in that case the man under the influence of passion would be a legion of demons."

76. *Hom. in Jesu Nave* XII.3. Cf. Völker, *op. cit.* 36f.

77. *Hom. in Jesu Nave* XV.5.

78. *De princ.* III.5.7–8. Cf. de Faye, *op. cit.* (n. 49), vol. 3, 261f.; E. Ferguson, "Divine Pedagogy: Origen's use of the Imagery of Education," *Christian Teaching: Studies in Honor of LeMoine G. Lewis* (Abilene, TX, 1981), 357–60.

79. *Hom. in Jesu Nave* XV.6.

80. *Hom. Num.* XXVII.8: "It seems to me that vengeance is exercised against the demons when a man, attracted by their seductions to the worship of idols but converted by the word of the Savior, renders to God the worship which is due him; by the fact itself of this conversion a vengeance is exercised against the Deceiver. . . . The demons are punished by our reformation and conversion."

81. Adolf Harnack, *The Mission and Expansion of Christianity* (New York, 1962 reprint), 125–46.

82. *C. Cels.* VIII.34.

Part IV

Worship and Assembly

15

Justin Martyr and the Liturgy[1]

Study of the historical basis of the Christian liturgy can do no better than to begin with Justin Martyr's account of the worship assembly of Christians at Rome in the mid-second century. The description contained in Justin's *Apology I*, 67, is thoroughly representative of Christian practice in Justin's lifetime. He knew Christianity in Asia as well as Rome, perhaps in Palestine as well.[2] He wrote as one representing the church to the Roman authorities. He may not tell all, he may even be mistaken on some things, and he certainly tailors the wording of his account to his intended imperial readership, but for his purposes he would not deliberately distort. Where he can be checked by other second-century sources, those sources accord with his account.[3] Justin, therefore, provides historically valid information and a precious piece in the history of worship. Justin was not an official minister, and he gives his account from the perspective of a participant but not a leader—a fact which adds greatly to its interest.

> After baptism we continually remind one another of these things. Those who have provide for all those in need. We are always

together with one another. For all the things with which we are supplied we bless the Maker of all through his Son Jesus Christ and through his Holy Spirit. On the day called Sunday there is a gathering together in the same place of all who live in a given city or rural district. The memoirs of the apostles or the writings of the prophets are read, as long as time permits. Then when the reader ceases, the president in a discourse admonishes and urges the imitation of these good things. Next we all rise together and send up prayers. And, as I said before, when we cease from our prayer, bread is presented and wine and water. The president in the same manner sends up prayers and thanksgivings, according to his ability, and the people sing out their assent, saying the "Amen." A distribution and participation of the elements for which thanks have been given is made to each person, and to those who are not present [the elements] are sent by the deacons. Those who have means and are willing, each according to his own choice, gives what he wills, and what is collected is deposited with the president. He provides for the orphans and widows, those who are in need on account of sickness or some other cause, those who are in bonds, strangers who are sojourning, and in a word he becomes the protector of all who are in need. We all make our assembly in common on Sunday, since it is the first day on which God changed the darkness and matter and made the world, and Jesus Christ our Savior arose from the dead on the same day. For they crucified him on the day before Saturn's day, and on the day after (which is the day of the Sun) he appeared to his apostles and disciples and taught these things, which we have offered for your consideration.[4]

Preliminaries

Before Justin's description of the Sunday assembly itself is examined, notice should be taken of his preliminary statements.

1. "We continually remind one another of these things," and "We take care of those in need." The account of the liturgy is set in the context of mutual

concern and care. Justin has just described the baptismal ceremony that brings deliverance from the power of demons (chs. 61–65).[5] Redemption was a matter of constant reminder. Christians remembered one another and remembered their needs. The Sunday assembly was part of this remembrance of redemption and relief of needs, and these themes are prominent in the account of the assembly itself. The assembly was part of the total corporate life of the Christian community. Justin thus reminds us that liturgy and life belong together. Services and service are not sharply distinguished.

2. "We are always together." Sunday was not the only time that Christians were together. Christians in a missionary situation are either "always with one another," or they do not survive. The fellowship, the association, the common life of Christians extended to all activities; and the common assembly was but one expression of that togetherness, even though it was the supreme expression.

3. "We are thankful"; "we bless the Creator." This is the fundamental biblical response to God. Justin brings together the humanward and Godward directions of the Christian life. Christians were mindful of one another, and they acknowledged the source of all they had. Both concerns become evident in the liturgy. There have been tendencies from time to time to shift the emphasis to one, to the neglect of the other, but both the Godward and the humanward directions must be present. The thanksgiving to God was directed through Jesus Christ and the Holy Spirit. Here was expressed the trinitarian structure of worship. The place of the Son and the Spirit provided the distinctive doctrinal foundation of Christian worship.

4. "We hold our common assembly on Sunday." A host of references back to the New Testament confirm this statement.[6] The phrase "in the same [or one] place" is used frequently in the New Testament and Apostolic Fathers with connotations of "in church, in one assembly, in community."[7] "Sunday" was the pagan name for the day of the week, used because Justin was addressing a pagan audience. "First day of the week" was the Jewish name. "Lord's day" was the peculiarly Christian designation for the day.[8] In the earliest Christian literature, exhortations to Christians to be present at the assembly relate the assembling together to eschatology.[9] The meeting was with reference to the final assembling of the saints at the Lord's coming. Justin adds at the

close of the passage a connection of Sunday with creation as well as with redemption. In this he may have been influenced by the Jewish view of the Sabbath, which connected it both with God's rest following creation and with redemption from Egypt at the exodus.[10] Justin connected the Christian day of meeting with the beginning of the physical creation and with the beginning of the new creation at the resurrection.

Activities in the Assembly

Justin mentions four activities in the common assembly each Sunday: Scripture reading and sermon, prayer, Eucharist, and contribution. The standard theory on the origins of the Christian liturgy runs something like this: The liturgy of the church resulted from a combination of the Jewish synagogue service with the Christian observance of the Lord's Supper.[11] The synagogue service had two foci: prayer and the reading and study of the Scriptures. There were various prayers, principally the *shemoneh esreh* ("Eighteen Benedictions"), but the recitation of the *shema* and the priestly benediction may also be included under the heading of prayer. There were readings from the Law and the Prophets, and if someone qualified was present, an address related to those scriptures. In addition to the two foci, the synagogue service may have included psalm chants and almsgiving, at least on occasion. The student can see in the developed Christian liturgies a twofold structure: the synaxis, which contains the synagogue's elements of the Word and prayer, and the Eucharist, with its own scriptures, prayers, and formulae. The theory is eminently reasonable, and it fits Justin's evidence quite well. The early history of the liturgy, however, may not have been everywhere so neat, and recent study is more cautious about generalization and points to greater variety in early Christian practice.[12] Regardless of theories, Justin's evidence is explicit about what was done at his time.

The modern liturgical movement has said much about "primitive wholeness." That is particularly descriptive of Justin's account. There is a balance about his brief description, a four-cornered solidity about the service that he describes. It is common to refer to the emphasis on the Mass at the expense of other activities in the medieval church as compared to the emphasis on preaching at the expense of other activities in the Protestant Reformation.

Justin permits us to go behind these aberrations to something more satisfying.[13] The balance was preserved because these activities were all engaged in every Sunday.[14] Justin's wording indicates that the order in his account was the actual order in which each activity was done.

1. *The Ministry of the Word*

Scripture reading and sermon may be discussed together, because Justin indicates that they were especially closely related.[15] The Scripture reading was from either the New Testament or the Old Testament or both. The "memoirs of the apostles" would be particularly the Gospels. The "prophets" was a standing designation among Christians for the entirety of the Old Testament.[16] But the prophetic books in the narrower sense had a special meaning and relevance for the early Christians beyond the other parts of the Jewish Bible, and they may well have been, in fact, the part of the Old Testament most frequently read. The Gospels and Prophets may have been a Christian counterpart to the Jewish readings from the Law and the Prophets.

Justin does not say whether the reading was part of a continuous cycle of readings (a lectionary) or was chosen specifically for the day. The phrase "as long as time permits" implies that the reading was not of a fixed length, but it does not have to mean a random selection. There is a third possibility: the reading may have been continuous from Sunday to Sunday, taking up where the reading left off the last week, but not of a predetermined length. The indication is that the readings were rather lengthy. In that day readings in church provided the principal opportunity for the average person to become familiar with the contents of Scripture.

The sermon was given by the "president." The word need mean no more than the "presiding brother," but it can also mean "ruler" and there seems no reason to doubt that this individual was the functionary we know elsewhere under the title "bishop."[17] In Justin's time he was a congregational overseer or pastor, not a diocesan bishop. He presided at the liturgy and administered the finances of the church as well as preached. He was a different person from the reader.

The sermon was expository in nature, based on the scripture reading of the day and making a practical application of that scripture to the lives of those present. As an apologist, Justin stresses the moral content of the preaching: "the imitation of these good things." That, nonetheless, accords with much that we know about the content of the preaching in the early church.[18]

2. Prayer

Justin gives a brief note about the posture for prayer: The congregation was standing. Other sources tell us about the significance of this posture. A person kneeled or made prostration to express humility, contrition, repentance, or confession of sin. Standing, on the other hand, was a sign of joy and boldness.[19] It expressed the freedom of the children of God to come openly and boldly into his presence. On the first day of the week, standing had a special reference also to the resurrection. This was the characteristic Christian attitude in prayer, as literary texts and archaeological sources combine to confirm.[20] Standing meant for the early Christians the special privileges that were theirs through Christ in coming to God as Father. To stand in the presence of God meant to be accepted by him and so the right to speak freely.

The prayer referred to at this point in the assembly was the corporate or common prayer.[21] It was evidently a free prayer. Justin may give some idea of the typical content in his words in chapter 13:

> We praise the Maker of the universe as much as we are able by the word of prayer and thanksgiving for all the things with which we are supplied.... Being thankful in word, we send up to him honors and hymns for our coming into existence, for all the means of health, for the various qualities of the different classes of things, and for the changes of the seasons, while making petitions for our coming into existence again in incorruption by reason of faith in him.

This summary statement accords with the general pattern to be found elsewhere—beginning with an address to God as Father and Creator, praising him for his mighty acts, moving from thanksgiving to petition, and closing with a doxology. The whole was done with reference to the mediation of Christ. Other sources would permit a greatly expanded list of topics covered in Christian prayer, whether corporate or private. Justin himself in chapter

65 mentions that the Christians prayed for themselves, the newly baptized, and all everywhere. He adds, "We pray that we who have learned the truth may be counted worthy and may be found good citizens through our works and keepers of his commandments so that we may receive eternal salvation." The apologetic purpose is no doubt behind the stress on good conduct.

This is the best place to mention the congregational ratification of the prayer in a unison "amen," although Justin mentions it in connection with the eucharistic prayer. The word "amen" is Hebrew and is explained by Justin in chapter 65 as meaning "May it be so." The congregational "amen" at the conclusion of prayer or in response to a doxology was taken over from the synagogue in the very earliest days of the church (1 Cor. 14:16). It was the congregation's confirmation of what had been said by another and so was a way of making the prayer pronounced by one person the joint prayer of the whole people. Justin seems to have been much impressed with this element of congregational participation. He describes its rendition with a word which has a double meaning: to make acclamation, or to sing. I have tried to bring out both meanings in the translation "sing out their assent." We should think of a chantlike, unison acclamation. It was shouted out, not mumbled.

Justin does not mention hymns in chapter 67. Other sources provide ample reason to assume their presence at this time,[22] and it is often suggested that Justin makes reference to them in chapter 13. It is possible that "hymns" in that chapter has the more general meaning of "praises" without reference to the manner of their rendition, but the normal way in the ancient world to verbalize praise to a deity was through melodic words or chant. Hymns, therefore, may have been present under Justin's headings of either Scripture reading or prayer. In favor of including them with the Scriptures would be the later practice of interspersing psalms among the different scripture readings and the fact that most of the singing was of the Psalms or of psalm-like compositions.[23] In favor of subsuming hymns under prayer would be the consideration that they had in common the elements of praise and address to God. Moreover, the prayers of the synagogue, like the scripture readings, were recited in a chant, and Christians may have followed this practice, so that the distinction made today between prayer (prose) and hymn (poetry or song) would not have been evident.

3. Eucharist[24]

Justin mentions in his account of a baptismal Eucharist (ch. 65) that following the common prayers and before bread and wine were brought, "We salute one another with a kiss."[25] The "holy kiss" or "kiss of love"[26] was particularly appropriate in a baptismal context, but may also have been employed at other observances of the Eucharist. It was an expression of brotherly love; it welcomed the newly baptized into the family of God. Justin emphasizes that "it is not lawful for any other one to partake" of the Eucharist (ch. 66) than one in the full fellowship of the church.[27] The exchange of the kiss was the sign of being in that fellowship.

Justin does not make much of the bringing in of the bread and wine, so it is difficult to say how much ritual significance was assigned to this act. He refers to "wine and water." It has been suggested that there were separate cups, and of course this is possible. I rather think, however, that Justin is referring in a loose manner to the practice of mixing wine and water. One of his statements in chapter 65 refers to "water and the mixture." The common table beverage in the ancient world was wine diluted with water.[28] Justin thus counters pagan stories about the Christian meal by saying that Christians ate ordinary bread and drank the common table beverage (not something more intoxicating).

The bread and wine may have been ordinary food, but they had no ordinary significance to Christians. For Justin, the two highlights of the eucharistic celebration were the consecration and the communion. According to Judaism, something was dedicated to a proper purpose "by the word of God and prayer."[29] The president's thanksgiving made the bread and mixed wine no longer "common bread and common drink" (ch. 66). Our liturgical study need not explore eucharistic theology nor enter the debate about the import of Justin's words connecting the bread and wine with the body and blood of Jesus. Those words have been controverted nearly as much as the words of institution in the Gospels.[30] It is sufficient for liturgical purposes to note that it was by the words of Jesus and by prayer that ordinary food and drink acquired new meaning and new use. Justin tells us that by the Word of God (Jesus) and by prayer (of thanksgiving) the bread and wine were now set apart, consecrated, given a new significance.

The name itself given to the food—Eucharist (ch. 66), which means thanksgiving—points to the most important feature. It was a thank-offering.[31] Although the New Testament uses as its common terminology "the breaking of bread,"[32] second-century Christian writers adopted the name "eucharist."[33] Breaking of bread and a prayer of thanksgiving went together in the Jewish ceremony of beginning a meal. In a Gentile context, "breaking of bread" was no longer meaningful as a title. The other, and more general aspect, received the emphasis—the prayer of thanksgiving, and hence the name which was adopted. Justin makes much of thanksgiving throughout his writings. This was the Christian sacrifice. Rather than the bloody offerings of paganism, Christians offered to God the pure spiritual sacrifice of prayers and thanksgivings.[34]

The president made the prayer "according to his ability." The phrase occurs also in chapter 13 for the praise offered by all Christians to God. The idea seems to be that human thanksgiving is inadequate to the greatness of God's goodness, but all, insofar as they are able, try to express their gratitude. In Justin's day the prayer was extemporaneous, but the presence of some formulae recurring with great frequency is not to be ruled out.[35] Some indications of the contents of the prayer are to be found elsewhere in Justin's writings.[36] Chapter 65: The president "sends up praise and glory to the Father of all through the name of his Son and of the Holy Spirit and makes thanksgiving at length for the gifts we were counted worthy to receive from him." *Dialogue* 41: "We thank God for having created the world with all things in it on behalf of man, and for having delivered us from the evil in which we were and completely overthrowing the principalities and powers by the one who suffered according to his will." The main theme, therefore, was praise and thanksgiving to God for his gifts, and these included both creation and redemption, but especially redemption, which was explained in terms of Justin's thought world.[37]

The deacons then distributed, for the communion of the members, the elements consecrated by prayer. Each person participated in both the bread and mixed wine. One was either in communion, or he was not. Sharing the bread and wine expressed the fellowship of the believing community. The deacons even carried the consecrated elements to those who were sick and unable to be physically present. This practice preserved a sense of corporate identity and fellowship with the total body among those in confinement.

4. Offering

Although we know from other sources about offerings in produce by the faithful, Justin describes a monetary contribution.[38] He gives particular emphasis to the voluntary nature of the gifts. The money deposited with the president was not an assessment. The congregational contribution, therefore, was unlike the "dues" of the clubs and private associations that were so much a part of life in the Hellenistic and Roman worlds. It was a freewill gift.

The contribution was a way of doing good for those in need. The persons who benefited from the almsgiving—orphans, widows, sick, prisoners, and strangers—are often mentioned in Christian texts and were traditional categories of needy persons.[39]

Evaluation

The service described by Justin calls us back to fundamentals. These were basic activities of every Sunday assembly in Justin's day and have so remained through the ages: the Word of God (read and preached), corporate prayer (including psalmody), communion of the bread and wine, and an offering of one's possessions.

An assembly that engaged in these activities manifested some liturgical principles. Justin has described a liturgy in which there are two balanced pairs of activity. In the service of the Word, God speaks to human beings. In prayer human beings speak to God. The Word of God to us calls forth the response of our words to him. In the second pair, the Eucharist represents the gift of God to his creatures, that is, spiritual life through Christ. The offering or contribution represents the gifts of his people to God. God gives, and we give. The first pair centers in words; the second pair, in actions.

Or another way of schematizing Justin's service would be to say that God addresses his people through his Word, and they respond in praise (prayer), thanksgiving (Eucharist), and giving.

Justin, as noted, has much to say about spiritual sacrifice. These activities in the congregational assembly were the rational service, which in Christianity replaced the usual material offerings of paganism and Judaism. No disrespect to Justin is meant in taking a parallel from the Valentinian Gnostic Ptolemy, a man with whom Justin on other points would have had notable differences.[40] Nevertheless, Justin's own concept of sacrifice is well summarized in the following statement from Ptolemy, who was close to Justin's time and who in this, and in much else, belonged to the same thought world: "The Savior commanded us to offer oblations, not those of irrational animals or incense, but of spiritual praises, gloryings, and thanksgiving, and of fellowship and doing good to our neighbors."[41] Justin could have ratified that with his own "amen."

*Originally printed in *Restoration Quarterly* 36 (1996): 267–78, "Special Issue: Studies in Honor of Thomas H. Olbricht on the Occasion of his Sixty-fifth Birthday."

Chapter 15 Endnotes

1. This article began as a paper read on September 15, 1977, as part of the Gorman Lectures on the Liturgy at the University of Dallas. A popular version—abridged, rearranged, and omitting footnotes—appeared under the title "How We Christians Worship" in Issue 37 (Vol. XII, No. 1) of *Christian History* and is used by permission. The full text with notes is offered here as a tribute to Thomas H. Olbricht—onetime colleague, longtime friend, ever-faithful Christian scholar—whose rare competence in biblical studies, theology, history, and communications is expressed in being a loyal churchman with an interest in the church's worship.

2. Several works have studied Justin's life and thought, e.g., L. W. Barnard, *Justin Martyr: His Life and Thought* (Cambridge: University Press, 1967); E. F. Osborn, *Justin Martyr* (BHT 47; Tübingen: J. C. B. Mohr, 1973); N. Hydahl, *Philosophie und Christentum: Eine Interpretation der Einleitung zum Dialog Justins* (ATDan 9; Copenhagen, 1966); J. C. M. van Winden, *An Early Christian Philosopher, Justin Martyr's Dialogue with Trypho,* Chapters 1–9 (Leiden: Brill, 1971); O. Skarsaune, *The Proof from Prophecy: A Study in Justin Martyr's Proof-Text Tradition* (Leiden: Brill, 1987); further bibliography in Theodore Stylianopoulos, "Justin Martyr," *Encyclopedia of Early Christianity* (2nd edition; ed. E. Ferguson; New York: Garland [Taylor & Francis], 1990), 649–50, to which add S. Parvis and P. Foster, eds., *Justin Martyr and His Worlds* (Minneapolis: Fortress, 2007). Justin's information about the liturgy has not received such detailed and systematic study, but see J. A. Jungmann, *The Early Liturgy* (Notre Dame: University of Notre Dame Press, 1959), 40–49; and A. Hamman, "Valeur et signification des renseignments liturgiques de Justin," *Studia Patristica* 13 (1975): 364–74.

3. For other accounts of worship services, see my *Early Christians Speak* (3rd ed.; Abilene: ACU Press, 1999), 79–89.

4. *Early Christians Speak,* 66, 79–80, 92. The translation is my own, but it is intentionally conventional.

5. George H. Williams, "Baptismal Theology and Practice in Rome as Reflected in Justin Martyr," *The Ecumenical World of Orthodox Civilization, Russia and Orthodoxy, III: Essays in Honour of George Florovsky* (eds. A. Blane and Th. E. Bird; The Hague, 1974), 9–34; C. I. K. Story, "Justin's *Apology* I.62–64: Its Importance for the Author's Treatment of Christian Baptism," *VC* 16 (1962) 172–78; Everett Ferguson, *Baptism in the Early Church: History, Theology, and Liturgy in the First Five Centuries* (Grand Rapids: Eerdmans, 2009), 237–44.

6. W. Rordorf, *Sabbat und Sonntag in der Alten Kirche* (Traditio Christiana 2; Zurich: Theologischer Verlag, 1972); E. Ferguson, *Early Christians Speak,* 65–78.

7. E. Ferguson, "'When You Come Together': *Epi To Auto* in Early Christian Literature," *Restoration Quarterly* 16 (1973): 202–8.

8. W. Rordorf, *Sunday* (Philadelphia: Westminster, 1968); D. A. Carson, ed., from *Sabbath to Lord's Day: A Biblical, Historical, and Theolgical Investigation* (Grand Rapids: Zondervan, 1982).

9. Heb. 10:25; *Barn.* 16; *Did.* 16; *2 Clem.* 17.

10. Exod. 20:8–11; Deut. 5:12–15.

11. L. Duchesne, *Christian Worship* (London: SPCK, 1949), 46–50; G. Dix, *The Shape of the Liturgy* (London: Dacre, 1945), 36–47; J. Jungmann, *The Early Liturgy* (Notre Dame: University of Notre Dame Press, 1959), 43; T. Klauser, *A Short History of the Western Liturgy* (2nd ed.; Oxford: University Press, 1979), 1–8; C. W. Dugmore, *The Influence of the Synagogue Service upon the Divine Office* (Westminster: Faith, 1966). For further bibliography on the early liturgy, see E. J. Kilmartin, "Liturgy," *Encyclopedia of Early Christianity* (2nd edition; ed. E. Ferguson; New York: Garland [Taylor, & Francis],1997), 686–87, and the articles reprinted in E. Ferguson, ed., *Studies in Early Christianity,* Vol. XV: *Worship in Early Christianity* (New York: Garland [Taylor, & Francis], 1993).

12. Paul F. Bradshaw (*The Search for the Origins of Christian Worship* [Oxford: University Press, 1992]) shows that less can be known about early Jewish practice than earlier scholars assumed and that there was not a straightline development of Christian practice, but rather a variety only later standardized. This was certainly true of details, if not of the broad categories of activities.

13. On the primitive balance of word and eucharist, see S. M. Gibbard, "Liturgy as Proclamation of the Word," *StudLit* 1 (1962), 6–20, repr. in *Studies in Early Christianity,* Vol. XV: *Worship in Early Christianity,* 68–82.

14. J. O. Cobham, "Sunday and Eucharist," *StudLit* 2 (1963), 8–28.

15. Evidence abounds from the early church for this practice of following the scripture reading with a lesson related to the reading: 1 Tim. 4:13; *2 Clem.* 19; Irenaeus, *Adv. Haer.* IV.xxxiii. 8; Tertullian, *Apol.* 39, and *On the Soul* 9. Clement of Alexandria's *Who Is the Rich Man?* is based on Mark 10:17–31; Melito *On the Passover* opens with a reference to the preceding reading from Exodus; Pseudo-Cyprian's *Against the Jews* begins with comments on the parables of the wicked husbandmen and of the wedding feast (cf. Dirk van Damme, *Pseudo-Cyprian Adversus Iudaeos: Gegen die Judenchristen, Die älteste Lateinische Predigt* [Paradosis 22; Freiburg, 1969]). Other references to reading are Clement of Alexandria, *Misc.* VI.xiv.113; Tertullian, *Praesc.* 36, 41. Other references to preaching include Clement of Alexandria, *Paed.* III.xi.80; *Acts of John* 106f. Reading of the Gospels and a sermon based on it in the assembly occurs in *Acts of Peter* 20–21.

16. E.g., Clement of Alexandria, *Misc.* I.ix; VII.xvi; Origen, *Princ.* IV.ii.7.

17. T. G. Jalland, "Justin Martyr and the President of the Eucharist," *Studia Patristica* 5 (1962), 83–85.

18. Cf. *2 Clem.*

19. Origen, *On Prayer* 31.1, 3; Tertullian, *On the Crown 3; On Prayer* 17.23; For bowing or prostration, see Justin, *Dial.* 90; and for bending the knee, *Acts of Paul and Thecla* 24.

20. E. Ferguson, "The Liturgical Function of the 'Sursum Corda,'" *Studia Patristica* 13 (1975), 359–63, with special reference to the Eucharistic prayer.

21. A. Hamman, *La Prière*, II. *Les trois premiers siècles* (Tournai, 1963). Some references to congregational prayers include Ign. *Eph.* 5; Clement of Alexandria, *Misc.* VI.xiv.113; Tertullian, *On the Soul* 9 and *Apol.* 39; *Acts of John* 108. For a sampling of some early prayers, see my *Early Christians Speak*, 133–44. A more complete collection is in A. Hamman, *Early Christian Prayers* (Chicago: Henry Regnery, 1961).

22. Josef Kroll, *Die Christliche Hymnodik bis zu Klemens von Alexandreia* (Darmstadt, 1968; repr. of 1921); Lucien Deiss, *Hymnes et prières des premiers siècles* (Paris: Fleurus, 1963); H. Darre, "De l'usage des hymnes dans l'Eglise des origines à S. Gregoire le Grand," *Etudes Gregoriennes* 9 (1968), 25–36, repr. in *Studies in Early Christianity*, Vol. XV: *Worship in Early Christianity*, 255–66. A few early hymns are translated in my *Early Christians Speak*, 145–62.

23. John Alexander Lamb, *The Psalms in Christian Worship* (London: Faith, 1962).

24. I follow Justin's own name, Eucharist, for what others have called the Lord's Supper, communion, or the breaking of bread. For other accounts and their interpretation, see my *Early Christians Speak*, 91–123.

25. K. M. Hofmann, *Philema Hagion* (Gutersloh, 1938); K. Thraede, "Ursprung und Formen des 'Heiligen Kusses' in frühen Christentum," *JAC* 11/12 (1968/69) 124–80; J. Quasten, "Der Kuss des Neugetauften in altchristlicher Taufliturgie," *Liturgie, Gestalt, und Vollzug* (Festschrift for J. Pascher; ed. W. Durig; Munich, 1963), 267ff.; E. Kreider, "Let the Faithful Greet Each Other: The Kiss of Peace," *Conrad Grebel Rev* (1987): 29–49; L. E. Phillips, *The Ritual Kiss in Early Christian Worship* (Bramcote: Grove, 1996); M. Penn, *Kissing Christians: Ritual and Community in the Late Ancient Church* (Philadelphia: University of Pennsylvania Press, 2006).

26. Holy—Rom. 16:16 et passim; love—1 Pet. 5:14.

27. W. Elert, *Eucharist and Church Fellowship in the First Four Centuries* (St. Louis: Concordia, 1966).

28. E. Ferguson, "Wine as a Table-Drink in the Ancient World," *Restoration Quarterly* 13 (1970): 141–53.

29. 1 Tim. 4:5. For the Christian practice of consecration by a prayer of thanksgiving see E. G. C. F. Atchley, *On the Epiclesis of the Eucharistic Liturgy and in the Consecration of the Font* (Oxford: University Press, 1935); N. A. D. Scotland, *Eucharistic Consecration in the First Four Centuries* (Oxford: Latimer House, 1989). G. A. Mitchell (*Eucharistic Consecration in the Primitive Church* [London, 1948]) argues that the original consecration through thanksgiving ceased to be understood, and so other elements were introduced into the prayer. E. Mazza, *The Origins of the Eucharistic Prayer* (Collegeville: Liturgical Press, 1995).

30. J. Hamilton, "Justin's *Apology 66*: A Review of Scholarship and a Suggested Synthesis," *ETL* 48 (1972), 554–60. For representative older scholarship, see A. J. MacDonald, *The Evangelical Doctrine of Holy Communion* (Cambridge: University Press, 1930), ch. 2, and Darwell Stone, *A History of the Doctrine of the Holy Eucharist*, Vol. 1 (New York: Longmans, Green, 1909), 23–41. Cf. more recently, G. W. H. Lampe, "The Eucharist in the Thought of the Early Church," *Eucharistic Theology Then and Now* (Theological Collections 9; London: SPCK, 1968); Maurice Jourjon, "Justin" in W. Rordorf, et al., *The Eucharist of the Early Christians* (New York: Pueblo, 1978), 71–85; P. F. Bradshaw, *Eucharistic Origins* (Oxford: Oxford University Press, 2004).

31. W. Rordorf, "Le sacrifice eucharistique," *TZ* 25 (1969), 335–53, repr. in E. Ferguson, ed., *Studies in Early Christianity*, Vol. XV: *Worship in Early Christianity*, 193–211; R. P. C. Hanson, *Eucharistic Offering in the Early Church* (Bramcote: Grove, 1979). For the meaning of the word *eucharistia* see T. Schermann, *"Eucharistia und Eucharistein* in ihrem Bedeutungswandel bis 200 n. Chr.," *Philologus* 69 (1910), 375–410; P.Schubert, *Form and Function of the Pauline Thanksgivings (ZNW* Beiheft 20; Berlin, 1939); J. Laporte, *Eucharistia in Philo* (New York: Edwin Mellen, 1983).

32. Luke 24:53; Acts 2:42; cf. 20:7; 1 Cor. 10:16; 11:24; Mark 14:22.

33. *Did.* 9(cf. 14); Ign. *Philad.* 4 and *Smyrn.* 8; *Acts of John* 86; 109–110; *Acts of Peter* 2; Tertullian, *Praesc.* 36; Origen, *C. Cels.* VIII.57.

34. Justin, *1 Apol.* 13, and *Dial.* 41; 116–18. Odo Casel, "Die *Logikē Thusia* der antiken Mystik in christlichliturgischer Umdeutung," *Jahrbuch für Liturgiewissenschaft* 4 (1924), 41–44; M. H. Shepherd, "The Early Apologists and Christian Worship," *JR* 18 (1938), 60–79; E. Ferguson, "Spiritual Sacrifice in Early Christianity and Its Environment," *ANRW* II.23.1 (Berlin: Walter de Gruyter, 1980), 1151–89, esp. 1167–69, 1173–74, 1178–79, 1182–83, 1185, 1187–88.

35. R. P. C. Hanson, "The Liberty of the Bishop to Improvise Prayer in the Eucharist," *VC* 15 (1961), 173–76; without use of Justin, Thomas J. Talley, "The Eucharistic Prayer of the Ancient Church According to Recent Research: Results and Reflections," *StudLit* 14 (1982), 34–51, both repr. in *Studies in Early Christianity*, Vol. XV: *Worship in Early Christianity*, 83–86, 88–108.

36. Louis Ligier, "The Origins of the Eucharistic Prayer," *StudLit 9* (1973), 161–85. There may be liturgical fragments in various places in Justin's writings—see David Gill, "A Liturgical Fragment in Justin's *Dialogue* 29.1," *HTR* 59 (1966), 98–101; and the creedal passages noted in J. N. D. Kelly, *Early Christian Creeds* (2nd ed.; London: Longmans, 1960), 70–76.

37. E. Ferguson, "The Demons According to Justin Martyr," in Wil C. Goodheer, ed., *The Man of the Messianic Reign and Other Essays: Festschrift in Honor of Dr. Elza Huffard* (Wichita Falls: Western Christian Foundation, 1980), 102–12.

38. Contributions of produce—*Did.* 13; of money—Tertullian, *Apol.* 39; the voluntary nature of giving—L. Vischer, *Tithing in the Early Church* (Philadelphia: Fortress, 1966).

39. Gerhard Ulhorn, *Christian Charity in the Ancient Church* (New York: Scribner's, 1883); Adolf Harnack, *The Mission and Expansion of Christianity* (New York: Harper, 1962; repr. of 1908) 147-98; selection of texts and further references in my *Early Christians Speak*, 203-14.

40. Gerd Luedemann ("Zur Geschichte des ältesten Christentums in Rom," *ZNW* 70 [1979], 97-114) argued that the Gnostic Ptolemy is the same as the Ptolemy mentioned in Justin's *2 Apol.* 2, but this must remain speculative.

41. *Ad Floram* 3 (Epiphanius, *Heresies* XXXIII.5).

16

"When You Come Together"

Επι το αυτο in Early Christian Literature

J. W. Roberts made his greatest contribution to scholarship in the grammatical insights which he brought to bear on the interpretation on the New Testament. The subject matter of this article is thus a fitting tribute to a friend who remained my teacher even after I became his colleague.

J. D. Thomas contributed a note on "'Added to the Church' Acts 2:47" in *Restoration Quarterly* 4.4 (1960), 238–40, in which he discussed the difficulties interpreters have felt with *epi to auto* in Acts 2:47. He rejected, with most scholars, C. C. Torrey's conjecture that the phrase was a mistranslation from an Aramaic original,[1] and he contended that the ordinary meaning of the Greek phrase "together" fitted the passage quite adequately.

The phrase *epi to auto* is defined by Bauer (following the fifth-century lexicographer Hesychius) as "together, at the same place."[2] It occurs in an author as classical as Thucydides, who uses it in 1.79 for coming to the same opinion or same conclusion.³ The meaning of the phrase in inscriptions and papyri is "in all," "total,"⁴ and Liddell-Scott cites a second-century papyrus with the meaning "added together," "making a total."⁵ Professor A. J. Malherbe points me to a passage where the meaning "together" almost means "public."⁶

More frequent than the classical and popular occurrences are its appearances in works by Jewish and Christian authors. The Septuagint offers a very large number of occurrences, and the frequency of *epi to auto* here perhaps reflects a Semitic background to the early Christian usage. Psalm 132 (133):1 may be an important text for early Christian usage. The phrase ends a sentence in Psalm 33:4 (34:3, English) as it does in the best manuscripts of Acts 2:47. It is used in 3 Maccabees 3:1 with *sunagō* ("to gather together in one place"), a combination frequent in early Christian writers. Henry J. Cadbury made an examination of the usage of *epi to auto* in the Greek psalter and offered this classification: community of place and action (Ps. 2:2, a frequently cited passage in the early church), association in time (4:9, English 4:8), and various intensive senses (18:10, English 19:9; 40:8, English 41:6; 121:3, English 122:3).⁷ Max Wilcox translates the phrase in Psalm 2:2 "in coalition" or "in alliance." He further observes that the Hebrew underlying the Septuagint translation is *yahad*, which is also rendered in the Greek version *hama* or *homothumadon*.⁸

The publication of the Dead Sea Scrolls has strengthened the case for a Semitic origin of the New Testament usage of *epi to auto*, particularly in Acts 2:47. *Yahad* has a frequent and peculiar use in the Dead Sea Scrolls for the "community."⁹ One of the occurrences of *yahad* in this sense is the *Rule of the Community* (1QS) V. 7, where Wilcox finds the Hebrew phrase "to join the congregation" equivalent to the Greek *prosetithei epi to auto* ("added together") in Acts 2:47.¹⁰ He concludes that *epi to auto* in Acts is not really a Septuagintalism and not a mistranslation. Rather it was a quasi-technical term meaning "in unity" or "in fellowship." If the phrase entered Luke's knowledge and use from Psalm 2:2, the factor determining its meaning was the peculiar nuance with which the early church endowed the phrase, a nuance warranted by the usage of the Dead Sea Scrolls. Wilcox translates Acts 2:47, "The Lord was day by day incorporating into the Fellowship those who were being saved."¹¹ By following the Qumran equivalent we could translate, "God joined [added] to the community."

The idea of a community or a definite assembly does not seem to be present in Hellenistic Jewish use of *epi to auto*. The calling together "in one place" for a speech in Josephus, *Wars* II.346 is not significantly different from coming "together" (intentionally) in Joshua 9:2 and (accidentally) in Susannah 14, or being in the same place (living there) in Deuteronomy 25:5 and (after a shipwreck) in *Testament of Naphtali* 6.6.

Before the discovery of the Dead Sea Scrolls, scholars had seen in Christian usage, however, an emphasis on community. A. A. Vazakas, in an early reply to Torrey's hypothesis, directed attention to the way the New Testament and apostolic fathers laid stress on the unity of the church in passages employing *epi to auto*. He concluded that in these documents the phrase signified the union of the Christian body in one society. Although noting that Ignatius, *Philadelphians* 6.2, referred to the "common assembly," he did not follow up the suggestion in the other references given.[12]

W. F. Howard accepted Vazakas's point about "union in the Christian body" and suggested that the phrase might be translated "in church." He further called attention to the parallelism of *en ekklesia* and *epi to auto* in 1 Corinthians 11:18, 20 ("when you come together in church," "when you come together at the same place") with the indication that the two phrases are synonymous.[13] An examination of the phrase *epi to auto* in the apostolic fathers permits Howard's suggestion to be carried further.

First Clement 34.7 exhorts, "When we have come together in one place (*epi to auto*) in harmony and with a good conscience, let us cry out earnestly as from one mouth to him in order that we may be partakers of his great and glorious promises." Ignatius warns the Ephesians: "The one who does not come to the assembly (*epi to auto*) is already puffed up and has condemned himself" (*Eph*. 5.3). Later he exhorts them, "Give diligence therefore to come together more frequently for thanksgiving (*eucharistia*) and praise to God. For whenever you are together (*epi to auto*) frequently, the powers of Satan are destroyed" (*Eph*. 13.1).

Ignatius speaks in the same way to the Magnesians: "Even so you are to do nothing apart from the bishop and the elders. Do not attempt to make an appearance of being right in your own eyes, but let there be in common (*epi to auto*) one prayer, one petition, one mind, one hope in love, in blameless joy"

(*Magn.* 7.1). Ignatius's exhortation to the Philadelphians is the same: "All of you are to be together with undivided heart" (*Philad.* 6.2). He further instructs them, "It is fitting for you as a church of God to appoint a deacon to be an ambassador of God to Antioch in order that you may rejoice together with them when they come together (*epi to auto*) and may glorify the name" (10.1).

The *Epistle of Barnabas* 4.20 expresses similar concerns: "Do not retire within yourselves and live alone as if you were already justified, but come together in one place (*epi to auto*) and seek what is profitable in common."

Every one of these passages refers to the public or common assembly of the church. The worship context is especially evident and could be confirmed by a detailed analysis if necessary. We might appropriately translate *epi to auto* in every case "in the assembly." Thus, instead of a more general reference to unity or fellowship, there is a more specific reference to a definite expression of that unity: the assembly of the church, more particularly the worship assembly of the church. If not a "technical" term, the phrase is a regular one for the gathering for worship of the community. The full force of this seems not to have been pressed by those who have considered the evidence of the extra-canonical Christian literature on the usage of *epi to auto*.

The *Epistle of Barnabas* uses *epi to auto* in two other passages, meaning "in the same place," in the same passage of scripture (11.8), and describing the coming of Israel together in the same place to make a petition to Moses (12:7). The three occurrences in the *Shepherd of Hermas*—"in one place" (the heart—*Mandates* V.i.4) and "together" (*Mandates* X.iii.3; in the heart—*Vision* III.ix.8)—have no special significance.

The use of *epi to auto* with reference to the liturgical assembly appears also in Justin Martyr. He introduces his description of early Christian worship with the statement "On the day called Sunday there is a meeting in one place (*epi to auto*) of all those who live in the cities and country, and the memoirs of the apostles or the writings of the prophets are read as long as time permits. . . ." (*1 Apol.* 67.3).[14] Justin elsewhere uses *epi to auto* only in 40.11 as part of a quotation from Psalm 2:2. When he refers to a chance meeting "in the same place," in *Dialogue* 3, he uses *en to auto*.

Should more weight be given to the background or the foreground in interpreting the New Testament usage of *epi to auto*? The New Testament uses the phrase in some passages with the meaning of "together" without any special significance. Two of these are quotations from Psalm 2:2 (Matt. 22:34; Acts 4:26). It means "together" or "at the same place" in Luke 17:35 and refers to husband and wife being together sexually in 1 Corinthians 7:5.

Other New Testament passages can be taken as referring to the assembly of the church. That this is the coming together for public worship is clear in 1 Corinthians 11:20 (as seen above) and 14:23 ("when the whole church comes together in one place," or in the assembly). Acts 1:15 may more naturally be read with the papyri "the multitude of persons was *in all* about one hundred and twenty," but there is the possibility that the idea is "there was a multitude of persons in one place (in an assembly) about one hundred and twenty." No doubt would seem to attach to Acts 2:1, "they were all together (*homou*) in one place" or "in assembly." Similarly Acts 2:44, "all the believers were together and had all things common," may be understood as "all the believers were a community," that is, "were in assembly." Manuscript D gives a different version of Acts 2:46, including another occurrence of *epi to auto*: "All continued in the temple, and in their houses together (*epi to auto*—in their own assembly in houses?) they broke bread."

That brings this study back to Acts 2:47, where the several variant readings indicate the difficulties scribes found with the text. The manuscripts which put *epi to auto* with 3:1 only transfer the problem to another sentence where "together" is even more awkward. Or one may continue to translate 2:47, "The Lord added together daily those who were being saved." Our evidence, however, points to the possibility of the rendering, "The Lord added daily those who were being saved to the assembly."[15] The addition "to the church" found in several manuscripts (principally D) may be adduced in support. Howard is probably right in seeing the phrase as first a marginal gloss by a scribe who recognized that "in the church" was the meaning of "in one place."[16] It found its way into the text as an interpretive addition, in this case a correct one. The value of the other evidence adduced for the usage of *epi to auto*, however, is in no way dependent on the correct solution of the textual and interpretive problems of Acts 2:47.

The principal expression of "togetherness" for the early church was in the public worship assembly. That the use of *epi to auto* for such an assembly is ultimately derived from Qumran is less than certain, but it is probable that this application does come from Jewish usage, where "together" had come to refer to "community" or "assembly." Either a quasi-technical meaning of *epi to auto* (or only of the underlying Hebrew) was already present in New Testament times and almost supplanted other uses of the phrase in early Christianity, or Paul's use of the phrase in reference to the public assembly led to a "technical" use. The frequent occurrence of the phrase is one more indication that early Christianity did not envisage itself apart from a visible community, an assembly which demonstrated its nature in coming together for worship. Such a conclusion is in keeping with J. W. Roberts's emphasis on the church.

*Originally printed in *Restoration Quarterly* 16 (1973): 202–8, a volume "In Memoriam: J. W. Roberts."

Chapter 16 Endnotes

1. *The Composition and Date of Acts* (Cambridge: Harvard University Press, 1916), 10.

2. *A Greek-English Lexicon of the New Testament*, ed. F. W. Arndt and W. F. Gingerich (Chicago, 1957), 123 and cf. 288; 3rd edition revised and edited by F. W. Danker (Chicago, 2000), 153, 363.

3. Cf. Dio Chrysostom, *Discourses* 33.9, "Frequenting the theatre for this very thing" (*ep' auto touto*).

4. In addition to Bauer's references, note F. Blass and A. Debrunner, *A Greek Grammar of the New Testament*, trans. and ed. Robert Funk (Chicago, 1961), 122.

5. *Greek-English Lexicon*, 9th edition (Oxford, 1940), 283.

6. Ps.-Crates, *Ep.* 21 (Hercher, *Epistolographi Graeci*, 212).

7. "Luke—Translator or Author?" *American Journal of Theology* 24 (1920): 454.

8. *The Semitisms of Acts* (Oxford, 1965), 95.

9. Bruno W. Dombrowski, "*Ha Yahad* in 1QS and *To Koinon*: An Instance of Early Greek and Jewish Synthesis," *Harvard Theological Review* 59 (July, 1966): 293–307; Ralph Marcus, "Philo, Josephus, and the Dead Sea *Yahad*," *Journal of Biblical Literature* 71 (1952): 207–9.

10. *Op. cit.* 96. If there should be some connection between the Therapeutae described by Philo and the Qumran sect, then it may be noted that when Eusebius paraphrases Philo's account of the "common assemblies" of the Therapeutae, he speaks of their meetings "at the same place" (*epi tauton*). Likely Eusebius is simply reflecting Christian usage (*H. E.* II.17.21).

11. *Op. cit.* 99, 100. His views are accepted by Matthew Black, *An Aramaic Approach to the Gospels and Acts* (3rd Edition; Oxford, 1967), 10. So also O. F. Payne, "Semitism in the Book of Acts," *Apostolic History and the Gospel*, ed. W. W. Gasque and R. P. Martin (Exeter, England, 1970), 1928. I would rather stress the assembly idea than the community idea.

12. "Is Acts I–XV.35 a Literal Translation from an Aramaic Original?" *Journal of Biblical Literature* 37 (1918): 105–10. See below for references to the apostolic fathers.

13. "Semitisms in the New Testament," *A Grammar of New Testament Greek*, by J. H. Moulton and W. F. Howard (Edinburgh, 1929), Vol. II, 473. The translation "in church" for *epi to auto* is cited with approval by Wilcox, *op. cit.*, 94, 98.

14. Cf. *Martyrdom of Justin* 3.1 (Rec. B); Origen, *On Prayer* 31.5.

15. Cf. Wilcox, *op. cit.*, 100, with the change from "fellowship" to "assembly."

16. Howard, *op. cit.*, 473. I have elsewhere argued that Codex D preserves a knowledge of Palestinian (even Qumran) terminology—"Qumran and Codex D," *Revue de Qumran*, June, 1972, 75–80.

17

Τόπος in 1 Timothy 2:8

Many commentators understand 1 Timothy 2:1–15 to refer primarily to public (older writers would say "social") worship. Dibelius and Conzelmann,[1] although acknowledging that the regulations for women "here doubtless intended for the worship service, originally referred to the behavior of women in general,"[2] point to the structural parallels between 1 Timothy and the nearly contemporary church order known as the *Didache*: prayer and worship, followed by ethical requirements of the worship service, followed by regulations for church officers.[3] Other indications that the setting envisioned for these instructions was the assembly of the church are the general description and specific contents of the instructions. Support for this understanding may be found in a more detailed look at the phrase "in every place" in 1 Timothy 2:8. After all, Greek had an adverb, πανταχοῦ, for the general meaning "everywhere." So, what does "in every place" refer to?

Some commentators see the reference of 1 Timothy 2:8 to the worship assemblies of Christians. Gordon Fee writes, "This is to be so in every church service, or perhaps more likely, 'in every place where believers gather in and around Ephesus' (the house-churches)."⁴ Walter Lock writes, "'Wherever you meet for public worship'; or more probably the writer means the rule to be universal for all churches under his influence."⁵ C. K. Barrett is the most explicit and most helpful: "'Such prayer is to be made everywhere', better 'in every place' (ἐν παντὶ τόπῳ). This is no mere literalism, for in Jewish usage 'place' meant 'meeting-place', 'place of prayer'; and there is evidence (especially 1 Cor. 1:2; 1 Thess. 1:8) that it became Christian usage too. The author means 'in every Christian meeting-place'. Cp. also Mal. 1:10f."⁶ This paper will present some of the evidence to support this more precise interpretation offered by Barrett.

Τόπος was the general word for any "place" (it gives English "topography" and, in reference to a place in a literary work, "topic"). The Jews, however, used τόπος (place) in some instances in a specialized sense for the temple or a synagogue. As they used προσευχή ("prayer") for "(house of) prayer" (full phrase in Matt. 21:13 and parallels) or "place of prayer" (Acts 16:13, 16), so they used simply "place" for "place of prayer" or "place of meeting." Bauer-Arndt-Gingrich-Danker consider the possibility that τόπος may mean "temple," as a short form of "holy place" but do not recognize the meaning "synagogue" and define ἐν παντὶ τόπῳ in 1 Timothy 2:8 as *"everywhere* that men or Christians live."⁷ This is inadequate, for a stronger statement may be made to the effect that among Jews "place" acquired in some contexts a technical reference to the "place of worship." This seems to have been the result of connotations acquired by the Hebrew *maqom* and Aramaic *âtar*.⁸

Helmut Koester notes that "place was seldom used in classical Greek literature for holy places; whereas in Hebrew this was common."⁹ Only the Septuagint developed τόπος into a technical term for the holy place.¹⁰ Among the passages where the Septuagint uses τόπος to refer to the temple are the account of its dedication by Solomon in 1 Kings 8:29, 30, 35, 42 (particularly notable because the Hebrew has the word "house" [="temple"], but the Greek says simply τόπος) and the Psalms, notably 75:3 (Heb.76:2), where God's "place" is parallel to his "dwelling (place) in Zion," and 131:5, 7 (Heb. 132:5, 7), where "place" is equivalent to God's "tent." The "holy place" is common in the books of Maccabees for the temple (e.g., 2 Macc. 5:19–20; 3:2, 18, 38; 13:23).¹¹

Despite the hesitance of the Bauer Lexicon, there seems no reason to take John 11:48 other than as a reference to the "temple and nation" of the Jews. There is no doubt that the phrase "holy place" in Matthew 24:15 means temple; the dropping of "holy" in Acts 6:14 and 21:28 in the same context where "holy place" also occurs (Acts 6:13; 21:28) agrees with the tendency in 2 Maccabees for the single word "place" to suffice for the fuller phrase in reference to the temple.

Perhaps as part of the tendency to transfer language of the temple to synagogues, Jews in Palestine applied the phrase "holy place," or simply "place," to their synagogues.[12] Note these two synagogue inscriptions in Hebrew: "May peace be in this place and in all the places of his people Israel" (from 'Alma) and "May peace be in this place and in all the places of Israel" (from Bar'am).[13] A synagogue at Bethshean of the Roman-Byzantine period contains a mosaic pavement ascribed to the sixth century AD with an accompanying Aramaic inscription that refers to the repair of the "holy place" (*dátarah [qedi]shah*). A nearby room contains a Greek inscription naming the person who "made the mosaic of this place [τόπου],"[14] presumably the synagogue. From near the same period a Samaritan synagogue at Ramat-Aviv in Israel includes a Greek inscription that reads, "Blessing and peace to Israel and to this place [τόπῳ]. Amen."[15] The terminology of "holy place" (ἁγίῳ τόπῳ) for the synagogue occurs also in the Dispersion, as in a third-century inscription from Stobi.[16] This use of "place" was much earlier.

The *Rule of the Community* (perhaps late second century BC) from the Dead Sea Scrolls uses the Hebrew word for "place" to refer to the gathering of ten men that formed the basic unit of the sect: "And in every place where there are ten persons of the Council of the Community"; "and in the place where the ten are" (1 QS vi.3, 6).[17] Philo provides the Greek terminology. In describing the Essenes he says, "[On the seventh day] they abstain from all other work and proceed to sacred places [ἱερούς τόπους] that they call synagogues [συναγωγαί]."[18] Elsewhere Philo uses τόπος for the temple[19] and προσευχή for synagogue.[20]

Josephus, in his collection of Roman decrees from the time of Julius Caesar (first century BC) guaranteeing privileges to the Jews, quotes two decrees that use "place" in the sense of "synagogue." One "to the magistrates, council and people of Sardis" notes that the Jews "from the earliest times ... have had an association of their own in accordance with their native laws and a place of their own [τόπον ἴδιον]" (*Antiquities* 14.235). The other, a "Decree of the people of Sardis," states that the Jews may "come together and have a communal life and adjudicate suits among themselves, and that a place [τόπος] be given them in which they may gather together with their wives and children and offer their ancestral prayers and sacrifices to God" and "a place [τόπον] shall be set apart by the magistrates for them to build and inhabit" (14.259–261).[21] Although these are official decrees, the language betrays Jewish terminology, the result either of the terms in which the Jews had phrased their petitions to the authorities (more likely) or of Josephus's (re)wording of the decrees.

The usage of "place" to refer to the "place of meeting" was taken up by Christians.[21a] Particularly impressive is Paul's use of the phrase ἐν παντὶ τόπῳ. With the Jewish meaning in mind, the four occurrences in Paul's writings take on a special significance. First Corinthians is addressed not only to "the church of God that is in Corinth" but also to "all those who call on the name of our Lord Jesus Christ in every place [ἐν παντὶ τόπῳ]" (1:2).[22] "To call on the name" is Old Testament language for worship, and the assembly would be where the name of Christ was invoked. Τόπῳ is parallel to ἐκκλησίᾳ. Paul wants his instructions to apply to every Christian assembly or church, every meeting place that acknowledges Jesus as Lord and calls on him in worship (cf. 11:16; 14:33). First Thessalonians 1:8 says that the faith of the Thessalonian Christians in God "has gone forth in every place [ἐν παντί τόπῳ]."[23] It was not among pagans that the faith of the Thessalonians had become famous, but "in all the churches," "in all the meeting places" of Christians (whether Jewish assemblies are to be included is doubtful). Second Corinthians 2:14 less obviously reflects the meaning we have found, but it is possible even here: "Thanks be to God ... who manifests the fragrance of the knowledge of him through us in every place." If the technical sense is intended, then Paul refers to his experiences spreading the blessing of the knowledge of Christ (or of God) to every congregation. In view of the usage in these passages, 1 Timothy 2:8 surely indicates the practice to be observed in the place of meeting, the assembled church.

The phrase ἐν παντὶ τόπῳ occurs in the Septuagint of Malachi 1:11 and likely came into Christian usage from that text. "Therefore, from the rising of the sun to its setting my name has been glorified among the Gentiles, and in every place [ἐν παντὶ τόπῳ] incense and pure sacrifice are offered in my name." Whether the Septuagint translators were thinking in terms of "in every synagogue" is doubtful, but the association with place of sacrifice is notable.[24] Christians who appropriated this text took it as a reference to Christian meetings of Gentile believers, whose sacrifice was acceptable to God, whereas God rejected the sacrifices of Jews (1:10).

Malachi 1:11 was the Old Testament text most frequently cited in early Christian literature with reference to the Lord's Supper.[25] The usage was probably suggested because of the reference to the "table of the Lord" in 1:12. The passage was the point of entry for the application of sacrificial terminology to the Lord's Supper. Thus *Didache* 14 prescribes:

> Each Lord's day of the Lord come together, break bread, and give thanks, having earlier confessed your sins so that your sacrifice may be pure.... For this is what was spoken by the Lord, "In every place [ἐν παντὶ τόπῳ] and time offer to me a pure sacrifice, because I am a great king, says the Lord, and my name is marvelous among the Gentiles." (Mal. 1:11, 14)

The compiler of the *Didache* adds "time (of meeting?)" to "every place," in his quotation, perhaps because of his emphasis on meeting "every Lord's day." Only the context (coming together to break bread and give thanks) gives an association of "every place" with the meeting of Christians. Otherwise, Malachi serves as a simple explanation of the Christians' sacrifice, pure by reason of being offered by those who are reconciled to each other, since quarreling defiles the offering of spiritual worship to God (14.2).

Malachi 1:10–11 serves as an anti-Judaic text in Justin Martyr (mid-second century), with a specific contrast between Jewish worship and Gentile Christian observance of the Lord's Supper, the "pure sacrifice." In his *Dialogue with Trypho* 28, Justin applies Malachi 1:10–12a to God's rejection of Jewish sacrifices. Elsewhere, he uses this passage to go beyond God's rejection of Jewish worship to affirm God's acceptance of Christian worship. In *Dialogue*

41 he speaks of "the bread of the eucharist" and the contents of the prayer of thanksgiving and then proceeds to quote Malachi 1:10–12a with slightly different wording from chapter 28 but beginning and ending at the same point. Justin's application is pertinent: "He speaks beforehand then concerning us Gentiles who in every place offer sacrifices to him, that is the bread of the eucharist and the cup similarly of the eucharist, since he said that we glorify his name but you [Jews] profane it." "In every place" refers to sites where (Gentile) Christians take the bread and cup of the Eucharist and so glorify God. Justin's fullest discussion of spiritual sacrifice occurs in *Dialogue* 116–117. Justin affirms that Christians are the "true high priestly race of God, as even God himself bears witness, saying that in every place [ἐν παντὶ τόπῳ] among the Gentiles pure and well-pleasing sacrifices are offered to him" (116.3). God, he continues, anticipated the sacrifices in the Eucharist of the bread and cup presented by Christians "in every place" of the earth but rejected the sacrifices of the Jews, quoting again from Malachi 1:10–12 (117.1). Justin considers then the Jewish interpretation of Malachi as referring to the prayers offered in the Dispersion "in every place" (117.4). He responds that the Jews did not extend from the rising to the setting of the sun, but he claims that "there is not one single race of men ... among whom prayers and giving of thanks are not offered through the name of the crucified Jesus" (117.5). The universality in the Malachi passage is argued according to the phrase "from the rising to the setting of the sun," not from the phrase "in every place." That phrase is part of the dispute over whose prayers are the "pure sacrifices" of Malachi. Justin's argument reflects the rival claims as to whose meeting places for prayer (the Jewish synagogues or the Gentile Christian churches) represented the "in every place" of Malachi.[26]

Irenaeus at the end of the second century used the bread and the cup of the Eucharist as part of his argument against the Gnostics for the goodness of creation. This was the offering predicted in Malachi 1:10–11, which indicated that "the former people will indeed cease to make offerings to God, but in every place (*omni loco*) a sacrifice will be offered to him, and that a pure one; and his name is glorified among the Gentiles" (*Against Heresies* 4.17.5). The connection between the "every place" of Malachi and the prayers in the church is made explicit in Irenaeus's conclusion:

> Since, therefore, the name of the Son belongs to the Father [so the glorifying of Christ is the glorifying of God] and since in the omnipotent God the church makes offerings through Jesus Christ, on both these grounds he says well, "And in every place incense is offered to my name and a pure sacrifice." Now John, in the Apocalypse, says that incense is "the prayers of the saints." (4.17.6)[27]

Irenaeus continues by identifying the oblation of the church offered throughout all the world as the pure sacrifice acceptable to God (4.18.1). (If the phrase "the whole world" [*in universo mundo*—4.18.1 and 4.17.5] is based on Malachi's "in every place," then either Irenaeus or his Latin translator has misinterpreted, but in view of the other statements and the explicit application in Justin Martyr, the universality, if derived from Malachi, probably comes from the phrase "from the rising to the setting of the sun.") Irenaeus returns once more to make explicit that it is the church which offers the "pure sacrifice," neither the Jews (whose hands are stained with blood) nor the "gatherings" (*synagogae*) of heretics (who do not acknowledge the Creator—4.18.4). It is **the church** that fulfills the prophecy of Malachi.

The phrase ἐν παντὶ τόπῳ does occur in early Christian literature without any clear allusion to Malachi 1:11. Although the association of words is suggestive, there is not likely any special Christian use in *Martyrdom of Polycarp* 19.1, where the martyred Polycarp (mid-second century) is said to have been spoken of "by the Gentiles in every place" (cf. the address, κατὰ πάντα τόπον in prol.). *First Clement* (end of the first century) has the phrase ἐν παντὶ τόπῳ, also with no indication that Malachi 1:11 is in mind, but with explicit reference to worship. The statement is made that God in the Old Testament commanded sacrifices to be offered only in Jerusalem and "not in every place" (41.2); only the sanctuary in Jerusalem was recognized. *First Clement* also used τόπος by itself with reference to the place of assembly of the church. When the author counsels the leader of the insurrection at Corinth to depart rather than cause schism in the church, he promises him that "every place will receive him" (54.3), meaning that every other church will welcome the person who subordinates his interests to the welfare of the group.

A check through the *Thesaurus Linguae Graecae* shows how seldom in Christian literature of the early centuries the phrase ἐν παντὶ τόπῳ occurs apart from biblical quotations (Old and New Testament).[28] Even where these biblical quotations are interpreted in the sense of "everywhere" (the distinctive Jewish usage apparently becoming lost in the Gentile church),[29] the fact that the phrase apart from these contexts was so rare argues against its having been a normal idiom for the adverb "everywhere."

Although the background of "place" as "place of meeting" in Christianity goes back to Judaism, the significance for Christians was not "holy place." Christian authors frequently contrasted the Old Testament's emphasis on a single holy place as the place of sacrifice with the Christian practice of "in every place"[30] (this, of course, conveniently overlooked the development of Jewish thinking in connection with the prayers of the synagogue as a sacrifice). Already 2 Maccabees had reversed Greek notions by declaring, "But the Lord did not choose the nation for the sake of the holy place, but the place for the sake of the nation" (5:19). Christians carried this thinking further: "For it is not the place that sanctifies the man, but the man the place" (*Apostolic Constitutions* 8.34.8).

The Jewish and early Christian usage surveyed in this paper make a strong case that ἐν παντὶ τόπῳ in 1 Timothy 2:8 should be understood as a reference to men [ἄνδρας] leading in prayer "in the Christian assemblies." The result makes this passage a very close parallel in meaning to 1 Corinthians 14:33–35.

*Originally published in *Restoration Quarterly* 33 (1991): 65–73.

Chapter 17 Endnotes

1. *The Pastoral Epistles* (Hermeneia; Philadelphia: Fortress, 1972), 35–49.

2. Ibid., 45

3. Ibid., 6. Cf. J. N. D. Kelly's heading for 1 Tim. 2:1–15, "The Ordering of Public Worship," in *The Pastoral Epistles* (Black's New Testament Commentaries; London: A. & C. Black, 1963), 59.

4. *1 and 2 Timothy, Titus* (A Good News Commentary; San Francisco: Harper, 1984), 34

5. *The Pastoral Epistles* (International Critical Commentary; Edinburgh: T & T Clark, 1924), 30. See also C. Spicq, *Saint Paul, Les Épîtres Pastorales* (Paris: J. Gabalda, 1969), 372; A. T. Robertson, *World Pictures in the New Testament* (Nashville: Broadman, 1931), 4.569; William Henrikson, *New Testament Commentary: Exposition of the Pastoral Epistles* (Grand Rapids: Baker, 1957), 102–3; E. K. Simpson, *The Pastoral Epistles* (London: Tyndale, 1954), 45.

6. *The Pastoral Epistles* (New Clarendon Bible; Oxford: Clarendon, 1963), 54.

7. *A Greek-English Lexicon of the New Testament and Other Early Christian Literature*, 3rd ed. (Chicago: University of Chicago, 2000), 1011. The addition of *Paraleipomena Jeremiou* 5.32 to the documentation in earlier editions does not affect matters. Neither it nor *Testament of Dan* 6.7 conclusively excludes the meaning "every place of worship," and a non-technical use of τόπος and even ἐν παντὶ τόπῳ is not in doubt. The question is whether in every instance the general meaning must be understood.

8. I. Sonne, "Synagogue," *Interpreter's Dictionary of the Bible*, ed. G. A. Buttrick (New York: Abingdon, 1962): 4.477.

9. "Τόπος," *Theological Dictionary of the New Testament,* ed. G. Friedrich, trans. G. W. Bromily (Grand Rapids: Eerdmans, 1972), 8.189, 195–199. A. D. Nock, "The Gild of Zeus Hypsistos," *Harvard Theological Review* 29 (1936): 46, notes the common use of τόπος for the place of meeting of an association and its common use in the Apocrypha for the temple.

10. Ibid., 198. Despite the evidence he introduces for Jewish usage of τόπος, Koester takes ἐν παντὶ τόπῳ in the New Testament as the adverb "everywhere"—ibid., 203. In the *Acts of John* 95.37–42 τόπος=οἶκος=ναός.

11. ἐν παντὶ τόπῳ refers to a place of sacrifice in Exod. 20:24; Deut. 12:13; "in every place of God's power" in Ps. 103:22; "in any [or every] place" in Num. 18:31; Deut. 23:16; 1 Macc. 1:25 (RSV, "in every community"); literal also in 1 Kings 21:19; Esther 8:11; Prov. 15:3; Jer. 8:3; 24:9; 45:5; 48:37 (English references in each case). Apart from Mal. 1:11, considered below, and possibly the references to sacrifice, it does not seem that the phrase had any special meaning in the Septuagint. Τόπος is "place of sacrifice" in Prayer of Azariah (Dan 3:38), where καρπow has its LXX meaning of "offer sacrifice."

12. W. Schrage, "Συναγωγή," *Theological Dictionary of the New Testament*, ed. G. Friedrich, trans. G. W. Bromiley (Grand Rapids: Eerdmans, 1971), 7.898–899; S. Krauss, *Synagogale Altertümer* (Hildesheim: Georg Olms, 1966 repr. of 1922 ed.), 24–25. T. W. Manson, "St. Paul in Ephesus (3) The Corinthian Correspondence," *Bulletin of the John Rylands Library* 26 (1942): 119–20, lists the uses known then where "place" means synagogue.

13. J. B. Frey, *Corpus Inscriptionum-Judaicarum,* Vol. II (Rome: Pontificio Instituto di Archeologia Cristiana, 1952), 973 and 974.

14. Lee I. Levine, ed., *Ancient Synagogues Revealed* (Detroit: Wayne State University, 1982), 82–85.

15. G. H. R. Horsley, *New Documents Illustrating Early Christianity* (North Ryde: Macquarie University, 1983), 122; J. Kaplan, "Chronique Archeologique: Ramat-Aviv," *Revue Biblique* 84 (1977): 284–85.

16. J. B. Frey, *Corpus of Jewish Inscriptions* (New York; KTAV, 1975 repr. of 1936 ed.), 694; studied by M. Hengel, "Die Synagogeninschrift von Stobi," *Zeitschrift für die neutestamentliche Wissenschaft* 57 (1966): 145–83, esp. 173–76.

17. A. Dupont-Sommer, *The Essene Writings from Qumran* (Cleveland: World, 1962), 85.

18. *Every Good Man Is Free* 12.81.

19. *Embassy to Gaius* 318.

20. *Flaccus* 7.45, 47, 48, 49 (the occurrence of τόπος in 49, although occasionally cited in this connection, does not seem to me to be technical). Cf. *Hypoth.* 7.12–13.

21. Translation by Ralph Marcus (LCL; Cambridge: Harvard University Press, 1943): 7.575, 589.

21ª A Christian letter from the late third century by a bishop Sotas uses τόπῳ for church—POxy XII, 1492, line 11, discussed by L. Michael White, *The Social Origins of Christian Architecture*, vol. 2 (Valley Forge: Trinity Press International, 1997), 162–64.

22. Manson, *op. cit.*, 103, suggests that the difficult phrase which follows, "theirs and ours," be related to the sentence in this way: "every church—theirs (founded by others) and ours (founded by Paul)." G. D. Fee, *The First Epistle to the Corinthians* (New International Commentary on the New Testament; Grand Rapids: Eerdmans, 1987), 34, and C. K. Barrett, *A Commentary on the First Epistle to the Corinthians* (Black's New Testament Commentaries; London: A. & C. Black, 1968), 33–34, although translating "every meeting place," as they do in their commentaries on the Pastorals cited above, follow the conventional understanding in construing "theirs and ours" with Lord.

23. The commentaries have not so readily recognized the possibility of the meaning "every meeting place" in this passage. Ernest Best, *A Commentary on the First and Second Epistles to the Thessalonians* (Black's New Testament Commentaries: London: A. & C. Black, 1972), 81, echoes many in describing Paul's words as "a pardonable exaggeration." Recognition of a technical sense would relieve some of the

embarrassment. Abraham J. Malherbe, *The Letters to the Thessalonians* (Anchor Bible; New York: Doubleday, 2000), 117, considers the Christian usage, but seems to favor the geographical meaning.

24. See note 11 above.

25. E. Ferguson, *Early Christians Speak*, 3rd ed. (Abilene: ACU Press, 1999), 117–18.

26. The only place Justin uses ἐν παντὶ τόπῳ without clear allusion to Mal. 1:11 is *Dial.* 113.6.

27. Cf. Fragment 37 cited in *Ante-Nicene Fathers* 1.574.

28. E.g., Clement of Alexandria, *Instructor* 2.5.47; *Miscellanies* 7.7.35; Eusebius of Caesarea, *Commentary on the Psalms* (PG 23.1044).

29. Origen, *On Prayer* 31.4; Eusebius of Caesarea, *Proof of the Gospel* 1.6 (one passage where Mal. 1:10–11 is not interpreted as the eucharist but as prayer and good works); but in 8.4 "in every place" is referred to as "the churches of Christ in each place." Strasbourg Papyrus 254 in a eucharistic prayer.

30. In addition to Justin Martyr, above, note the anti-Jewish use of Mal. 1:11 and of the OT limitation of worship to the place where God recorded his name in Tertullian, *Answer to the Jews* 5.4,7; *Against Marcion* 4.1.8 (cf. 3.22.6 where Mal. 1:11 is said to agree with Ps. 68:26); Cyprian, *Testimonies* 1.16; Lactantius, *Institutes* 4.11.8; Eusebius, *Proof of the Gospel* 1.3; 1.7; 1.10; 2.3; *Commentary on Psalms* (PG 23.25, where Mal. 1:10f. is quoted in interpreting Ps. 29 as applying to the church; 23.420; 23.784; 23.1272).

18

Sabbath: Saturday or Sunday?
A Review Article

Bacchiocchi, Samuele. *From Sabbath to Sunday: A Historical Investigation of the Rise of Sunday Observance in Early Christianity.* Rome: Pontifical Gregorian University Press, 1977.

Beckwith, Roger T. and Wilfrid Stott. *This is the Day: The Biblical Doctrine of the Christian Sunday.* Greenwood, SC: Attic Press, 1978.

These two books, seemingly so different, have some things in common beyond their subject matter. Both take a sabbatarian position, only differing whether Saturday or Sunday is the Sabbath. They agree that the Christian Sabbath goes back to creation as part of the universal natural law, not the Mosaic law, and is, moreover, not a day of inactivity but a day for worship, fellowship, and ministering to the needs of others. Both books contain valuable material and many helpful insights, yet I am convinced that the main thesis of both is wrong. Both contend that the Sabbath has continuing validity and that Christians changed the day of keeping the Sabbath, Beckwith and Stott say in the first century with divine approval, and Bacchiocchi says in the second century by church authority. Both works are based on doctoral dissertations. Bacchiocchi, himself an unusual person as the first "separated brother" to earn a doctorate at the Pontifical Gregorian University in Rome and taught at Andrews University, Berrien Springs, Michigan, presents a condensation, rearrangement, and popularization of his dissertation. Part Two of the latter book (two-thirds of the whole) is based on Stott's dissertation at Oxford. (In view of the relative space, the subtitle of this book should be "The Early Christian Doctrine of the Christian Sunday.") The two works were apparently undertaken without knowledge of each other (Stott's unpublished dissertation is included in Bacchiocchi's bibliography). Each is a useful corrective to the other, yet both need the correction of Willy Rordorf's *Sunday* (see *Restoration Quarterly* 11 [1968], 203ff.), against which both argue successfully in some points but whose main thesis, in the judgment of this reviewer, still stands.

This Is the Day derives its name from Psalm 118:24, frequently ascribed in patristic sources to the Lord's Day. Part One, by Beckwith, deals with "Biblical and Jewish Evidence." It notes that the Sabbath in the Old Testament was a memorial of the world's creation and of Israel's redemption. Hellenistic Jewish sources, more correctly Alexandrian Jewish authors such as Aristobulus and Philo, connected the Sabbath (and all of the law) with universal principles; whereas, Palestinian Judaism saw them as peculiar to Judaism. Beckwith concludes that the New Testament agrees with Hellenistic Judaism here, but the closest statements are found in the later Alexandrian Christian school of thought which similarly interpreted the Old Testament in a universalistic sense. Actually, the distinction is overdrawn. Beckwith does not recognize the difference between an apologetic thrust and legal definition: The rabbinic sources defined the practice expected; whereas, the Greek authors were commending the Jewish law to outsiders and probably did not have a different understanding of its peculiar relation to Judaism. In view of Paul's argumentation, it is strange that Beckwith sees the New Testament as agreeing more with Philo. The best he can do with Paul is to say, "It is possible that Paul means to preserve the substance of the Sabbath in the Lord's day" (27).

Most of the biblical argumentation and the explanation of the patristic sources depend on a distinction between the universal Sabbath authorized at creation and the Mosaic Sabbath. Yet the distinction is never explicitly made in the New Testament and early Christian sources, and is a theory advanced to interpret the evidence. There is much that counts against this fundamental point which is never treated in the book: the lack of a specific command for men to keep the Sabbath before the time of Moses, the absence of New Testament teaching that Sunday is the Christian Sabbath, the failure of the early Christian sources to treat the Sabbath as anything other than a Jewish institution, and the failure of the Jews themselves to consider the Sabbath binding on Gentiles.

The argument is made that the Ten Commandments were a restatement of the natural moral law and hence still binding. Since the other nine commandments were repeated in word or substance in the New Testament, it is argued that it is certainly strange if the fourth does not have equal status, even if it must be reinterpreted in the Christian context (this reinterpretation meaning the transfer to another day). The absence of the repetition of the fourth commandment could be interpreted as pointing in another direction, namely, that it was put in the same category with other ceremonial regulations of the law. If silence here gives consent, does not that consent include the Mosaic seventh day? Was it not Moses who delivered the Ten Commandments? Would it not take a positive declaration, as the Seventh Day Adventists contend, to change the day? In fact, the New Testament is far from silent about the abrogation of the "Ten Commandments" insofar as they are part of the Mosaic law (Rom. 7:1–7; 2 Cor. 3:1–18; Col. 2:13–17).

The Lord's Day is presented in the New Testament, according to Beckwith, as a memorial of Christ's resurrection, as a day of worship, and as a day of rest. On this basis, extensive parallels are drawn between the Sabbath and the Lord's Day. There is good evidence for the first two points, but the best that can be mustered for Sunday as a day of rest in the New Testament is presumption based on analogies which may or may not have been in an author's mind in the use of certain terminology. Even if the analogies were intended, the conclusions drawn remain without supporting testimony.

Since Christ kept other things in the Mosaic law not expected of his followers, Beckwith's elaborate argumentation really does not come out confirming that Christ made a distinction between the creation Sabbath and the Mosaic ceremonial Sabbath. Both books take exception to Rordorf's claim that Christ in his ministry "simply annulled" the Sabbath. A better expression would be that Christ by implication, as he did in making "all foods clean" (Mark 7:19), annulled the Sabbath.

Part Two, "The Evidence of the Fathers," considers their attitude on the Sabbath, their attitude toward Sunday, how Christians spent the Lord's Day, the theology of the Christian Sunday, and the attitude of the early church regarding the Ten Commandments.

It is correctly noted that the Fathers looked on the Sabbath as a Jewish institution and as such opposed it. But the argument is made that the Sabbath in its spiritual meaning was still seen as of great importance for Christians. The inference drawn from the positive appreciation of the Sabbath found in some passages is that the Saturday day of rest had merged into the Christian Sunday. Our attention here may center on the contention that Sunday was viewed as a day of rest. The argument once more proceeds by analogies and presumptions: Cessation of work was a feature of pagan and Jewish feasts (here it is noted that for the church it was laborious work, as on the feast days of the Old Testament, that was avoided, not all work, as was included in the Sabbath prohibition—a contention that would seem to challenge the basic argument that Sunday was a Christian version of the Sabbath); "eighth day" stands for the rest of the world to come, an idea that could not have developed unless Sunday was a day of rest (more likely the influence is in the reverse direction); the lengthy Christian services would have required that the day be free from ordinary work. The few passages in the early centuries which bring in "rest" on the Lord's day are a nonliteral accommodation to Old Testament texts being commented on (and then spiritualized in terms of contemplation of divine things) or else have as their main thrust the attendance at divine service (which everyone agrees was the principal activity on the Christian Sunday). The alternatives are not limited to a mystical versus a literal interpretation; sometimes the terminology is simply an accommodation to an Old Testament text. That there was a Christian counterpart to circumcision, temple, sacrifices, etc., is not the same as making Sunday a Sabbath; these very "analogies" would argue for making the Lord's Day considerably more different from its Old Testament shadow than the authors' terminology allows.

It is noted that there was no direct appeal during the first four centuries to the Decalogue to support an observance of the Christian Sunday. I would conclude, therefore, that the high regard for the Ten Commandments in early Christianity did not carry over to the Sabbath.

When examining the discussion of how Christians spent the Lord's Day (aside from exaggerations) and the early Christian theology of Sunday (a very useful chapter), I am not actually that far away from the authors. "The rest of the Christian Sunday is not the inactivity associated with the Jewish Sabbath, but the restful activity of service of God" (117). If this represented the authors' whole mind, I would have little to disagree with except the contention over a name. But would not rabbinic Jews, for whom the seventh day was the principal day for synagogue worship, have said the same thing, without the negative stricture, for their Sabbath? If it were not for the effort to present the Sabbath rest as a part of Christian theology, one could appreciate the authors' conclusion that each Christian must decide in terms of his own situation the appropriate way to keep the Lord's Day as a holy day to the Lord.

These two books give us on a more historical and scholarly level the old debate between the Reformed and the Seventh Day Adventists. Beckwith and Stott do not take the SDA arguments seriously; where mentioned, they are dismissed without consideration. The authors do not seem to realize the vulnerability of their position to the SDA interpretation. Their position rests on the assumption of the continuing validity of the Sabbath with a change in the day of its observance. It is this double assumption which provided the framework for Bacchiocchi's study.

Seventh Day Adventists have recently become aware of the considerable church historical evidence against their position and the impossibility of the claim made in their older literature that Constantine in the fourth century changed the Sabbath to Sunday. Professor Bacchiocchi gives a comprehensive and broadly researched study, offering a hypothesis of how the historical evidence may be interpreted from a sabbatarian viewpoint. The author's SDA background perhaps makes him more conscious than other students of the Jewish background of the early church and more attune to certain features in the Sabbath passages in the New Testament. Nonetheless, I cannot accept his central hypothesis, which is that Sunday observance began in Christianity in the early second century under the sponsorship of the church at Rome as part of a broader program to distinguish Christians in the eyes of pagans from Jews and that this day, rather than some other day, was chosen because of its association with the sun god and light symbolism.

Bacchiocchi argues in chapter 2 for a positive assessment of the Sabbath by Jesus and its continued observance by the early Christians. The interpretations are similar to Beckwith's in their conclusion. Jesus' healings and other breaches of the Sabbath were not abrogations of the Sabbath but a restoring of it to its original divine value and function (redemption, joy, and service—a theology of which is deduced, it seems, as much out of rabbinic literature as out of the Old Testament prohibitions). He sees Hebrews 4:9 as indicating a present observance as well as an eschatological fulfillment. To him Matthew 24:20 implies that Christ took for granted the permanence of the Sabbath after his death; but as page 71 acknowledges, he was only discussing hindrances to flight and not what was unlawful on the Sabbath.

Differences from the other book become more pronounced in chapter 3, which begins the assault on the evidence for an early observance of Sunday by denying that the New Testament makes a connection between the resurrection appearances and the observance of the first day. The Lord's Supper commemorates the death and coming again of Jesus, not his resurrection. But does not Paul stress the connection with the death because of the Corinthians' overenthusiastic identification with the spirit of the resurrected Christ? And who else is believed to come again than the resurrected Jesus, and what else gave the eschatological note to the Lord's Supper than the resurrection? It still remains as primary data that the resurrected Jesus met with his disciples on the first day of the week and that the New Testament repeatedly underscores the first day of the week as the day of the resurrection. If the New Testament authors were only interested in giving chronological data, there was more meaningful information to be given. Generally information is given that was relevant to the life of the communities.

So, chapter 4 tries to get rid of the New Testament references to the first day of the week. First Corinthians 16:1–3, by enjoining a private collection, suggests that on the first day there were no regular public services conducted. Why then a reference to the first day of the week? The lame answer is that the contribution was to be set aside at the beginning of the week before other priorities emerged. Acts 20:7–11 receives extensive treatment: the view is advanced that this was an extraordinary fellowship supper occasioned by Paul's departure the next day and had nothing to do with a regular first-day-of-the-week service or of the Lord's Supper. Several of the considerations advanced depend on verse 11 referring to the same things as verse 7 (it may, but one cannot simply assume it). Of course, there is "no evidence" for the Lord's Supper if one denies it or gives another meaning when it is there. If the passage had occurred in the late second century, there apparently would have been no problem in taking the passage at face value; such is done with *Acts of John* 106 and 109 and other references to "breaking of bread," but these are no less problematical than Acts 20:7, only less uncomfortable to the theory.

Professor Bacchiocchi argues that the Lord's day as the Christian designation for Sunday occurs undisputedly for the first time near the end of the second century in the apocryphal *Gospel of Peter*. His list of references here omits the *Acts of John* 106, which would push the undisputed references earlier. He advocates the reading "Lord's life" instead of "Lord's day" in Ignatius, *Magnesians* 9, for Ignatius was contrasting ways of life, not days. *Didache* 14 is more difficult to eliminate: He argues that "doctrine," not "day," is the noun to be supplied after the adjective "Lord's," on the basis that "according to the [Lord's] commandment" is a common phrase in the document. But in the passages using this phrase, the word "commandment" is there and does not have to be supplied. The discussion of different interpretations of the passage overlooks the obvious possibility that *kata* with the accusative has its common distributive use, "every Lord's day." The adjective "Lord's" without a noun was the common Christian designation for Sunday. Professor Bacchiocchi's refusal to accept the church historical evidence and common Christian usage as valid for the meaning of *Didache* 14 or Revelation 1:10

is characteristic of his approach but is methodologically wrong, because it excludes the evidence closest at hand in favor of a speculative hypothesis. He takes Revelation 1:10 as referring to the "day of the Lord" because of the eschatological associations of the context: "John felt himself transported by the Spirit to the future glorious day of the Lord" (124). One need only read the verse to realize that is not what John said. Bacchiocchi can find no other example of the "Lord's day" meaning "day of the Lord" but advocates an "exception" (127) in John's usage. And so one gets rid of embarrassing early evidence by adopting a variant reading, by assuming error in transmission, by giving an exceptional meaning, and in general by ruling out of court the later established usage (but eighteen centuries closer to the situation than anyone now).

Chapter 5 argues against the widely held position that Sunday observance began with the primitive church in Jerusalem. The theological orientation of the Jerusalem church, its attitude toward Jewish worship services and liturgical calendar, and its adherence to Jewish customs are taken to mean that it would not have instituted Sunday observance. Although the author argues against it, the fact remains that the Sabbath was not one of the things imposed on the Gentile converts by Acts 15:20f. (as it was not included in God's commands to Noah), and the whole drift of his material would indicate that the Sabbath was among the "customs" Paul was charged with teaching Jews to forsake (Acts 21:22—the charges were false with references to Jews but true in reference to his teachings to Gentiles), uncomfortable facts to Beckwith and Stott as well. It is quite damaging to the sabbatarian position that the Jews themselves did not consider the Sabbath binding on the Gentile world. More fundamentally, the author's argument presupposes an incompatibility of Sabbath and Sunday, as if both could not have been observed (Beckwith and Stott are more preceptive here). Nevertheless, in his conclusion Bacchiocchi recognizes the "basic difference between Sabbath and Sunday" (318). But if these were two different kinds of days, with different meanings and observed in different ways, the whole argument—that if the Jerusalem church kept the Sabbath it could not have observed Sunday—loses cogency. We know from Eusebius that later there were Jewish Christians who kept both days. Bacchiocchi makes much of the statements of Justin Martyr and

Epiphanius about Jewish Christians observing the Sabbath without saying anything about their keeping Sunday, but both authors were talking about their differences from Gentile Christians. So silence on this count leaves the presumptions that their practice was the same as other Christians in regard to Sunday.

With chapter 6 Bacchiocchi comes to the positive part of his thesis: The Roman church, predominantly Gentile, during the reign of Hadrian took the lead in severing ties with Judaism by substituting for the Sabbath and Passover new religious observances (the weekly Sunday and the annual Easter). The anti-Jewish attitude of the church in this period is shown by the *Preaching of Peter,* Aristides' *Apology*, and the *Epistle to Diognetus;* but each of these works is no more anti-Jewish than anti-pagan and hardly adopts an "attitude of reconciliation toward the empire" (178). That Quadratus wrote against the Jews is pure supposition. Irenaeus traced Easter Sunday back to Bishop Sixtus of Rome, but his traditional dates are 116–126, hence before Hadrian's anti-Jewish laws. Here Bacchiocchi throws up a smoke screen about the general period of time, without coming to grips with the fact that the occasion for the church's differentiation from Judaism which he posits (Hadrian's legislation) does not match the specific time given for the innovations in the evidence he adduces (about which one could certainly be as skeptical, with more reason, as he is about Acts 20:7). To the question "Did the church of Rome in the second century already exert sufficient authority through her bishop to influence the greater part of Christendom to accept new festivities?" he answers "Yes." This conclusion no doubt favorably impressed Bacchiocchi's Roman Catholic professors, but will it impress others? The situation in the first third of the second century was not the same as at the end of that century, yet Victor's efforts to impose the Sunday Easter against the Quartodeciman practice of Asia met strong resistance and considerable controversy. Could the Roman bishop at the beginning of the second century have carried through a change that left no trace in the historical record (the hypothesis should not be mistaken for the facts on which it rests or which it seeks to explain) and no immediate controversy and resistance comparable to that of Easter later? Nothing indicates Rome had that much influence around AD 130; indeed, when at the end of the century the Roman church was undoubtedly stronger, Victor was able to get his way only with great difficulty. It is questionable that Rome had a monarchical bishop at all until somewhere about this time; after all, this was when Hermas was writing in Rome. The triumph of the Sunday Easter presupposes a long history of a weekly Sunday observance of the resurrection.

Chapter 7 adduces the anti-Judaism of the Fathers as the reason for the rejection of the Sabbath: Ignatius, Barnabas, and Justin are primarily discussed. Barnabas gives, according to the author, the first explicit reference to the observance of Sunday (denominated the "eighth day"). He accepts as the date of Barnabas ca. 135, but that date rests on tenuous grounds.

Chapter 8 considers why Sunday, rather than some other day, was chosen to evidence the Christian separation from Judaism. Pagan sun worship is seen as the primary reason. Reflexes of sun worship on Christianity are seen in the depiction and symbolism of Christ as the sun, the acceptance of December 25 as the birthday of Christ, and eastward orientation in prayer. The evidence for these practices, later than the period assumed for the introduction of Sunday worship, only establishes that Christians were later open to the influence of the pagan sun cult, which, although present, did not become a powerful force in Rome until the third century. May not the direction of thought have been the reverse of what the author posits (indeed this seems clearly the case in Justin): because Christians met on Sunday, an identification of Christ with the sun was facilitated and this used to apologetic advantage for Christianity? Whether one faced toward Jerusalem or toward the east in prayer was the same for all points west of Jerusalem; Christian and Jewish practice would have been the same, only the interpretation different, and Christians made no effort at distinction here.

Chapter 9 considers the theology of Sunday developed in early Christian writers to justify the "new" practice. Although the resurrection became the dominant reason for Sunday observance, the earliest references (Barnabas and Justin) give it as the "secondary reason." The author makes the curious and mistaken assumption that when two reasons are given, the reason stated second is less important than the first. The other theological reasons were creation and the typology of the eighth day. The latter Bacciocchi finds as the principal theological consideration, although he labels the reasoning associated with it "bizarre and irrational" (219 and frequently). He betrays either his lack of familiarity with patristic exegesis or his modern prejudice here, for what he so labels was typical patristic argumentation. The "symbology" of the eighth day would not "degrade the seventh day" (306) unless that was already so; institutional symbolism comes after the institution. The earliest theological justifications were *a posteriori* considerations (302). The author seems not to realize that this statement, designed to denigrate the early Christian theology of Sunday, is actually an admission that Sunday-keeping was much earlier than he says. If Barnabas, writing in the 130s in Alexandria, was developing after-the-fact arguments to justify the Christian practice of observing Sunday, how could the church at Rome have initiated a change from the Sabbath to Sunday about the same time? Barnabas and Justin do not sound as though they were arguing for a new practice or defending an innovation; they were speaking of common traditional Christian practice, a practice earlier than those authors in which Bacchiocchi finds the first evidence for this practice.

In summary, Bacchiocchi still represents the SDA view that the Roman Catholic Church changed the day of worship, a claim the Catholic Church has been glad to acknowledge, only he has moved the date back earlier than the Adventists. He is wrong on two major counts: The Roman church did not have power to make such a change at this early date, and the nature of the evidence does not suggest a new change but accepted practice. Beckwith and Stott argue the Reformed view that finds its Christian theology and the Christian covenant in the Old Testament. They are no more successful in vindicating this view from the New Testament and early Christian literature. These books are much more sophisticated and historically knowledgeable than anything earlier in support of the respective views. Those who deal with the SDA and the Reformed should be acquainted with these two books, for they will be hearing more of the arguments contained in them.

The view that the Sabbath is binding on Christians rests on no explicit text in the New Testament or early Christian literature. It is surpassingly strange that a supposedly central Christian religious duty depends on the interpretation of an Old Testament text. Rather than seeing a continuing validity of the Sabbath, which was changed from Saturday to Sunday, whether legitimately by the apostles in the first century or illegitimately by the church in the second (or Constantine in the fourth), it is better to see the Sabbath command as a part of the superseded Mosaic institution and the Lord's day as a different type of day, a day of assembly and worship. The idea of a weekly day of rest is obviously sound, but any principle of cessation or limitation of work on Sunday is ancilliary to the prior obligation of Christians to assemble for edification and fellowship.

*Originally printed in *Restoration Quarterly* 23 (1980): 172–81.

Note: A major study supporting the viewpoint expressed in this review has since appeared: D. A. Carson, ed., *From Sabbath to Lord's Day: A Biblical, Historical and Theological Investigation* (Grand Rapids: Zondervan, 1982).

Part V

Church Music

19

Jewish Religious Music in the First Century—
Temple, Synagogue, Home, and Sect

First-century Judaism provides the historical context of the beginning of Christianity. A proper interpretation of New Testament texts requires an understanding of their historical background and of the subsequent development of the church. This material defines the historical parameters of what was possible and what was probable in the situation of the time. The present essay will survey Jewish religious music in the first century with a view to defining the practices with which early Christians would have been familiar. Four settings must be considered: the temple, the synagogue, the home, and Sect.[1]

Temple
There is an absence of contemporary sources for the music at the temple in the century before its destruction in AD 70. Information from both before

and after the first century, however, permit a fairly detailed description of the temple liturgy.[2] The account of the rededication of the temple under Hezekiah in 2 Chronicles 29 mentions that the Levites stood with their "cymbals, harps, and lyres" and "the priests with their trumpets," and "when the burnt offering began, the song to the Lord began also, and the trumpets, accompanied by the instruments" (2 Chron. 29:25–28). There is a similar account of the rededication of the altar by Judas Maccabee in 165 BC with songs, harps, lutes, and cymbals accompanying the sacrifices (1 Macc. 4:52–56). The songs were presumably the Psalms: "Hezekiah . . . commanded the Levites to sing praises to the Lord with the words of David and of Asaph the seer" (2 Chron. 29:30).[3] This is made explicit in the rabbinic remembrances of temple worship written down after its destruction. The Mishnah[4] and the Talmud[5] preserve lists of which psalms were sung on each day of the week by the Levites in the temple. Otherwise, the Hallel Psalms (113–18) are most frequently referred to in connection with the temple.[6] At the daily sacrifice, the singing was accompanied by stringed instruments, with cymbals (to keep time?) and a pipe to close the melody.[7] At every break in the singing there was a blast on the trumpet and prostration by the people (*Tamid* 7.3). The Levites who sang stood on the fifteen steps that led from the Court of the Women to the Court of the Israelites, and those who "played upon harps, lyres, cymbals, and all instruments of music" were in the chambers beneath the Court of the Israelites which opened into the Court of the Women.[8] The type of pipe called the *halil* was played on twelve days in the year at set feasts. It was the use of this instrument which provoked the rabbinic discussion whether playing an instrument overrode the prohibition of work on the Sabbath (*b. Arakhin* 10a; *b. Sukkah* 50b–51a). Those instruments mentioned in the Bible which accompanied the sacrifice did override the prohibition of work, but an instrument on another occasion did not.[9] This could have some bearing on the absence of instruments from the synagogues.[10] One rabbi suggested that there was no water organ in the temple because it would interfere with the song (*t. Arakhin* 1:13; *b. Arakhin* 10b). This accords with other indications that the vocal music was primary and the instruments accompanied the song.[11] Music, vocal and instrumental, was closely connected with sacrifice at the temple and was sometimes considered essential to it (*b. Arakhin* 11b–12a; *b. Sukkah* 51a; *b. Ta'anit* 27a).

Synagogue

There is a similar lack of first-century sources for musical practices in the synagogues. Here the situation is more controversial, however, because there are first-century references to other activities in the synagogues. It is generally agreed that instrumental music was absent from the synagogue meetings, but some have argued that singing too, and particularly psalm-singing, was also absent.[12] The argument from the silence of first-century sources about psalmody proves too much. The sources cited[13] mention only scripture reading and its interpretation; if these sources were all we had to go on, we would have to omit prayer from the synagogue service in the first century. No one does so, and for good reason; but to include it, one has to adduce other sources. There are special reasons why Philo and Josephus mention only instruction in the scriptures and do not give a complete account. On the other hand, there are indications of the use of the Psalms in the synagogue. If rabbinic sources, some of them going back to the second century, although written later, are accepted as preserving the liturgy of the temple, then their descriptions of synagogue practice may also go back to the first century. Representatives from the towns of Israel met for prayer at the times of the daily sacrifices in the temple; this practice gave the names to the times of prayer in the synagogues. At these gatherings, the Hallel Psalms were recited (*Ta'anit* 4.4; 3.9).[14] The practice originated while the temple was still standing and would seem to be the origin of the use of the same psalms in the synagogues as in the temple. The Mishnah, compiled around AD 200, gives instructions about the congregational reciting of the Hallel.[15] The tractate *Rosh HaShanah* 4.7 refers to reciting the Hallel before the ark where the Torah scrolls were kept in the synagogues. The argument is made that the accounts of "reciting" do not refer to "singing," but it must be remembered that cantillation, a kind of chanting, was employed in scripture reading (*b. Megillah* 32a; *Sopherim* 3.13), prayer (*b. Ta'anit* 16a), and reciting the Shema (*Abot de Rabbi Nathan b.* 44).[16] In the context of the times we must describe the Hallel as "sung," not "read."

Philo himself gives another indication that singing was part of the synagogue service. In his account of the persecution of the Jews in Alexandria under Flaccus, the prefect of Egypt, Philo relates that at the Feast of Tabernacles the Jews learned of the arrest of Flaccus. In their homes "with hands outstretched to heaven [the Jews] sang hymns and led paeans to God." Then, "all night long they continued to sing hymns and songs, and at dawn pouring out through the gates, they made their way to the parts of the beach near at hand, since their places of prayer [synagogues] had been taken from them" (*Flaccus* 121–122). It is rightly observed that this was an exceptional circumstance and not a service nor in a synagogue.[17] The very fact that it was an exceptional circumstance argues that the Jews were accustomed to singing religious songs. They had learned these hymns to God somewhere, and they would have gathered in their synagogues on this occasion if they had been able to do so. Concerning a similar situation of crisis from an earlier time (ascribed to third century BC but written probably in the first century BC), 3 Maccabees 7:16 speaks of the Jews as a group joining in "songs of praise and melodious hymns" to celebrate their deliverance. These songs included "psalms" (6:35) and "the song of their fathers" (6:32).

It seems reasonable to conclude that at least some of the psalms were sung at least on some occasions in the synagogue meetings. But this was not the only setting in Judaism for the practice of unaccompanied song.

Home

It has recently been argued that Jewish religious activities in the family and home provide the pattern for early Christian assemblies. Noting that early Christian assemblies resembled Jewish private gatherings by meeting in houses, including a meal with their worship, and holding vigils at night, J. A. Smith has observed these further similarities between the church and Jewish private religious assemblies: they were informal but not disorderly, there were no musical instruments, and there was no exclusion of women.[18]

We are best informed about the Passover. Although the lambs were sacrificed at the temple, the Passover meal itself was eaten at home. The Passover was a celebration by families or small groups. Once more the most detailed accounts come from rabbinic literature, that is, later than the New Testament.

The Hallel Psalms were sung in the Passover ritual in the home (*Pesahim* 9.3; 10.6). The rabbis could not conceive of the Passover without uttering song (*b. Pesahim* 117a; 118a; cf. 85b; *Pesahim* 7.11). Other songs were sung in addition to the appointed Psalms of the *seder* (*Pesahim* 10.6). In regard to the Passover, we have the confirmation of the New Testament for the first-century practice of singing (Matt. 26:30).

There is also first-century evidence for the practice of singing the Psalms in families on other occasions. A faithful mother reminded her children that their father "sang to you the psalm of David" in the home (4 Macc. 18:15).

Musical instruments did continue to have a place in the family observances of weddings and funerals. There was singing for joy at weddings (*Sotah* 9.11; 3 Macc. 4:6–8) and songs of lamentation at funerals (*Mo'ed Qatan* 3.8ff.). The Mishnah refers to "pipers for a bride or for a corpse."[19] Again there is New Testament confirmation: pipe players at a funeral in Matthew 9:23 and pipe playing at a (wedding) dance in 11:17.

There is some indication that some of the rabbis sought to eliminate or restrict instrumental music from banquets in the home (*b. Gittin* 7a; *b. Sotah* 48a), but this effort belonged to a later period.

Sect

There is another context in Jewish religious life in the first century that must be considered: sectarian Judaism. The musical practices of the Qumran community that produced the Dead Sea Scrolls are not clear, but some evidence is suggestive. The Qumran documents include scrolls of the Psalms which contain psalms in addition to the canonical psalms. An intriguing hypothesis about these supplementary psalms is that they were written so that each of the twenty-four courses of Levites would have a different psalm for each day of its week on duty (twenty-four courses times seven days required a total of 168 psalms).[20] If this hypothesis should hold up, it would give significant new evidence about the use of the Psalms at the temple. Whether there was some effort to preserve this psalm usage at Qumran must remain uncertain, but a note in one of the Psalm Scrolls (1Q Psa) on David's compositions envisages four liturgical uses for the Psalms: daily, Sabbaths, thirty holy days, and exorcisms.

The Thanksgiving Scroll (*Hodayoth*) contains hymns that may have been employed in community worship. The use of the first person singular is not necessarily a barrier to this use. One of the hymns declares, "Into my mouth Thou hast put songs of thanksgiving and on my tongue [a song of pr]aise, and Thou has circumcised my lips in the abode of rejoicing that I should sing Thy favors" (1QH xi.3). A reference to instruments in the *Rule of the Community* may be metaphorical for the human body: "I will sing in knowledge (cf. 1 Cor. 14:15), and my whole lyre shall throb to the glory of God, and my lute and harp to the holy order which he has made. I will raise the flute of my lips because of His righteous measuring-cord" (1QS x.9).[21]

The Therapeutae, a sect in Egypt perhaps related to the Essenes, are known from Philo's treatise *On the Contemplative Life* (early first century).[22] At one of the sacred banquets of the sect:

> The president rises and sings a hymn composed as an address to God, either a new one of his own composition or an old one by poets of an earlier day who have left behind them hymns in many measures and melodies [Psalms ?] . . . After him all the others take their turn as they are arranged and in the proper order while all the rest listen in complete silence except when they have to chant the closing lines or refrains, for then they all lift up their voices, men and women alike. (*Contemplative Life* 80)

And an all-night vigil:

> They form themselves into two choirs, one of men and one of women, the leader and precentor chosen for each being the most honored among them and also the most musical. Then they sing hymns to God composed of many measures and set to many melodies, sometimes chanting together, sometimes taking up the harmony antiphonally, hands and feet keeping time in accompaniment, and rapt with enthusiasm reproduce sometimes the lyrics of the procession, sometimes of the halt and of the wheeling and counter wheeling of a choric dance. . . . Then they mix and both together become a single choir, a copy of the choir

set up of old beside the Red Sea in honor of the wonders there wrought. This wonderful sight and experience ... so filled with ecstasy both men and women that forming a single choir they sang hymns of thanksgiving to God their Savior, the men led by the prophet Moses and the women by the prophetess Miriam. (*Contemplative Life* 83–87)[23]

This description has a special importance for the study of Christian origins. It shows the types of vocal music available in the Judaism at the time of the beginning of Christianity. Therapeutae employed solo, responsive (the congregation chanting refrains following one person's rendition), antiphonal (the group divided into two choirs singing alternately), and unison singing. These same four types of vocal rendition are attested in Christian usage in the fourth century.[24] Furthermore, the description sounded so much like Christian practice that Eusebius thought Philo was describing Christians (*Ecclesiastical History* 2.17.22).

Conclusion

The Christians' practice of singing in their assemblies would have had its ultimate roots in the psalmody of the temple. The transfer of the use of the Psalms to a congregational setting apart from material sacrifice and without instrumental accompaniment presumably occurred in the synagogues. The influence of synagogue practices in general upon the early church makes this a likely historical source for the Christian practice of unaccompanied song. The most explicit evidence from the first century, however, of religious songs without instrumental accompaniment pertains to religious exercises in homes and in sectarian groups. Whatever the exact Jewish antecedents, the Christian practice of unaccompanied singing of the Psalms and other religious songs is well attested and would have been quite at home in the context of the Judaism of the first century.

*Originally printed in *Missions in Crisis: Challenge and Opportunity* (ACU Lectureship, 1988), 208–20.

Chapter 19 Endnotes

1. For surveys see Everett Ferguson, *A Cappella Music in the Public Worship of the Church,* 3rd ed. (Fort Worth: Star Bible, 1999); Bill Flatt, ed., *The Instrumental Music Issue* (Nashville: Gospel Advocate, 1987). More extensive treatments, based mainly on rabbinic and later sources are found in A. Z. Idelsohn, *Jewish Music in its Historical Development* (New York: Tudor, 1944); Eric Werner, *The Sacred Bridge,* 2 vols. (New York: Columbia University Press, 1959; New York: KTAV, 1984); Karl Erich Groezinger, *Musik and Gesang in der Theologie der fruehen Juedischen Literatur* (Tübingen: J.C.B. Mohr, 1982).

2. See my *A Cappella Music,* 29–31 for some of the evidence.

3. A. Buechler, "Zur Geschichte der Tempelmusik and der Tempelpsalmen," *Zeitschrift fuer die alttestamentliche Wissenschaft* 19 (1899): 344, correctly notes that the Chronicler says nothing about Psalm singing, but seems unduly skeptical about the extent of the usage of the Psalms at the Temple, especially in view of indications within the psalms themselves. See Jack P. Lewis, "New Testament Authority for Music in Worship," *The Instrumental Music Issue,* ed. Bill Flatt (Nashville: Gospel Advocate, 1987), 20–22.

4. *Tamid* 7.4

5. *b. Rosh HaShanah* 30b, citing R. Akiba, early second century; cf. *b. Shabbath* 118b; *Song of Solomon Rabbah* 4.4.6.

6. *Pesahim* 5.7; *Sukkah* 3.9; 4.1; Buechler, *Z.N.W.* 20 (1900): 131–35, would limit the use of these.

7. *Arakhin* 2.3–6, which gives the minimum and maximum number of each instrument and of singers.

8. *Middot* 2.5, 6; cf. *Sukkah* 5.4 on instruments and *b. Menahoth* 44b on psalms sung over the drink offering.

9. Groezinger, 128, 228.

10. James W. McKinnon, "The Exclusion of Musical Instruments from the Ancient Synagogue," *Proceedings of the Royal Musical Association* 106 (1979–1980): 82.

11. Groezinger, 128ff. Cf. Sirach 40:21.

12. McKinnon, 84f; J. A. Smith, "The Ancient Synagogue, the Early Church and Singing," *Music and Letters* 65 (1984): 1–16.

13. Philo, *Hypothetica* 7–13; *Quod omnis probus* 12 (81) on the Essenes; Josephus, *Apion,* 2.17 (175); cf. Luke 4:16ff.; Acts 13:15f. See Smith, 7f.

14. See *A Cappella Music,* 32–33, and H. Danby, *The Mishnah* (Oxford: University Press, 1933), 794, note on Maamad.

15. If a slave, woman, or a minor says it, others must repeat the words; if the person reciting is of age, then others may respond only with "Hallelujah" (*Sukkah* 3.10ff.). The later *Sukkah* 38a–b gives directions for the responsive singing of Hallel Psalms.

The different types of congregational participation in *b. Sotah* 30b (see *A Cappella Music*, 33ff.) corresponds with the practices in the church—Basil, *Ep.* 207.

16. McKinnon, after saying that the references "give much more the impression of a simple recitation than a melodious psalmody" (84ff.), then must grant that "the recitation of Scripture in the ancient Synagogue was not a dry reading in the modern sense, but rather some sort of elemental declamation or cantilation" (85). There seems to be nothing more than a quibble over what constitutes "melody."

17. Smith, 4f.

18. Smith, 12–15.

19. *Bava Metzi'a* 6.1; for funerals cf. *Shabbath* 23.4 and Josephus, *War* 3.9.5(437).

20. R. T. Beckwith, "The Courses of the Levites and the Eccentric Psalms Scrolls from Qumram," *Revue de Qumran* 11.44 (1984): 499–524.

21. Eric Werner, "Musical Aspects of the Dead Sea Scrolls," *Musical Quarterly* 43 (1957): 21–37.

22. For Philo's own musical views, see *A Cappella Music*, 15, 36–40, and my "The Art of Praise: Philo and Philodemus on Music," in J. T. Fitzgerald, T. H. Olbricht, and L. M. White, eds., *Early Christianity and Classical Culture: Comparative Studies in Honor of Abraham J. Malherbe* (Leiden: Brill, 2003), 391–426.

23. Cf. *Sukkah* 5.4 for dancing and song as part of the celebration of the Feast of Tabernacles.

24. Basil, *Epistle* 207; for comparable practice among Jews, see *b. Sotah* 30b.

20

The Theology of Singing

Society at large thinks of music in terms of aesthetics or feelings. Most of our attention to music in Churches of Christ has been negative (the non-use of instrumental music) or practical (how to sing better). Little attention has been given to the doctrinal meaning of our singing. Hence, this essay is a preliminary effort to encourage thought. I do think that it is important to ask, "What are we doing when we sing?" I suggest eight points which may be found in biblical passages about singing.

1. In *praise* we share in *heavenly eschatological* activity. The heavenly beings are constantly singing praise to God (Rev. 4:8, 10, 11; 5:8–12; 14:2, 3; 15:2, 3). The harps I take as symbolic of singing, even as the incense represents the prayers of the saints (5:8; and note that the harpists are described only as singing—5:9; 14:3; 15:3).

In song, therefore, we share in a heavenly activity. The barriers between earth and heaven, time and eternity, are temporarily lowered. We are brought into the presence of the divine in a special way. We participate in the activities of the end of time. Now our praise is imperfect; then it will be perfected. Yet we can now anticipate the end time. We are transported in spiritual songs into the realm of angels and share their praise. Christian song is a heavenly activity.

2. *Praise* in song is a *spiritual sacrifice.* Hebrews 13:15f. presents praise and benevolence as the sacrifice acceptable to God.

The Christian offers to God the fruit of lips instead of the fruits of the earth or the offspring of flocks and herds. The phrase "fruit of lips" comes from the Old Testament—as in Hosea 14:2. The Old Testament had presented thanksgiving as a sacrifice: Psalm 26:6 (accompanying sacrifice); Jonah 2:9 and Psalm 141:2 (the equivalent of sacrifice); Psalm 50:14, 23 (in place of sacrifice). The idea of vocal praise as a sacrifice was much developed in Judaism (as may be seen in intertestamental literature, Dead Sea Scrolls, and rabbinic literature). Pagan philosophers also developed the thought of spiritual sacrifice in opposition to bloody sacrifices, instrumental music, and even song. Judaism and Christianity, although using the language of spiritual sacrifice, did not go along with the idea of "silent song" (although some have misunderstood Colossians 3:16, "singing in your hearts," as meaning this).

New Testament thought connects singing with the spirit (1 Cor. 14:15). It is a spiritual activity: note the "spiritual songs" of Ephesians 5:19 and Colossians 3:16. Singing thus comes in the category of spiritual sacrifice, even as prayer does. It takes the place for Christians of the offerings brought to God under the old law. It is a sacrifice which is *continuously available* (Heb. 13:15).

3. Song is a *confession* of faith. Hebrews 13:15 adds that the lips "acknowledge" his name, or make confession of him.

This word, which can be translated "acknowledge," "confess," or "praise," is often brought into connection with the word "sing" in the Psalms. Notice especially Psalm 18:49, which is quoted in Romans 15:9, and 138:1.

Singing is a way of acknowledging God—praising him and confessing our faith in him. We do this when we give thanks or express gratitude. Song is to be with thankfulness (Eph. 5:19f.; Col. 3:16; cf. James 5:13). Thanksgiving acknowledges God as the source of blessings.

4. Singing gives expression to the *indwelling Spirit* and *word of Christ.* Ephesians 5:18, 19 associate singing with being filled with the Spirit; Colossians 3:16 associates singing with the indwelling word of Christ. There is no need to interpret one passage in terms of the other, as if the one is what the

other means. Both statements are true and belong together: singing is the result of the presence of the Spirit and of the word of Christ.

Praise is a consequence of being filled with the Spirit and possessing the word of Christ. When the Spirit and word of Christ dwell in a person, it finds expression in song. The knowledge of salvation in Christ, the acceptance of God's grace, the receiving of the Holy Spirit as the firstfruits of redemption—this leads to song. Notice James 5:13.

Another phrase from Hebrews 13:15 may be mentioned here: the sacrifice of praise is "through him," that is, through Christ. It is the relationship to Christ that gives the special character to Christian song; it is done "in the name of the Lord Jesus Christ" (Eph. 3:20; Col. 3:17).

5. Singing is a way of *preaching* Christ. We have just seen how Christ, through his word and Spirit, is the ground or basis of Christian singing. It should now be observed that Christ is also the content of Christian song. Christians sing about Christ. If they sing about God, it is what God has done through Christ; if about the Holy Spirit, it is the Holy Spirit as the gift of Christ; if instruction to one another, it is about the life in Christ. But mostly Christians sing about Christ.

The hymns of early Christians which have been identified in the New Testament have as their content Christ. Such are Philippians 2:6–11 and 1 Timothy 3:16.

Christ, therefore, must be the standard by which we judge the content of our songs in our assemblies which occur in his name. We ought to examine our songs by this standard.

6. Singing is for mutual *edification* as well as praise. When we sing, we are edifying one another. Singing has reference to our neighbors as well as God. We not only honor God in song, but we also aim to profit others. This combination of praise and instruction had been a characteristic of the synagogue.

Ephesians 5:19 and Colossians 3:16 mention not only that singing is to the Lord, or God; it is also "addressing one another." 1 Corinthians 14:26 declares that our psalms and whatever we do in the assembly is to be for edification. Here is another standard by which we can judge our songs.

We have stated that song is confession and proclamation. We teach as well as praise through song. Both contribute to community edification.

Edification is not what makes one feel good, but is related to instruction. It requires understanding of what is said (1 Cor. 14:17, 19). Melody, therefore, is secondary to the words. The melody must support and deepen the message and not obscure it. The musical aspects may add to the emotional impact, but the emotion is not the main thing. Singing is not for the sake of the beauty of the music. It certainly should be our best; anything we do for God should be our best. But quality must be related to the purpose of edification.

7. Singing involves the *whole person*. Singing engages mind, heart, and the organs of speech; the intellect, the emotions, and the physical self are involved. A human being is a symbol of unity. The physical body is not to be devalued as it was in some strands of pagan thought and in Gnosticism. Hence, the tongue—the physical body—is the instrument on which God is praised. This is done from the heart, and it is done intelligibly.

Notice the emphasis on wholeness in a passage like 1 Corinthians 14:15; Ephesians 5:19 and Colossians 3:16 mention the heart. There is an Old Testament background for linking the lips and the soul in passages like Psalm 71:23.

The mind understands; the heart responds in thankfulness; the tongue expresses it. All are involved in song.

8. Singing exemplifies the *unity of the church*. Romans 15:5, 6 is often overlooked in discussions of church music. Singing together symbolizes the one body in Christ. The "one voice" expresses the unity of the church. There was a great emphasis in the ancient church on unison singing. The difference of pitch of male and female, children and adult voices means this was not absolutely unison. The point was unity and harmony in which all participated. That is an important message for the church today.

Singing together is a beautiful and specific way of showing that we are the church, the one body, united to the Lord and to one another. The corporate or body life of the church, which is the reason for assembling, finds expression as we mingle and blend our voices in song.

*Originally printed in *How Great Thou Art*, Harding University Lectureship, 1978 (Austin: Firm Foundation, 1978), 77–81.

21

The Case for A Cappella Music in the Christian Assembly

The Argument from New Testament Texts

The New Testament clearly teaches that Christians sang in their congregational assemblies. The corporate meeting is undeniably the setting for Paul's instruction in 1 Corinthians 14 ("in church," v. 19; "the whole church assembles," v. 23). In that context, he speaks of singing "with the spirit" and "with the mind also" (v. 15). Particularly explicit is verse 26, "When you come together, each one has a hymn, a lesson, a revelation, a tongue, or an interpretation." In view of this practice, we can understand the Epistle to the Hebrews quoting the words of Hebrews 2:12 as spoken by Jesus, "I will proclaim thy name to my brethren, in the midst of the congregation I will praise [hymn] thee."

Ephesians 5:19 reads, "addressing one another in psalms and hymns and spiritual songs, singing and making melody to the Lord with all your heart." Colossians 3:16 says, "As you teach and admonish one another in all wisdom, and as you sing psalms and hymns and spiritual songs with thankfulness in your hearts to God." It may be objected that neither of these passages specifically refers to the assembly. While it is true that the context deals with ethical instructions, the concern is with the Christians' corporate life and their mutual relations. The instructions apply to the appropriate situation, whenever that might be. It would be when Christians meet together that there would be the opportunity to address one another and teach and admonish one another.

On the other hand, there is no mention in the New Testament of the use of instrumental music in the Christian assemblies. And here let it be said that the non-use of instrumental music among churches of Christ is based on the theological principle of silence and not because the words themselves employed in the New Testament exclude an instrument.

The Argument from Psallō

The effort to break through the wall of silence in the New Testament texts has centered on the Greek word *psallō* and its related words. It is pointed out, and correctly so, that the word was used for playing on a stringed instrument by classical Greek authors and by the Jewish historian Josephus, who wrote for a pagan audience. This "classical" use of the word continued among pagan authors until after New Testament times.

There was, however, another usage of the word. The Jews came to use *psallō* and its cognate words to describe the non-instrumental rendition of their religious songs. This usage is reflected in some passages of the Septuagint, the Greek translation of the Old Testament. It is characteristic of the apocryphal books (2 Macc. 1:30; Sir. 47:8–10; 50:18) and is particularly clear in the *Psalms of Solomon* from the first century BC (3.1, 2; 15.3).

How did the New Testament authors use the word *psallō*? Most New Testament translators and lexicographers have concluded that this intertestamental Jewish usage, "to make melody" or "to sing," governs the meaning in the New Testament. This conclusion is supported by the context of the New Testament references to *psallō*. The word is used in close association with vocal activities. It is in parallel with "pray" in James 5:13 and 1 Corinthians 14:15; with "sing" in Ephesians 5:19; with "praise" ("confess") in Romans

15:9, quoting Psalm 18:49. These associations definitely suggest vocal and not instrumental music.

The usage of *psallō* for vocal praise in the New Testament is confirmed by early Christian authors. Although aware of the classical meaning, Christian authors after New Testament times used *psallō* with the meaning "sing." It is my contention that the early Christians best understood the meaning of the words in their sacred texts. Their uniform testimony expressed in the way they used *psallō* is decisive for the New Testament meaning. This word usage agrees with the historical testimony about Christian musical practice.

The Argument from Christian History

Early Christian texts, as the New Testament, refer to singing when Christians met in their public assemblies. Those texts, once more as is true with the New Testament, are silent about an instrument. We are not left for long, however, with inferences from the historical evidence. Eventually Christian authors commented on the absence of instrumental music from the Christian assemblies, an absence which contrasted with the use of instruments in Old Testament and in pagan worship. Christian writers in the fourth century and after were not only explicit about the exclusively vocal nature of Christian music, but they also offered explanations for it. An abundant number of texts could be quoted. I select only one—from Eusebius of Caesarea, the church historian, whose wide acquaintance with Christian practice in his own and earlier times permits him to speak for many others.

> Of old at the time those of the circumcision were worshipping with symbols and types it was not inappropriate to send up hymns to God with the psalterion and kithara and to do this on Sabbath days.... But we in an inward manner keep the part of the Jew, according to the saying of the apostle.... (Romans 2:28ff.). We render our hymn with a living psalterion and a living kithara, with spiritual songs. The unison voices of Christians would be more acceptable to God than any musical instrument. Accordingly in all the churches of God, united in soul and attitude, with one mind and in agreement of faith and piety, we send up a unison melody in the words of the Psalms. We are

> accustomed to employ such psalmodies and spiritual kitharas because the apostle teaches this saying, "in psalms and odes and spiritual hymns." Otherwise the kithara might be [understood as] the whole body, through whose movements and deeds the soul renders a fitting hymn to God. The ten-stringed psalterion might be the worship performed by the Holy Spirit through the five senses of the body (equaling the five powers of the soul).
> *(Commentary on Psalms* 91.2, 3)

The historical argument about Christian practice on this subject is particularly strong. Many centuries passed before instruments were played in the catholic liturgy. They are still absent from the Eastern Churches. Our brethren in the instrumental churches of Christ have never faced the full force of the historical testimony against the presence of mechanical instruments in the early Christian assemblies.

The Argument from the Jewish Synagogue

Where did the practice of the Christian assemblies have its origin? An understanding of the historical context of early Christian practice requires a look at the synagogue. The nature of the synagogue will also prepare the way for a consideration of the theological reasons behind Christian practice.

Explicit testimony concerning musical practice in the synagogue comes from later than New Testament times. It confirms what may be inferred from the testimony which is contemporary with New Testament times concerning what was done in the synagogue meetings. Instrumental music was absent, in contrast to the temple worship. Instruments accompanied the animal sacrifice at the temple. The synagogue employed a non-sacrificial worship. Its service was built around prayer to God and instruction from the scriptures for those present. The use of the Psalms in this kind of a service left no place for instrumental accompaniment.

It is generally agreed that the Jewish synagogue provided the most important antecedent from which the Christian assembly was developed. From the historical standpoint this was a normal development. It would both explain the absence of the instrument from Christian assemblies and provide a supporting argument for that absence.

The Argument from the Nature of the Christian Assembly

The non-use of instrumental music in the assemblies of the early Christians was more than simply a historical development. It rested on doctrinal considerations which are still valid. A principal purpose of the Christian assembly is edification. Vocal music serves this purpose. Instrumental music can contribute nothing to it and may interfere with it.

Edification in its biblical meaning refers to teaching, instruction. It means to build up and strengthen, not through a feeling of uplift or what makes one feel good, but through what confers a benefit. Edification requires that understanding be involved.

Paul gives his most extensive instructions on the Christian assembly in 1 Corinthians 14. He argues against speaking in tongues in the assembly unless there is an interpreter. Throughout the chapter he sets edification as the standard for what is done (note verses 4, 5, 12, 17, and 26). Edification requires that the speech be intelligible (verses 9, 16, and 19). On this basis prophecy is superior to speaking in tongues (verses 3, 6, 24, and 31).

The principle which is developed in 1 Corinthians 14 may be applied to the question of vocal versus instrumental music. Vocal music, singing, has the possibility of edification. It can teach, admonish, encourage, and build up in the faith. Instrumental music can do none of these things. Accompanied singing may distract from these ends.

The Argument from the Nature of Human's Service to God

The Christian assembly exemplifies the relationship of humans to God. It honors God and is a model of human's praise to God.

God is a spirit, and a person is linked to God by his or her spiritual nature. Therefore, the New Testament emphasizes that the Christian's service to God proceeds from the highest part of his nature—his spiritual, intellectual, rational nature. "God is spirit, and those who worship him must worship in spirit and truth" (John 4:24). "Present your bodies as a living sacrifice, holy and acceptable to God, which is your spiritual worship" (Rom. 12:1). "Like living stones be yourselves built into a spiritual house, to be a holy priesthood, to offer spiritual sacrifices acceptable to God through Jesus Christ" (1 Pet. 2:5).

These verses draw on terminology and concepts used in early Christian times to express a worship that was non-sacrificial, non-material.

A person must live life in the world, but when the church comes together, it affirms the priority of spiritual values. The church in assembly confesses who God is and what its relationship to him is. In that setting its service to God is rational, spiritual. The tongue, the voice can give proper praise to God. That which is "lifeless" (1 Cor. 14:7), that which is mechanical cannot. Vocal music is an expression of the spiritual nature of the human person in a way that instrumental music never can be.

Conclusion

A cappella music was employed in the assemblies of the earliest Christians. There is no evidence that instrumental music was. A cappella music remained characteristic of Christian music for many centuries. A cappella music best accords with the purpose of the Christian assembly—edification—and with spiritual praise to God.

*Originally printed in *How Great Thou Art,* Harding University Lectureship, 1978 (Austin: Firm Foundation, 1978), 196–201.

22

Church Music in Ephesians and Colossians

Exegesis of Colossians 3:15–17

Some scholars suggest that the sequence of putting away sins (Col. 3:5–11), putting on the virtues of Christ (including worship—3:12–18), and assuming a code of conduct for the members of a household (3:18–4:1) were a part of instruction for new converts in early Christianity. Verses 15 and 16 have a similar grammatical form, each introduced by a third person singular imperative, "Let the peace of Christ rule in your hearts" and "Let the word of Christ dwell in you [...] with gratitude in your hearts." Christ—the peace of (v. 15), the word of (v. 16), and the name of (v. 17)—and thanksgiving are the dominant themes of this section, as they are of Colossians as a whole.

The peace that Christ gives is to hold sway over the whole of our lives. "Hearts" is used in the biblical sense of the center of intellect and will that governs the total person. God calls us to peace (1 Cor. 7:15). This calling takes place "in the one body" that is the church (1:18). The calling is collective, so it is in this one body where there is to be unity. With peace goes thanksgiving as characteristic of the church. The command calls for more than a grateful attitude: thanksgiving is to be expressed. Christians are to be a people who are thankful. On the theme of thanksgiving in Colossians see 1:3, 12; 2:7; and 4:2.

The reference to the collective church continues in 3:16. Compare 1:27, "Christ in you," with 3:16, the "word of Christ in you." In both cases the reference is not individual, "inside you" (although that would follow), but collective, "among you." The verse may refer to three elements of the corporate assembly: the announcing of the word (either by prophetic speech or reading), teaching and admonition, and singing. A corporate context is indicated by the "one another" who are taught and admonished. Although the term translated "one another" is the reflexive pronoun *(heautous,* literally "yourselves"), in usage it does not really differ from the reciprocal pronoun *(allelous,* "one another") and is frequently used in that sense, as in verse 13, where both occur together.

The "word of Christ" is the message that centers in Christ. It is not clear whether the genitive is subjective (Christ as the source of the word) or objective (Christ as the content of the word). Both ideas may be involved (cf. 2:6–7). Parallel expressions are "the word of the truth, the gospel" (1:5–6); the "word of God" (1:25; Acts 12:24); and "word of the Lord" (1 Thess. 1:8; 2 Thess. 3:1; Acts 8:25).

The richly indwelling word results in teaching and admonishing and in singing. These participles have the force of imperatives. Participles can be used as imperatives. Here the sentence begins with an imperative, "Let the word of Christ dwell in you," which sets the tone for the following construction. Compare verse 13, where "bear with one another . . . and forgive each other" are actually participles that get their imperative meaning from the main verb, "clothe yourselves," in verse 12.

There are two possible ways to construe verse 16: (1) May the word of Christ richly dwell in you in all wisdom, as in gratitude you teach and admonish one another with psalms, hymns, and spiritual songs, singing with your hearts to God; or (2) may the word of Christ dwell in you richly, as you teach and admonish one another in all wisdom, and as you sing with thanks in your hearts to God. Other arrangements of the words are possible, but the main choice is whether the teaching is done by the psalms, hymns, and spiritual songs or whether these songs are taken with the singing as a distinct activity from the teaching. The former construction is closer to Ephesians 5:19, but recent commentators favor taking the items sung with the participle "singing," and I give a cautious preference to this analysis.

Three prepositional phrases—"in wisdom," "in gratitude," and "in the name of Christ"—mark the three activities of teaching, singing, and giving thanks. Wisdom is a prominent theme in Colossians (1:9, 28; 2:3, 23; 4:5). "With gratitude" is literally "in grace [*charis*]." The word has three meanings: charm (graciousness), divine grace, and thanks. Either of the latter two are possible here (in a state of grace, or with thankfulness), but I have opted for the repetition of the theme of thanksgiving. The other prepositional phrase with "in," "in your hearts," is not silent worship but as in verse 15 refers to the center of one's being, "with your whole self."

Most modern commentators recognize that it is impossible to distinguish "psalms, hymns, and songs." If one were going to do so, the psalms would be primarily the Old Testament Psalms or compositions like them; hymns would be songs of praise; and songs (odes) would be the more general word. The words can be distinguished by their etymology, as was done by Gregory, bishop of Nyssa in the fourth century: "A psalm is the melody made by a musical instrument. An ode is a melodious expression made by the mouth with words.... A hymn is the honor rendered to God for the good things which are ours" *(On the Titles of the Psalms* 3.2). In spite of this etymologically correct definition, Gregory's own usage, like that of other Christians, was to refer "psalms" to vocal music. By the time of the writing of the New Testament, Christian and most Jewish usage had dropped instrumental associations from *psalmos*. The three terms are interchangeable in the titles appearing in Greek manuscripts of the Psalms and in other compositions, such as the *Psalms of Solomon* (first century BC). Philo and Josephus use "hymns" to mean "Psalms." It may be that "spiritual" modifies all three nouns, not just "songs" and is feminine because the nearest noun ("songs") is feminine.

Verse 17 shows that these injunctions are not limited to the assembly of the church. To do everything in the name of the Lord Jesus recalls 3:11,

"Christ is all in all." In the Old Testament one's "name" meant the person's self. To do all in Jesus' name is to proclaim that Jesus is Lord. "Giving thanks" is another imperatival participle. Linking Jesus with "everything" one does means to ask, "Can I do this in the name of Jesus?" "Can I thank God for the opportunity of doing this?" (Bruce, 160).

Exegesis of Ephesians 5:18–20

The three exhortations in the second person plural imperative in Ephesians 5:15–20 contain a "not . . . but" *(me . . . alla)* contrast: "Not as unwise but as wise" (5:15), "not be foolish but understand" (5:17), "not get drunk . . . but be filled with the Spirit" (5:18). As in Colossians, there is the sequence of renouncing the old life (4:17–5:14), walking in wisdom (including worship—5:15–20), and assuming a household code (5:21–6:9); but there is no confirmation that this was a standard sequence in early Christian instruction.

"Do not get drunk with wine" (5:18) quotes Proverbs 23:31 according to the Greek version. The comparison between drunkenness and being filled with the Spirit is that a person is under the control of an external power—spirits or the Spirit. Some suggest that the comparison occurs because of drunkenness in the worship of Dionysus, but there is no indication that such was a special problem for the readers. Drunkenness is probably introduced for the sake of making a contrast with the Holy Spirit.

"Be filled" with or by the Spirit—both are possible. To paraphrase, "Let your fullness come through the Holy Spirit" (Bruce, 379). The Spirit strengthens the inner person (3:16). Being filled with the Spirit, therefore, is the equivalent of the indwelling word of Christ in Colossians 3:16. The two ideas belong together, and it is not necessary to interpret one as really being the other. What is involved in being filled with the Spirit is indicated by five participles: speaking, singing, making melody, giving thanks, and submitting oneself (5:19–21). These are the results, not the means, of being filled with the Spirit.

The believers address one another in "psalms, hymns, and spiritual songs." Although the singing derives from the Spirit, it involves intelligible articulation, because the songs are addressed to one another as well as to God. *Heautois* is once more used not as a reflexive ("talking to yourselves") but in a reciprocal sense ("speaking to one another"), as it is in 4:32, where the two pronouns are interchangeable. The occasion where this was possible was the common meeting of Christians, for everyone was to take part. Although addressed to one another, the songs were still directed to the Lord.

The construction in verse 19 follows the phraseology of the Greek translation of the Psalms, where *ado* and *psallō* (the verb forms of two of the nouns naming what was sung) frequently occur together (Ps. 21:13; 27:6; 57:7; 101:1), sometimes in synonymous parallelism (Ps. 13:6; 59:16–17; 68:4, 32; 104:33). The Greek translation of the Old Testament contains the construction *psallō* with the preposition *en* and the name of an instrument and a reference to "the Lord" also in the dative case with the meaning "to play on the instrument to God" (Ps. 33:2; 71:22; 98:5; 144:9; 147:7; 149:3). If Ephesians follows this construction (some of the best manuscripts, however, lack the preposition *en),* then the heart is the instrument on which the music is made. One difference is that in Psalms, the "Lord" is God but in Ephesians it is Christ. Where the instrumental connotation of *psallō* is present in early Christian literature, it is with such a metaphorical meaning, but even that metaphorical usage is not the principal way the word is used. It is probably best, therefore, to take the combination of the verbs in Ephesians as an example of hendiadys, saying the same thing in two words joined with "and."

The melody comes from the heart; the presence of the pronoun "your" with "heart" rules out the possibility that *tē kardia* is adverbial "heartily." The heart in biblical language, unlike modern usage, does not refer primarily to the emotions. The thought is that the singing is to be with sincerity and conviction, rather than with heartiness.

A parallel to Ephesians 5:19 is found in the report the Roman governor Pliny sent to the emperor Trajan about AD 110 concerning what he had learned about Christian meetings: "They were in the habit of meeting on a certain fixed day before it was light, when they sang in alternate verses a hymn to Christ, as to a god" *(Letters* 10.96). The "alternate verses" might describe the "speaking to one another," but the specific interpretation of this activity as antiphonal singing is not necessarily the meaning of Pliny or of Paul. That the hymns were addressed to Christ is common to both statements.

Singing is associated with thanksgiving. Verse 20 reminds the readers that thanksgiving is to be made in all circumstances (cf. 1:16). It is made with reference to the name of Christ and directed to God the Father.

History of Interpretation

Clement of Alexandria (about AD 200) cited Colossians 3:16 in his chapter on conduct at banquets *(Instructor* 2.4.41–44). In this passage he condemned the pipe and *aulos* as instruments associated with revelry and unsuited to a temperate banquet. He gave qualified approval to the *kithara* and lyre in such a setting, but clearly his preference was for vocal music with emphasis on the words. He cited Colossians 3:16 in support of this vocal emphasis. Psalmody is the most suitable music at a Christian's meal. Clement associated psalmody with thanksgiving and said that the apostle (Paul) called the psalm a "spiritual song." It is characteristic of Clement to weave together texts about religious worship with his discussion of daily activities, so his use of Colossians 3:16 here is no indication that he thought it applied only (or even primarily) to a private social gathering.

Tertullian from Carthage, a younger contemporary of Clement of Alexandria, set singing to the Lord with psalms and hymns (Eph. 5:18–19) in contrast to drinking wine with drums and psalteries (Isa. 5:11–12).

The first commentary on either of these books for which there are significant remains is Origen's *Commentary on Ephesians* (first half of the third century). Origen applied the adjective "spiritual" to all three nouns in Ephesians 5:19. His comments on "psalms" imply the association he made elsewhere of psalms with the instrument known as a psalterion but applied, again as was his custom, to the human person. Thus in commenting on Psalm 33:2 he interpreted the ten-stringed psalterion as the body with its five senses and five powers of the soul and alluded to Ephesians 5:19: "The one who makes melody with the mind makes melody well, speaking spiritual songs and singing with his heart to God" (Ferguson, *A Cappella,* 52–53). He interpreted the Psalms by the New Testament, not vice versa.

Eusebius of Caesarea (early fourth century) made explicit what was implicit in Origen's allegorizing. Christians "employ spiritual psalmody and kitharas, since the apostle teaches this, saying 'psalms, odes, and spiritual hymns.'" Then he proceeded to contrast these with instruments, for the body is the kithara, the soul is a hymn, and the ten-stringed psalterion is worship performed by the Holy Spirit through the five senses and five powers of the soul *(Commentary on Psalms* 92:2–3).

John Chrysostom, the great preacher of Antioch and Constantinople at the end of the fourth century, gave full attention to our verses in his homilies on these books. His *Homily 9 On Colossians* in commenting on 3:16–17 takes the "teaching and admonishing" as being done "in all wisdom" by the psalms, hymns, and spiritual songs. These kinds of songs are to replace the "songs and dances of Satan." Hymns contain nothing human but are "a diviner thing." In keeping with a common patristic interpretation that gave a higher evaluation to hymns than to psalms because the etymology of *psalmos* had the connotation of physical activity in contrast to the higher activity of contemplation associated with songs (Ferguson, *A Cappella,* 62–67), Chrysostom says, "The powers above chant hymns, not Psalms." He offers different possible meanings of singing "with grace": God in his grace has given us these songs; singing is to be done with grace; admonishing is to be done in a gracious way; Christians had these gifts in grace; song comes from the grace of the Spirit. "In your hearts" means to sing not simply with the mouth but with heedfulness, not to the air but to God. It is not to be done for display. When a person is in the marketplace or walking, he can sing and pray in the heart.

Chrysostom's *Homily 19 On Ephesians* 5:18–21 comments, "They who sing Psalms are filled with the Holy Spirit, as they who sing satanic songs are filled with an unclean spirit." The phrase "with your hearts to the Lord" means "with close attention and understanding, for they who do not attend closely, merely sing, uttering the words, while their heart is roaming elsewhere." We should give thanks, he said, for everything that befalls us. We can even be thankful for hell itself, for the dread of hell is a bridle on our hearts.

Theodoret of Cyrus (fifth century) says on Colossians 3:16 that "the old law commanded continual meditation on the divine word" with Deuteronomy 6:7 quoted. "The divine apostle commands this so that we may always carry about the teaching of Christ in our soul, to praise him, and to sanctify the tongue with spiritual songs." We are to sing "not only with the mouth" but "with the heart" *(Commentary on Colossians* 3.16).

Theodoret interprets being filled with the Spirit in Ephesians 5:18 as "praising God continually, deferring to one another, and always stimulating the reasoning.... The one who makes melody with the heart moves not only the tongue but stimulates the mind to the understanding of the things said" (*Commentary on Ephesians* 5:18–19).

Thomas Aquinas (thirteenth century) wrote a commentary on Ephesians. He identified "Psalms, hymns, and spiritual canticles" as the subjects of meditative prayer. He followed patristic exegesis in interpreting psalms as concerned with good works, hymns with divine praises, and spiritual canticles with the hope of eternal realities. He responded to the error that the singing was to be only in the heart and not vocalized. The external expression has two purposes: it stimulates one's mind to devotion and it encourages others to become more devout. Singing, therefore, is addressed to three persons: God, one's neighbor, and one's self.

Aquinas's *Summa theologiae,* Question 91, dealt with two questions: "Whether God should be praised with the lips," and "Whether God should be praised with song." He affirmed both. It is interesting that the first of the objections to praising God in song to which Thomas responded was Colossians 3:16—God should be praised with spiritual, not bodily, canticles. Thomas's reply was that "the praise of the voice is necessary in order to arouse one's devotion towards God."

The interpretation of Colossians 3:16 as requiring "silent singing" was picked up by the early Anabaptists from the teaching of Zwingli. A letter from Conrad Grebel and his friends in Zurich to Thomas Müntzer, dated September 5, 1524, argued, among other things, against singing in church. Ephesians 5:19 and Colossians 3:16 were cited as teaching that we should speak to one another and only sing and give thanks in the heart.

John Calvin's *Commentary on Ephesians* (1548) included comments against silent singing: "'Speaking to themselves' is 'speaking among themselves.'" He added, "Nor does he enjoin them to sing inwardly or alone." "'Singing in your hearts'" he interpreted as, "Let your praises be not merely on the tongue, as hypocrites do, but from the heart."

Calvin's *Commentary on Colossians* offered the following explanation of how the three terms were "commonly distinguished":

A "psalm" is that, in the singing of which some musical instrument besides the tongue is made use of; a "hymn" is properly a song of praise, whether it be sung simply with the voice or otherwise; while an "ode" contains not merely praises, but exhortations and other matters. He would have the songs of Christians, however, to be "spiritual," not made up of frivolities and worthless trifles." "Singing in your hearts" he related to the disposition "that there may not be merely an external sound with the mouth." Paul did not intend everyone to "sing inwardly to himself, but he would have both conjoined, provided the heart goes before the tongue."

Although Calvin gave the common etymological definition of "psalm," he must have understood that the command was only to "sing" the Psalms. This conclusion follows from the fact that he elsewhere said that musical instruments such as were mentioned in the Psalms were no more to be employed than other practices of the Old Testament law "in the holy services of the church," where only understandable vocal music was to be used (*Commentary of Psalms*, 33:2).

The commentaries by J. B. Lightfoot on Colossians and B. F. Westcott on Ephesians have been justly influential for their solid philological and historical learning. Lightfoot understood the "psalms, hymns, and spiritual songs" as the instruments of the teaching and admonition (224). He distinguished them etymologically: "While the leading idea of *psalmos* is a musical accompaniment and that of *hymnos* praise to God, *ōdē* is the general word for a song" (225). He observed, However, that in the text the reference in *psalmois* "is specially, though not exclusively [. . .] to the Psalms of David." Lightfoot concluded that "the reference in the text is not solely or chiefly to public worship as such" (225). "In your hearts" indicated that "There must be the thanksgiving of the heart, as well as of the lips" (226).

On the three items to be sung, Westcott cited Jerome, who followed Origen (referred to above). He considered the passage to refer to the Christian congregation: "The same strains which set forth aspects of God's glory elevate the feelings of those who join in them" (82). The outward song is accompanied by the inward music of the heart (82).

Two substantial recent commentaries in the Word Biblical Commentary series may be noted as representing the current state of evangelical scholarship: Peter T. O'Brien on Colossians and Philemon and Andrew T. Lincoln on Ephesians. I drew extensively from them in the exegesis given above.

Theology of Singing

Most of the affirmations in the New Testament about the doctrinal significance of Christian song may be found in Colossians 3:15–17 and Ephesians 5:18–20 (Ferguson, *Church,* 268–73).

Christian songs are directed to God the Father (Col. 3:16, 17; Eph. 5:20). They are expressions of worship, praise, and petition to him who is Father of all, who is over all, through all, and in all (Eph. 4:6). This gives a sense of reverence and awe that should characterize all activities in the assembly.

Singing is also directed to Christ as the one Lord and Savior (Eph. 5:19). It is done in the name of the Lord Jesus (Col. 3:17), that is, as an act of worship to him, with reference to his saving work for us, and by his authority. Christ provides the motivation and essential content of Christian songs.

The songs Christians sing spring from being filled with the Holy Spirit (Eph. 5:18) and so are spiritual in nature (Col. 3:16; Eph. 5:19). As derived from the Spirit and his indwelling, songs are to express the spiritual nature of human beings, created with the capacity for rational, spiritual worship (Rom. 12:1). Christian enthusiasm comes not from artificial stimulation but from the presence of the Holy Spirit, who through the word of Christ makes us realize the greatness of God and the greatness of our salvation in Christ.

The predominant note in Christian song is thanksgiving (Col. 3:15–17; Eph. 5:20). This is because Christians know God as Father, have received salvation in Christ, and have received the gift of the Holy Spirit. So, there is a deep, underlying spiritual joy expressed in song—a joy that can be thankful to God for other people and thankful in all circumstances.

Christian song expresses one purpose of the assembly, namely mutual edification. In song we speak to one another (Eph. 5:19). Song results from the active presence of the word of the Lord in the gathering of God's people

(Col. 3:16). Hence, the singing involves intelligible words. It will support the teaching and admonishing expressed in the delivery of the word of Christ. The word of Christ will control the content of the songs.

Singing both expresses unity and contributes to unity (cf. Rom. 15:6). Christians meet as called by God into one body, where peace rules (Col. 3:15). Singing is a unifying activity.

Christian song proceeds from the heart (Eph. 5:19; Col. 3:16). It expresses concentration and intention. It is not mere words; it is not pretty melodies. It comes from the center of our beings and is concerned with basic spiritual truths.

Observations on Contemporary Practice

The teachings of Colossians 3:15–17 and Ephesians 5:18–20 have a practical application to our singing today. The instructions were addressed to the whole church and presuppose that all participate. Some practices ostensibly intended to improve the singing may actually work against congregational participation. Any practice that calls attention to certain singers, either visually or in volume, makes others want to watch or listen to them rather than to participate themselves.

Elaborations of the music that emphasize the musical quality at the expense of the words easily focus attention on the wrong thing and enhance aesthetics at the expense of instruction and edification. Melody is useful in deepening the impression of the words, making them memorable, and adding to their emotional impact, but the melody should not detract from the message and direct attention to itself and away from the words. The melody is subordinate to and supports the words, not the other way around.

The singing of rounds is particularly subject to this criticism, for they are destructive of communication and instruction to one another. Would we permit four men in the congregation to read simultaneously four different passages of scripture? The words would be scriptural, but would intelligible communication take place? Setting those words to beautiful music does not mean edification occurs.

The verbal content is primary in the texts of Ephesians and Colossians, both from what is expressly said and from the larger contexts of the verses studied. For something to be vocal does not necessarily mean that it corresponds to the teaching of these verses. Of course, instrumental sounds cannot do the things described in these verses. But neither do nonverbal sounds made by the voice or other parts of the body—only words that are rational, intelligible, and spiritual.

*Originally printed in *Exalting Christ in the Church: Unsearchable Riches in Ephesians and Colossians*, Freed-Hardeman University Lectureship, 2002 (Henderson, TN: Freed Hardeman University, 2002), 90–101.

Selected Bibliography

Aquinas, St. Thomas. *Commentary on Saint Paul's Epistle to the Ephesians.* Translated by Matthew L. Lamb. Albany: Magi Books, 1966.

———. *The "Summa Theologica" of St. Thomas Aquinas.* Translated by Fathers of the English Dominican Province. Vol. 11. London: Bums Oates & Washbourne, 1922.

Bruce, F. F. *The Epistles to the Colossians, to Philemon, and to the Ephesians.* New International Commentary on the New Testament. Grand Rapids: Eerdmans, 1984.

Calvin, John. *Commentaries.* Translated by James Anderson, John Pringle, and William Pringle. Vols. 8, 41, 42. Grand Rapids: Eerdmans, 1948.

Chrysostom, John. *Homilies on Ephesians; Homilies on Colossians.* Translated by W. J. Copeland and J. Ashworth. Nicene and Post-Nicene Fathers. Ser. 1, Vol. 13. New York: Christian Literature, 1889. Peabody: Hendrickson, 1994.

Dunn, James D. G. *The Epistles to the Colossians and to Philemon: A Commentary on the Greek Texts.* New International Greek New Testament Commentary. Grand Rapids: Eerdmans, 1996.

Ferguson, Everett. *A Cappella Music in the Public Worship of the Church.* 3rd ed. Fort Worth: Star, 1999.

———. *The Church of Christ: A Biblical Ecclesiology for Today.* Grand Rapids: Eerdmans, 1996.

Grebel, Conrad. "Letters to Thomas Müntzer." *Spiritual and Anabaptist Writers.* Library of Christian Classics. Edited by George H Williams and Angel M. Mergal. Vol. 25. Philadelphia: Westminster, 1957.

Lightfoot, J. B. *St. Paul's Epistles to the Colossians and to Philemon.* 1879. Grand Rapids: Zondervan, n.d.

Lincoln, Andrew T. *Ephesians.* Word Biblical Commentary 42. Dallas: Word, 1990.

O'Brien, Peter T. *Colossians, Philemon.* Word Biblical Commentary 44. Waco: Word, 1982.

Schnackenburg, Rudolf. *Ephesians: A Commentary.* Edinburgh: T. & T. Clark, 1991.

Schweizer, Eduard. *The Letter to the Colossians: A Commentary.* Minneapolis: Augsburg, 1982.

Westcott, B. F. *St. Paul's Epistle to the Ephesians.* 1906. Grand Rapids: Eerdmans, 1952.

23

Early Church History and the Instrumental Music Controversy

My assignment is to discuss the evidence of early Christian history concerning the kind of music employed in the early church. The testimony of early church history is clear and strong that early Christians employed vocal music but did not employ instrumental music in their assemblies. In making my argument, I am not saying that church history is our authority or that uninspired writers should determine what our practice today should be. I do not want to be misunderstood on this point. The New Testament is our authority. Christian authors and others in the early centuries function as witnesses to what Christians did. They gave testimony about what the New Testament taught and how the early Christians understood the apostolic teaching. They are not themselves the authority. They, as any other witnesses, must be questioned and cross-examined. Individually and collectively they certainly were wrong in many of their understandings and many of their teachings, but they were in a better position than we to know what words meant. They can show us how they used words. And certainly they knew what they did when they went to church every Sunday. The New Testament faith and practice are the standard, but, as I argued in the Festschrift for Jack Lewis,[1] the witness of early church history is evidence which should be heard in determining what the New Testament meant and what it teaches. Every time a person examines a lexicon or grammar in order to determine the meaning of a word or the teaching of a given verse, he is making use of historical evidence. The lexicon or grammar is not the authority; it is a means of determining the meaning of the Bible, which is the authority.

I propose to examine the evidence of early church history on five topics: (1) on singing in the assembly, (2) on how the singing was done, (3) on the meaning of the word *psallō*, (4) on the opposition to instruments of music, and (5) on the interpretation of instrumental music in the Old Testament.

Singing in the Assembly

The first description of Christian meetings outside the New Testament comes from a pagan source. Pliny the Younger, the Roman governor of Bythinia about AD 110, wrote to the emperor Trajan an account of his examination of Christians. He wrote that they "affirmed, however the whole of their guilt, or their error, was that they were in the habit of meeting on a certain fixed day before it was light, when they sang in alternate verses a hymn to Christ, as to a god, and bound themselves by a solemn oath."[2] The Christ-centered nature of early Christian song is attested by other sources.[3] The "alternate verses" are sometimes taken as indicating antiphonal singing, but I think they were more likely responsorial. These terms will be explained later.

The Christian sources agree about the presence of vocal music, song, in Christian gatherings. Ignatius, bishop of Antioch at about the same time as Pliny, exhorted the church at Ephesus as follows:

> For your deservedly famous presbytery, worthy of God, is attuned to the bishop as strings to a kithara. Therefore, by your concord and harmonious love Jesus Christ is being sung. Now all of you together become a choir so that being harmoniously in concord and receiving the key note from God in unison you may sing with one voice through Jesus Christ to the Father.[4]

The context is not that of a Christian assembly, but Ignatius was clearly drawing his language from an assembly setting (the same thing happens in the New Testament in Eph. 5:19 and Col. 3:16). It is not clear whether the instructions for the whole congregation to become a united chorus was a literal exhortation or a metaphor for the unity which Ignatius enjoined, but either way the basis of the instruction is the Christian practice of congregational song about Christ addressed to God. That is the experience of Ignatius's readers which gives meaning to the exhortation. The language of Ignatius has many affinities with the so-called *Odes of Solomon,* also from Syria and many think from about the same time period as Ignatius. Comparable to Ignatius's emphasis on the many singing with one voice and the use of an instrumental analogy for vocal music is the statement of the *Odes* "that . . . they may sing to [the Lord] with joy and with the harp of many voices."[5] The many voices are themselves the harp.

There are many passages about Christians' vocal praise, but I will limit myself here to those which explicitly have as their setting the congregational assembly. Clement of Alexandria late in the second century offered this criticism of the inconsistency of some Christians:

> After having paid reverence to the discourse about God, they leave within what they have learned. And outside they foolishly amuse themselves with impious playing, and amatory quavering, occupied with pipe-playing, and dancing, and intoxication, all kinds of trash. They who sing thus, and sing in response, are those who before hymned immortality—found at last wicked and wickedly singing this most pernicious palinode, "Let us eat and drink, for tomorrow we die."[6]

In the church, one hymned immortality. This is contrasted with the suggestive and immoral singing outside the assembly, which is put in the same company with pipe-playing, dancing, and drinking.

A few years later, at the beginning of the third century, Tertullian listed the activities in an assembly in Carthage: " . . . when the Scriptures are read, or the Psalms are chanted, or sermons are preached, or prayers are sent up."[7] He similarly connected "hymns and psalms" with prayer and the "altar" of communion.[8] His contemporary, Hippolytus of Rome, spoke of the "proper day . . . in the house of God" when "all are praying there and singing to God."[9]

A century later at the beginning of the fourth century, Eusebius offered a comparable summary of a Christian service: " . . . singing of Psalms and recitation of other such words as have been given us from God," "the ineffable symbols of the Savior's passion were present," and the church's rulers delivered orations, "inspiring the assembly."[10] The most striking testimony from Eusebius comes in his *Commentary on Psalms* 65.10–15:

> Throughout the world—in cities, in villages, and in the country—in all the churches of God the people of Christ, who have been chosen out of all the nations, send up, not to the native gods nor to demons but to the one God spoken of by the prophets, hymns and psalmody with a loud voice so that the sound of those singing can be heard by those standing outside.[11]

This passage pertains expressly to congregational assemblies and in some cases expressly to the Sunday assembly. More of these testimonies will appear later to establish other points.

The same vocal practice was observed at other gatherings of Christians. Tertullian told us that after the agape, or love feast, in the evening "each one who is able is called into the center to chant praise to God either from the holy Scriptures or from his own talents."[12] There were also daily meetings. "Assemble yourselves together every day, morning and evening, singing Psalms and praying in the Lord's house."[13]

Manner of Singing

These testimonies are sufficient to establish the presence of song in the meetings of Christians in the first centuries of our era. I want now to give some attention to the evidence from church history of how the singing was done.

Not a great deal is known about the melodies ancient Christians employed. There is a papyrus fragment of an early Christian hymn from the third century with notations for vocal rendition but none for instrumental accompaniment.[14] For the most part we are dependent on inferences from what is known about ancient Greek and Jewish music and from working back from Gregorian chants and Byzantine melodies to determine the musical aspects of early Christian song. That is not my interest here and is beyond my competence. Rather I want to adduce some of the evidence for the formal aspects of the manner of singing.

The solo singing of the Psalms was known in the daily services from monastic circles, and this probably continued earlier devotional practices of Christians at home. John Cassian described the custom: "As they were going to celebrate their daily rites and prayers, one rose up in the midst to chant the Psalms to the Lord. And while they were all sitting... with their minds intently fixed on the words of the chanter...."[15]

In communal gatherings, there was provision for congregational participation in the singing. One of the fullest accounts of the different ways of performing the Psalms is found in a record by Basil, bishop of Caesarea in Cappadocia, of all-night vigils from the second half of the fourth century:

> The customs which now obtain are agreeable to those of all the churches of God. Among us the people go at night to the house of prayer and, in distress, affliction, and continual tears, making confession to God, at last rise from their prayers and begin to sing psalms. And now, divided into two parts, they sing antiphonally with one another, thus confirming their study of the [scriptures], and at the same time producing for themselves a heedful temper and a heart free from distraction. Afterwards they again commit the prelude of the strain to one, and the rest take it up; and so after passing the night in various psalmody, praying at intervals as the day begins to dawn, all together, as with one voice and one heart, raise the psalm of confession to the Lord, each forming for himself his own expression of penitence.[16]

Basil's description covers three ways of rendering the Psalms: antiphonally, responsorially, and in unison. All can appropriately be called "congregational" singing, for the whole congregation was involved, but the manner of participation differed. Let us discuss each separately and in the order in which Basil mentioned them.

He described first a situation in which the congregation was divided into two parts. They alternated in singing to one another the verses of the Psalms. This demonstrated a knowledge of the total content of the Psalms by the whole congregation that permitted them to know where to come in and what to say. Basil had to defend this practice because it seems to have been a newer custom and was resisted by some as an innovation.[17] Have you ever had trouble trying to do something in a different way? The fifth-century church historian Theodoret placed the introduction of antiphonal singing in the mid-fourth century at Antioch: "Flavianus and Diodorus . . . were the first to divide choirs into two parts, and to teach them to sing the Psalms of David antiphonally. Introduced first at Antioch, the practice spread in all directions."[18]

Another source traces the practice of antiphonal singing to Ignatius of Antioch.[19] That report seems to have been motivated by a desire to give greater antiquity to the practice. On the other hand, there are problems with putting the introduction as late as the mid-fourth century. It was known among the Jewish sect of Therapeutae at the beginning of the Christian era,[20] and it was apparently practiced in the Syriac-speaking church. Antiphonal singing apparently did become popular in the Greek Church during the fourth century, and from the Greek Church it was introduced into the West by Ambrose at Milan.[21] A superficial reading of the ancient sources has led to statements that this marked the beginning of congregational singing in the church. That is not correct. Antiphonal singing did give a greater role to the congregation than did responsorial singing, and that fact accounts for its being described as "congregational," but this is not the beginning of congregational involvement in the singing.

The earliest definite form of congregational participation most widely attested was what is known as responsorial singing. According to this method, as Basil mentioned, a leader (the precentor or cantor) sang the first part and the people then responded to what he had sung. This response might have taken the form of a word (such as "Hallelujah" or "Amen") or a phrase (such as "His mercy endures forever") or the repetition of a refrain from the psalm or of the verse sung by the leader. This form of participation did not require prior knowledge of the psalm by the people nor extensive musical ability. I would insist that this too was genuinely "congregational singing" even if it was not in the form that we know today.

It may be good to cite some of the passages they sang. Tertullian referred to reciting the Psalms, at the close of which the company responded.[22] A fourth-century manual of church life instructed that during the Sunday assembly: "When there have been two lessons read, let some other person sing the hymns of David, and let the people join in the singing at the conclusions of the verses."[23] John Chrysostom referred to the practice of the congregation's singing together refrains to the Psalms in response as an old custom continued in his day.[24]

Basil gave as a third way of rendering the Psalms for all as with "one voice" to sing together so that the words became the confession of each individual. Many ancient authors made a special point of emphasizing the unison or corporate singing by the whole congregation. It is not always clear whether their references to unison singing had to do with the joint participation in responsorial or antiphonal singing or to something more like our congregational singing in which all sing the entire song. There is enough evidence from the Jewish background and Christian authors to indicate that Basil was not speaking of anything unusual. The *Martyrdom of Matthew* 8, inauthentic but nonetheless accurately reflecting current church practice, said: "Entering into the church they shared the eucharist.... And all those glorifying God were singing in the church the whole night." Ambrose, bishop of Milan in the late fourth century, said the following:

> What a labor it is to achieve silence in church while the lessons are being read. When one man would speak, the congregation makes a disturbance. But when the psalm is recited it makes its own "silence," since all are speaking and there is no disturbance. Psalms are sung by emperors; the common people rejoice in them. Each man does his utmost in singing what will be a blessing to all.... The singing of praise is the very bond of unity, when the whole people join in song a single act of song. The strings of the harp are of varying lengths, but the harmony is a unity. The musicians' finger, too, may often make mistakes on

the small strings, but in the congregation that great Musician, the Spirit, cannot err.[25]

Jerome identified the church as a chorus: "Wherever there is a choir many voices blend into one song. In the same way that separate chords produce a single effect, so, too, do separate voices harmonize as one. In other words, when the faithful gather together, they form the Lord's choir. Let them praise his name in choir."[26]

The emphasis on harmony in the singing reminds us that the singing in the early centuries was monodic or homophonic. Polyphony, as we know it in our four-part harmony, was developed later. Nonetheless, there was recognition of the different qualities of human voices. As John Chrysostom put it: "For indeed women and men, old and young, have different voices, but they do not differ in the word of hymnody, for the Spirit blends the voice of each and effects one melody in all."[27]

An instrument, however, would have introduced an unacceptable element of polyphony into the church's music. Before turning to passages dealing expressly with instrumental music, let us consider how early Christian writers used the words *psallō* and *psalmos*.

The Meaning of Psallō and Psalmos

Psallō ("to make melody" in Eph. 5:19) and *psalmos* ("psalm") have been the principal words controverted in the philological and lexicographical discussion of instrumental music because these words were used in classical Greek for instrumental music, specifically that produced on stringed instruments. The testimony of early church literature is important here for the Christian usage of these words and the meaning they were understood to have in the New Testament. Here, once more, the evidence shows a vocal practice.

Psallō was used by Christians with the meaning "to sing Psalms, to chant." Apart from Old Testament quotations (as *Barnabas* 6.16, quoting Ps. 22:22, notably using *psallō* for the Greek version's *humneō*), the first use of *psallō* by Christian writers outside the New Testament was by Justin Martyr in the middle of the second century. He used *psallō* in his *Dialogue with Trypho* 74.3, as does the New Testament, as a synonym for *adō* ("to sing") and with an express vocal content: "David sang [the words of God] in the Psalms."²⁸ Melito, bishop of Sardis around AD 180, in his *Homily on the Passover* 80, used *psallō* for the Jews' singing.

The most extensive use of *psallō* in early Christian literature was made by Clement of Alexandria. His most frequent usage of the word was to introduce quotations from the Psalms, so his ordinary meaning for the word was "sings" or "says in the Psalms." The vocal content is explicit in many passages, for instance, "The Word sings [*psalle*] through David concerning our Lord, saying..." followed by a quotation from the Psalms.²⁹ The hymn at the close of the *Instructor*, sometimes incorrectly called the earliest Christian hymn, is introduced with the words "Let us sing" (*psalomen*) followed by the words of the hymn. The associations of the word are shown by the phrase, "praising, hymning, blessing, *psallō*ing" in a passage that refers to activities in the assembly.³⁰ Clement normally allegorized the references to instruments in the Old Testament, but in one passage he gave a qualified approval of the use of a lyre or kithara, one of the rare favorable comments on instrumental music found in patristic literature: "Even if you wish to sing and make melody [or sing Psalms] to the accompaniment of the kithara or lyre there is no blame."³¹ The construction shows that playing instruments was not meant by the word *psallō*, which here has its usual vocal content as intended by Clement. The approval of the stringed instruments (not wind instruments) applied only to the banquet at home. Efforts to find in this statement an approval of instrumental music in the agape or even in church ignore the context and Clement's customary manner of writing. The passage is no exception to Clement's use of *psallō* for vocal music, nor to the early church's rejection of instruments in the assembly.

The vocal meaning of *psallō* continued to be normal for third-century and later writers. For example, Origen used *psallō* synonymously with hymning in commenting on 1 Corinthians 14:15.³² His opponent Methodius of Olympus was at one with him in word usage. Methodius spoke of "singing [*psallei*] the hymns."³³ Athanasius, in *Epistle to Marcellinus on the Interpretation of the Psalms*, repeatedly used *psallō* and *adō* as synonyms.³⁴ It is superfluous to cite further references for the meaning, which is so well attested by the patristic lexicons.

Some passages do preserve the etymological, classical meaning of *psallō*, but these are exceptional—either in talking about something other than the church's practice or in using the word in a metaphorical way.

It should be evident that the church itself is the best interpreter of its own language. Early Christian usage was decisive for the vocal meaning of the word *psallō* in the New Testament. The vocal meaning can be confirmed in the Septuagint, other Jewish literature of the intertestamental period, and from the context in the New Testament. The really conclusive argument, however, is Christian usage. Someone who wants to find another meaning in the New Testament must explain how early Christians uniformly came to use the word in reference to words and not to instruments.

The same situation applies even more thoroughly to the noun *psalmos*. Its overwhelming usage in early Christian literature, as in the New Testament, was in reference to the words of the book of Psalms. This was so common that to cite references is gratuitous; hence, I will instead look at the exceptions to the rule.

Several early Christian authors, in commenting on the Psalms, gave etymological definitions of *psalmos* and other musical terms. They pointed out that *psalmos* originally referred to the sound made by plucking on a stringed instrument. This meaning was then made the basis for an allegorical interpretation in order to give a moral lesson. Since there was physical activity involved in playing on a musical instrument, the use of the word "psalm" in the Old Testament was taken as teaching the need for physical activity along with meditation and contemplation in the spiritual life.[35] I will take only one passage as illustrative of what several writers did, and I will use an author to whom I have given considerable special study—Gregory, bishop of Nyssa in the late fourth century.

> There is a distinction between psalm, ode, praise, hymn, and prayer. A psalm is the melody of a musical instrument. An ode is a melodious expression made by the mouth with words. A prayer is a supplication brought to God with reference to something of concern. A hymn is the honor rendered to God for the good things which are ours. Praise includes a panegyric for the divine accomplishments, for a panegyric is nothing but an increase

of praise.... The interpretation which by these titles leads us to virtue is as follows. The psalterion is a musical instrument making its sound from the upper parts of its construction, and the music from this instrument is called "psalm." Therefore the Word which exhorts to virtue provides a significance from the very shape of the instrument's construction, for it admonishes you that your life which is not characterized by earthly sounds is a psalm. (I say "sounds" meaning "thoughts.") Rather it has the pure and audible sound produced from the upper and heavenly parts. When we read "ode," we understand through a figure the respectable life with reference to outward things.[36]

The passage continues in a similar vein. The point is that the definitions of the words are used only as a basis for moral and spiritual lessons. The definitions do not necessarily have anything to do with church practice or the author's normal use of the words. In Gregory's case, he used *psalmos* ninety-four other times and in every instance in reference to the book of Psalms, an individual psalm, or the title of a psalm.[37] Gregory's definition is of etymological interest but states nothing more than what everyone who has studied classical Greek knows about the meaning of the word. Here he has told us nothing about the Christian use of the word. For that, one must examine the rest of his writings. And these show the normal Christian usage. Apparently Gregory chose to stay with the proper "classical" meaning of the word in this one passage because it suited his allegorical purpose, not because it corresponded to church usage in his or any other time. Furthermore, Gregory has told us that by the sounds of the instrument he meant "thoughts," so the instrument he had in mind was the human body. There is no evidence that Gregory departed from the usual patristic opposition to instruments in church.

Opposition to Instrumental Music

Many patristic passages can be cited about the association of instruments with pagan immorality, and many sought to banish instruments from the daily life of Christians, recommending that the singing of psalms take the place of instruments at home, at weddings, at funerals, and for entertainment.[38]

This was not successful, but it shows how unlikely it would be to find patristic support for instruments in church. Since our concern is with the type of music employed in the assemblies of the church, we shall not pursue this aspect of the antagonism to instruments further but will direct our attention to Christian assemblies.

Christian authors not only referred to the practice of singing in the assemblies and made comments on how this was done and used *psallō* in reference to this singing, but they also made express statements about the Christian rejection of instrumental music in the praise of God. By the fourth century, Christian interpretation of the Psalms, reflection on the differences between Christian assemblies and pagan and Jewish cultic practices, and consideration of the implications of the Christian rejection of the Jewish religious practices in the Old Testament led to comments dealing expressly with the non-use of instruments by Christians. The reasons adduced are quite interesting.

Eusebius of Caesarea, the church historian at the beginning of the fourth century, wrote in his *Commentary on Psalms* 91.2–3:

> Of old at the time those of the circumcision were worshipping with symbols and types it was not inappropriate to send up hymns to God with the psalterion and kithara and to do this on Sabbath days.... We render our hymn with a living psalterion and a living kithara with spiritual songs. The unison voices of Christians would be more acceptable to God than any musical instrument. Accordingly in all the churches of God, united in soul and attitude, with one mind and in agreement of faith and piety, we send up a unison melody in the words of the Psalms.

Niceta, bishop of Remesiana in what is now Serbia, wrote one of the first treatises on church music. Apparently some had such a "spiritual" view of worship that they considered thoughts alone ("silent singing") the proper activity in worship and would have banished singing along with other outward ceremonies from the Old Testament. Niceta responded to them:

> It is time to turn to the New Testament to confirm what is said in the Old, and, particularly, to point out that the office of

psalmody is not to be considered abolished merely because many other observances of the Old Law have fallen into desuetude. Only the corporal institutions have been rejected, like circumcision, the sabbath, sacrifices, discrimination in foods. So, too, the trumpets, harps, cymbals, and timbrels. For the sound of these we now have a better substitute in the music from the mouths of men. The daily ablutions, the new-moon observances, the careful inspection of leprosy are completely past and gone, along with whatever else was necessary only for a time—as it were, for children. Of course, what was spiritual in the Old Testament, for example, faith, piety, prayer, fasting, patience, chastity, psalm-singing—all this has been increased in the New Testament rather than diminished.[39]

The anonymous treatise, *Questions and Answers for the Orthodox*, is now ascribed to Theodoret, bishop of Cyrhus in Syria. He dealt with a similar consideration:

107. Question: If songs were invented by unbelievers to seduce men, but were allowed to those under the law on account of their childish state, why do those who have received the perfect teaching of grace in their churches still use songs, just like the children under the law?

Answer: It is not simple singing that belongs to the childish state, but singing with lifeless instruments, with dancing, and with clappers. Hence the use of such instruments and the others that belong to the childish state is excluded from the singing in the churches, and simple singing is left. For it awakens the soul to a fervent desire for that which is described in the songs, it quiets the passions that arise from the flesh, it removes the evil thoughts that are implanted in us by invisible foes, it waters the soul to make it fruitful in the good things of God, it makes the soldiers of piety strong to endure hardships, it becomes for the pious a medicine to cure all the pains of life. Paul calls this the "sword of the Spirit," with which he arms the soldiers of piety against their unseen foes, for it is the word of God, and when it is pondered and sung and proclaimed it has the power to drive out demons.

The common perspective between Niceta and Theodoret, in two different languages and parts of the empire, is notable. Instrumental music, along with other ritual practices of the Old Testament, had been abolished for Christians. The singing of the Psalms of the Old Testament was continued in the church.

Interpretation of Instruments in the Old Testament

It was important to Christian authors to find an explanation of the instruments mentioned in the Old Testament, particularly in the Psalms, because the Psalms continued to be sung in the Christian assemblies. Eusebius, Niceta, and Theodoret took a historical or covenantal approach to interpreting the use of instruments in the Old Testament. Instruments were approved by God at one time as part of his covenant with the Jews, but they were not part of the new Christian dispensation. Other interpreters went further and explained that instruments were allowed in the Old Testament in order to lead the people away from idolatry. People were attracted to instrumental music and might partake in idolatrous worship where such was practiced. Theodoret himself adopted this explanation: "So it was not in any need of victims or craving odors that God commanded them to sacrifice, but that he might heal the sufferings of those who were sick. So he also allowed the use of instrumental music, not that he was delighted by the harmony, but that he might little by little end the deception of idols."[40] The association of instrumental music with animal sacrifice was quite common in the ancient world and thus in patristic comments on the religious use of instruments.

A more common approach, and one not antithetical to the covenantal explanation, since some authors adopted both, was to give a moral or allegorical interpretation to the instruments named in the Old Testament. Although there were some common interpretations, there was considerable variety according to each interpreter's ingenuity, as is characteristic of nonliteral exegesis. Origen was very influential on later allegorization. He explained that "The psalterion is the pure mind moved by spiritual knowledge; the kithara is the practical soul moved by the commandments of Christ."[41] It was particularly common to identify the instruments with the parts of the human body or with human activities. Psalm 150 offered ample opportunity for this kind of allegorization. I take one example:

> "Praise him with the sound of the trumpet," by his preaching. "Praise him with psalterion and kithara," hymning him by the grace of the Holy Spirit with heart, tongue, and your lips. "Praise him with timbrel and dance." Hymn him by putting to death your entire body. "Praise him with strings and organ." Strings, I think, are nerves. When these are dead, and attached to a certain piece of wood, and played by a musician, they make a sound. The organ is pipes which are brought together and share with one another the melody blown by the breath when someone plays on them. Praise him then in the light commandments and the hard.... "Praise him with pleasant cymbals." Hymn him with the lips of your body.[42]

This kind of interpretation kept the words of the Psalms as used in church but avoided a literal application of them, which would have been contradictory to the church's practice. We may not care for the kind of exegesis involved, but it speaks loudly and clearly as to the early Christians' understanding of their own praise to God.

Conclusion

The case is now complete; the witnesses have been called and questioned. Their testimony is unmistakable: early Christians sang unaccompanied by instrumental music in their assemblies.

My observation is that our brethren who support the use of instrumental music in worship have not faced the full force of the historical evidence against their position. The evidence of church history confirms the reading of the New Testament that is found among the noninstrumental churches of Christ. The historical argument is quite strong against early Christian use of instrumental music in church. What do I mean by a historical argument?

If something was present in the New Testament church, there should be some trace of it later in the practice of the church. If it is not to be found in the early centuries after the New Testament, there should be some clear and convincing explanation of why it disappeared or was discontinued. Where the early historical evidence is full—in this case virtually universal, uniform, and unanimous—about the church's practice, there is a strong presumption about apostolic practice and the New Testament teaching. The absence of the instrument in early Christian assemblies (as shown by the extracanonical evidence) creates a negative presumption about its presence in the New Testament. Instrumental music was abundantly available in the religious practices of pagan cults and was brought to consciousness by reading the Old Testament and remembering the temple ritual of the Jews. Where something was available and every assumption would seem to favor Christian adoption of the practice and yet there is complete evidence of the rejection of the practice in the post-apostolic period, there is every reason to look to a deliberate choice made in the apostolic age. A person must have a very good explanation in order to think that instruments were authorized in the New Testament but were not used by Christians for many centuries after the New Testament.

Two strategies are possible in order to avoid the force of this historical evidence. One approach is to say that the instrument really was there in the New Testament and early church. Some would argue that it was implicit in the word *psallō*; others point to etymological interpretations of *psallō* and *psalmos* by some church fathers or to isolated favorable statements about instruments as an indication that instruments had some use by Christians in religious contexts. There would then be a cultural explanation to be sought for the patristic statements enunciating a complete rejection of instruments in Christian worship. This cultural explanation is typically found in the association of instruments with pagan idolatry or with the immorality of the entertainment of the times. This hypothetical reconstruction breaks down before the actual evidence of the texts. That is not the explanation for the absence of instruments given by the ancient authors themselves. I must simply refer you to my presentation of the evidence and leave with you the determination of which account makes the most sense and best explains the data at our disposal.

Another strategy is to say that the absence of the instrument in the early centuries of the church is of no significance for present practice. Instrumental music may or may not be employed. On this view we are at liberty to choose which type of music we prefer or find most expedient. The early church made one decision; we have freedom to make another choice.

This latter response to the historical evidence brings us to a consideration of the theological arguments and the significance of the biblical teaching. I for one find the theological considerations advanced by the early church fathers more persuasive than the reasoning of our modern instrumental brethren. I find them more in accord with biblical teaching and believe they provide a better basis for Christian practice.

Without attempting here a complete theology of music from patristic literature, I will summarize some points from the texts I have garnered for my study.[43]

1. Instruments of music belonged to the childhood of the human race's spiritual development. They appealed to the senses and have now been abolished from the Christian assemblies with the other types and shadows of the Old Testament. Vocal music pertains to the spiritual nature of human beings.
2. The human body is the true instrument for praising God. Praise is to be offered with the voice, with the understanding, and with good works.
3. Psalm singing is a spiritual sacrifice, pleasing to God and beneficial to the one singing and the one listening. It lifts thoughts to God and calms the soul.
4. Congregational singing exemplifies the harmony of body and soul and the harmony of man with God, which is the goal of God's plan. It expresses the unity of the church.

Those are worthy theological reflections, and the attainment of their goals requires vocal song, unaccompanied by instruments.

*Originally printed in *The Instrumental Music Issue*, ed. Bill Flatt (Nashville: Gospel Advocate, 1987), 79–102.

Chapter 23 Endnotes

1. "Using Historical Foreground in New Testament Interpretation," *Biblical Interpretation: Principles and Practice. Studies in Honor of Jack Pearl Lewis*, ed. F. Furman Kearley, Edward P. Myers, and Timothy D. Hadley (Grand Rapids: Baker, 1986), 254–63.

2. Pliny, *Epistles* 10.96.

3. Eusebius, *H. E.* 5.28.6.

4. Ignatius, *Ephesians* 4.

5. *Odes of Solomon* 7.17. There are many references to a harp in the *Odes*: 6.1; 7.17; 14.8; 26.3. Some are clearly figurative, and likely all are; see the emphasis on lips and tongue in 40.

6. Clement of Alexandria, *Instructor* 3.11.80.4.

7. Tertullian, *On the Soul* 9.4.

8. Tertullian, *On Prayer* 28.

9. Hippolytus, *Commentary on Daniel*, PG 10.693D.

10. Eusebius, *H. E.* 10.3.3.

11. Eusebius, *Commentary on Psalms* 65.10–15.

12. Tertullian, *Apology* 39.18.

13. *Apostolic Constitutions* 2.59.2.

14. *Oxyrhynchus Papyri* XV.1786. A transposition into modern musical notation may be found in E. Wellesz's "The Earliest Example of Christian Hymnody," *Classical Quarterly* 39 (1945):34–45; C. Cosgrove, *An Ancient Christian Hymn with Musical Notation: PO 1786: Text and Commentary* (Tübingen: Mohr Siebeck, 2011).

15. John Cassian, *Institutes* 2.5; cf. 2.12.

16. Basil, *Epistle* 207.

17. E. Ferguson, "Psalm-Singing at the Eucharist: A Liturgical Controversy in the Fourth Century," *Austin Seminary Bulletin* 98 (1983): 52–77.

18. Theodoret, *H. E.* 2.19.

19. Socrates, *H. E.* 6.8.

20. Philo, *Contemplative Life* 83; cf. Eusebius, *H. E.* 2.17.22.

21. Augustine, *Confessions* 9.7; Paulinus, *Life of Ambrose* 4.13.

22. Tertullian, *On Prayer* 27.

23. *Apostolic Constitutions* 2.57.6.

24. John Chrysostom, *Homily 36 on 1 Corinthians* 14:33.

25. Ambrose, *On Psalm 1, Exposition* 9.

26. Jerome, *Homily 59 on Psalm 149*; cf. *Homily 65 on Psalm 87*.

27. John Chrysostom, *Homily on Psalm* 145:2; cf. *Exposition on Psalm* 150.

28. Justin, *Dialogue* 29.2.

29. Clement of Alexandria, *Instructor* 2.10.110.2.

30. Clement of Alexandria, *Miscellanies* 6.14.113.3

31. Clement of Alexandria, *Instructor* 2.4.43.3.

32. Origen, *On Prayer* 2.4.

33. Methodius, *Banquet* 4.2.

34. E. Ferguson, "Athanasius' Epistola ad Marcellinum in interpretationem Psalmorum," *Studia Patristica* 16.2 (Berlin, 1985): 295–308.

35. E. Ferguson, "The Active and Contemplative Lives: The Patristic Interpretation of Some Musical Terms," *Studia Patristica* 16.2 (Berlin, 1985): 15–23.

36. Gregory of Nyssa, *On the Titles of the Psalms* 2.3.

37. E. Ferguson, "Gregory of Nyssa and Psalmos," *Restoration Quarterly* 22 (1979): 77–83; a fuller study by me, "Words from the ΨΑΛ-Root in Gregory of Nyssa," *Studien zu Gregor von Nyssa und der Christlichen Spätantike*, ed. H. R. Drobner and C. Klock (Leiden: Brill, 1990), 57–68.

38. E. Ferguson, *A Cappella Music in the Public Worship of the Church*, 3rd ed. (Ft. Worth, 1999), 67–71. See also Tertullian, *To His Wife* 8 on singing at home and Cyprian, *Ep.* 1.16 on psalms at meals.

39. Niceta, *On the Utility of Hymn Singing* 9.

40. Theodoret, *On the Healing of Greek Afflictions* 7.16.

41. Origen, *Selections on the Psalms* in PG 12.1552D.

42. *On the Titles of the Psalms* 150, attributed to Athanasius but probably by Hesychius.

43. See my "Toward a Patristic Theology of Music," *Studia Patristica* 24 (1993): 266–83.

24

Congregational Singing in the Early Church[1]

According to Matthew 26:30 and Mark 14:26, at the conclusion of the Last Supper, Jesus and his disciples "sang hymns and went out to the Mount of Olives." Since this meal was apparently for Jesus and the disciples a Passover meal, these hymns were presumably the Hallel Psalms. According to later rabbinic literature, the Levites sang Psalms 113–118 during the slaughter of the lambs for the Passover offering. In the celebration of Passover at home, Psalms 113–114 were recited during the Passover meal, and at the conclusion of the meal the remaining Hallel Psalms (Pss. 115–118) were sung.[2]

How was the singing done? We do not have much information, but let us pursue what the sources that we do have tell us. The plural verbal form in the text of Matthew and Mark indicates that all participated. What form did this participation take? Did Jesus or someone else lead, and the others respond? Did they divide into two groups and alternate in the singing? Did they sing in unison?

Other statements in the New Testament do not offer much help. Ephesians 5:19 reads, "Speaking to one another in psalms, hymns, and spiritual songs, singing and making melody with your heart to the Lord." Colossians 3:16 reads, "Singing psalms, hymns, and spiritual songs with your hearts to God." The plural verbal forms once again indicate group participation. The "one another" is sometimes taken to indicate antiphonal or responsorial singing. That is possible as to the manner of rendition, as we shall see, but probably overinterprets the reflexive pronoun.[3] The singing was in some way mutual, reciprocal.

Paul describes his participation in the assembly in 1 Corinthians 14:15, "I will pray with the Spirit, and I will pray also with the mind; I will sing praise with the Spirit, and I will sing praise also with the mind." He individualizes his instructions to the Corinthians in order to correct their practices. As is true throughout 1 Corinthians 14, he describes his own practice in order to instruct the Corinthians on what they are to do in the assembly. He intends his practice to model what they are all to do. Hence, we should not be too quick to conclude that 1 Corinthians 14:26 refers to someone offering a solo in the assembly. Once more, Paul is individualizing group practices: "When you come together, each one has a psalm, each one has a teaching, each one has a revelation, each one has a tongue, each one has an interpretation. Let all things be done for building up." It should also be noted that Paul may here be speaking descriptively, not prescriptively; his prescription has to do with the purpose of edification, and how that is to be carried out is detailed later in the chapter. But, assuming that Paul is here giving instructions on what should be done, we may consider several possibilities of how each one brings a psalm to the meeting. One could make a selection out of the book of Psalms for the congregation to sing; one could bring a new composition to be taught to the congregation; or one could bring a new set of words to which a traditional response was given by the congregation. The psalm might not be sung strictly as a solo in the same manner that only one person at a time ought to give a teaching or a revelation; indeed we know that the Corinthians were not giving their revelations and messages in tongue one at a time, which was the confusing situation requiring the regulations in 14:27–31. Similarly, in Hebrews 2:12, Psalm 22:22 is quoted as describing Jesus "in the midst of the church" hymning praise to God. Whether a solo or some other method of singing was employed must be determined in part by what evidence we have from contemporary sources as to what Paul's words in 1 Corinthians 14:26 would have meant to his hearers.

So, let us go outside the New Testament to see if other sources offer us any help. I begin with one of the earliest notices of Christianity by a non–Christian, and it reports what Christians did when they met together. The governor of the Roman province of Bithynia in Asia Minor, Pliny the Younger, wrote a letter about the year 110 to the emperor Trajan. In it he states the practice of Christians "to come together on a certain fixed day before daylight and to sing in alternate verses a hymn to Christ as to a god."[4] Like the passages in Ephesians and Colossians, this description indicates all were involved but not necessarily in unison or simultaneously. Beyond that, one must speculate as to details, and many interpretations have been offered.[5] Although the passage is often translated so as to indicate a kind of antiphonal singing, the practice may have been responsorial, but we cannot be sure even what Pliny understood the practice to be, much less that he correctly understood what was told him.

Allow me to fast-forward to the fourth century and take a passage that, although late, in describing Christian practice at that time conveniently summarizes the options available for interpreting the first-century Christian practice. From it we will be in a position to work back to earlier evidence with more understanding. Basil was a presbyter (362–370) and then bishop (370–379) of the church at Caesarea in Cappadocia. His critics in the ecclesiastical conflicts of his time forced him to defend many of his practices. One of those charges was connected with psalmody, the singing of the Psalms, probably the practice of antiphonal singing, for there is no indication that the other ways of singing the Psalms were ever in doubt. In the following letter, he describes an early morning vigil of his church, probably not a regular Sunday service; but presumably the congregation did at the vigil things with which it was familiar on Sunday, just as Christians' Sunday practice is followed in many respects at midweek or other additional meetings.

> The customs we observe are in agreement and harmony with all the churches of God. At night our people are awake and go

to the house of prayer. In labor, affliction, and continuous tears they make confession to God. At last, arising from their prayers, they enter into psalmody. At one time, divided into two groups, they sing antiphonally to one another. This practice strengthens their recitation of the words, and at the same time controls their attention and keeps their hearts from distraction. Next, entrusting to one person the task of leading the melody, the others sing the response. Thus they pass the night in a variety of psalmody interspersed with prayers. When day begins to dawn, all in common—as if of one mouth and one heart—lift up the psalm of confession to the Lord, each one making the words of repentance his or her own.[6]

Basil had polemical reasons to want to emphasize that the practice of his church was not unique, so there may be rhetorical exaggeration in his claim that its customs agreed with those of "all the churches." Nonetheless, we must grant a substantial truth in his claim, for complete falsehood would have been too readily refuted. He is not describing an isolated practice. His description shows a variety of methods of engaging in psalmody, a variety that would have assisted in keeping people awake for an early morning service. These three kinds of singing are antiphonal, responsorial, and unison. In antiphonal singing, the congregation was divided into two parts, each group singing alternately. In responsorial singing, a leader carried the main part of the singing with the congregation responding either with a set phrase (like a refrain), which was more common, or with a repetition of what the leader had sung. In unison singing, the whole congregation "as if of one mouth and one heart" sang together the same words. The phrase "one mouth" did not mean unison in the sense of all singing the same note but was a phrase for joint participation in which all agreed in speaking the same thing.[7] Accordingly, I will use "unison" not for singing the same melodic line (although this may often have been the case) but for unified congregational singing.

Before saying something more about each of these forms of expression, I note that solo singing was known in a monastic setting. Thus John Cassian, who was influential in transferring the spirituality of Egyptian ascetics to western Europe (Gaul) in the early fifth century, relates the following story of the early leaders of Egyptian monasticism:

> As they were going to celebrate their daily rites and prayers, one rose up in the midst to chant the Psalms to the Lord. And while they were all sitting (as is still the custom in Egypt), with their minds intently fixed on the words of the chanter, when he had sung eleven Psalms, separated by prayers introduced between them, verse after verse being evenly enunciated, he finished the twelfth with a response of Alleluia.[8]

Earlier, about the year 200, Tertullian reported that solos were sung at love feasts. He says that after the meal the following occurred: "After the washing of hands and lighting of lamps, each one who is able is called into the center to chant praise to God either from the holy scriptures or from his own talents."[9]

So far as I know, explicit testimony for such solo recitation at the other church services is lacking, but it may have occurred in situations where only one was learned in the Psalms or skilled in music.

The use of antiphonal singing may be the specific practice Basil had to defend, for it is the manner of singing for which he gives an explanation of its value: It helps to strengthen the recitation of the words (it helps to say things together with others), and it helps to maintain the attention of the heart (since one has to pay attention when his or her part comes). Moreover, we know that there was some controversy over the introduction of antiphonal singing reflected in fourth-century sources. One historian testified that the practice was introduced at Antioch in the middle of the century.[10] Another historian, however, reported the claim of a greater antiquity of the practice, attributing it to Ignatius, bishop of Antioch at the beginning of the second century.[11] The practice of dividing into two groups and singing back and forth was almost certainly known earlier than the fourth century, as we shall see. Was the practice of antiphonal singing introduced at Antioch a revival of an earlier practice that seemed new at the time, or was there something new about the manner in which it was done?[12] We cannot be sure.

One reason that antiphonal singing seemed novel was that the common practice was responsorial singing. There is an abundance of evidence, of which we will cite only a sampling. The instructions concerning a Sunday assembly in the fourth-century *Apostolic Constitutions* include the following directions: "When there have been two lessons [from the Scriptures] read, let some other person sing the hymns of David, and let the people join in the singing at the conclusions of the verses."[13] John Chrysostom considered the practice to go back to apostolic times: "They all met together in old time and sang in response to the Psalms in common. This we do also now, but then among all there was one soul and one heart."[14] A work by Methodius, bishop of Olympus (d. about 311), entitled the *Banquet* in 11.2 contains a responsorial hymn sung by a group of virgins with the text of the song sung by the leader given in full and the refrain repeated by the others as a response after each verse. I am spending more time on the fourth century because our evidence is fuller and more descriptive, and so permits us to read the earlier evidence with greater clarity.

There is more evidence than is commonly recognized for unison or congregational song. In fact, one historian of church music argued that congregational singing was the oldest form of church music.[15] Some of the statements about everybody participating, however, could refer to antiphonal or responsorial participation. Some passages, nonetheless, do sound as if they were talking about everyone singing the whole psalm. Ambrose, bishop of Milan (374–397), has this to say:

> What a labor it is to achieve silence in church while the lessons are being read. When one man would speak, the congregation makes a disturbance. But when the Psalm is recited, it makes its own "silence," since all are speaking and there is no disturbance.... The singing of praise is the very bond of unity, when the whole people join in song a single act of song.[16]

The same passage continues with a defense of women singing in spite of Paul's words, "Let women keep silent in church" (1 Cor. 14:34), which, Ambrose says (and I think correctly), do not apply to group participation in song. Basil of Caesarea in his commentary on the Psalms discusses what psalmody accomplishes and comments on the whole congregation participating: Singing the Psalms together is a bond of unity, "uniting the people into the harmony of one chorus."[17] Eusebius, the church historian and bishop of Caesarea in Palestine (313–339), gives this impressive testimony from the early fourth century:

> Throughout the world—in cities, in villages, and in the country—in all the churches of God the people of Christ, who have been chosen out of all the nations, send up, not to the native gods nor to demons but to the one God spoken of by the prophets, hymns and psalmody with a loud voice so that the sound of those singing can be heard by those standing outside.[18]

A frequent expression for this common participation by all was "one mouth." It is already in the New Testament—Romans 15:6—but also in the passage quoted from Basil that provides a framework for our discussion of three types of congregational singing. An equivalent expression was "one voice." Niceta of Remesiana gives this advice: "Let us sing all together, as with one voice, and let all of us modulate our voices in the same way. If one cannot sing in tune with the others, it is better to sing in a low voice rather than drown out the others."[19] (I follow this advice.)

"One voice" or unison singing, as I said, referred to congregational participation, not the same pitch, for some passages make explicit that different ages and sexes participated. John Chrysostom writes: "[God] invites every age to sing: old men, mature men, youths, adults, women, all inhabitants of the world."[20] In another passage he speaks similarly:

> Our tongues are the strings of our kithara [a string instrument played by plucking—the body, as commonly in patristic sources, is the instrument[21]], putting forth a different sound yet a godly harmony. For indeed women and men, old and young, have different voices, but they do not differ in the word of hymnody, for the Spirit blends the voice of each and effects one melody in all.[22]

I would insist that all three of these methods of singing, not just the unison, are "congregational singing," for the whole congregation is involved even if not all at the same time. In neither case is there performance, whether by one person (although one person, the precentor or "song leader," has great prominence in responsorial singing) or by a chorus (actually two choruses comprising the whole congregation in antiphonal singing). In each instance the group that is silent part of the time is not simply listening but is actively engaged and must enter in at the appropriate time. We may compare, although not exactly equivalent, the practice of soprano, alto, tenor, or bass leads (or singing of one verse) and then other parts joining in. The congregation or one of the choruses might not sing the whole song.

In those passages where it is emphasized that the whole congregation was involved, can we tell more about how? Which of the three methods was involved in any given case? Here I think it is instructive to compare Basil's statement with a rabbinic passage that describes similar but not identical practice. The time of writing was nearly contemporary, but it cites earlier rabbis. The subject is the song of Moses and Miriam in Exodus 15, and the discussion is how the singing was done. The passage compares different ways in which the congregation participated in a synagogue service:

> Our Rabbis taught: On that day R. Akiba [early second century] expounded: At the time the Israelites ascended from the Red Sea, they desired to utter a song; and how did they render the song? Like an adult who reads the *Hallel* (for a congregation) and they respond after him with the leading word. (According to this explanation) Moses said, "I will sing unto the Lord," and they responded, "I will sing unto the Lord"; Moses said, "For He hath triumphed gloriously" and they responded, "I will sing unto the Lord." R. Eliezer [mid-second century], son of R. Jose the Galilean, declares, like a minor who reads the *Hallel* (for a congregation), and they repeat after him all that he says. R. Nehemiah [second century] declares: Like a school-teacher who recites the *Shema* ["Hear, O Israel"] in the Synagogue, viz., he begins first and they respond after him. On what do they differ? R. Akiba holds that the word "saying" refers to the first clause; R. Eliezer, son of R. Jose the Galilean, holds that "saying" refers to every clause; and R. Nehemiah holds that "and spake" indicates that they sang all together "and saying" that Moses began first.[23]

The passage describes two types of responsorial participation and one type of unison participation. In the first type, the response is with a key phrase repeated as a refrain each time; in the second type, the response is to repeat the words of the leader (who might be a minor);[24] and in the third type, the leader starts and everyone joins in unison. The whole congregation is involved in all three types. The passage would indicate various types of singing were known among the Jews in the period shortly after the beginning of the church. Can we go back earlier? The interpretation of the Song of the Sea in Exodus 15 points us to a Jewish writer on the eve of the New Testament, Philo of Alexandria.

Philo describes a Jewish sect known as the Therapeutae, who lived as a kind of monastic community composed of both men and women not far from Alexandria. The following passage describes their celebration on the fiftieth day (presumably Pentecost).

> [Following a discourse by the president,] The president having stood up sings a hymn addressed to God, either a new one composed by himself or an old one by poets of an earlier time [one of the Psalms?], for they have left behind in many meters and melodies verses in trimeters, hymns for processions, at libations, and at the altars, and careful metrical arrangements for the stops and varied movements of choruses.[25] After him the others [sing] in proper order according to their rank, while all the rest listen in great silence except when they must sing the closing phrases or refrains, for then all, both men and women, lift up their voices. [When each has finished his hymn, the meal is served.]

[Then came an all-night vigil of the community that was spent in song.]

> They all rise together in the midst of the dining room and first form two choruses, one of men and one of women. For each chorus the most honored and most musical is chosen as precentor and leader. Then they sing hymns to God composed in many meters and melodies, sometimes singing together and at other times with antiphonal harmonies, motioning with their hands

> and dancing, inspiring in turn processional odes and then performing the stops, turnings, and movements of a choric dance. Then when each of the choruses has taken its own part in the feast, ... they combine and out of the two become one chorus, a copy of what was constituted at the Red Sea on account of the marvelous things done there.... [At that time (Ex. 15)] filled with divine enthusiasm, the men together with the women, becoming one chorus, sang thanksgiving hymns to God their Savior, the prophet Moses leading the men and the prophetess Miriam the women. On this model the male and female members with responsive and antiphonal strains, blending the bass sound of the men with the treble of the women, perform a harmonious and truly musical symphony. Truly beautiful are the thoughts, truly beautiful the words, reverent are the chorus members. The goal of the thoughts, the words, and the choruses is godliness.[26]

Philo adopts the terminology of the choral music and dances of the Greek theater and religious festivals. My interest here is not in the possible bodily movements he describes as accompanying the singing but what he says about the way the singing was done. He mentions a solo by the president of the assembly, community responses to songs (both new and old) sung by the various members, antiphonal choruses (one of men and one of women),[27] and unison singing of all together. The passage has the great interest of describing the extensive musical practices of a Jewish community contemporary with the beginnings of Christianity. It would be supposed that Jewish musical practices would provide the pattern for those of Christians. That supposition and the interest of the passage for historians of early Christianity are confirmed by what the church historian Eusebius says about it.

Eusebius, in the early fourth century, thought that Philo in the first century in writing about the Therapeutae was describing early Christians. He singles out one aspect of Philo's account of their musical practices as agreeing with the church music of his own day.

> What need is there in connection with these things to speak of their meetings together, ... the exercises even now customarily

accomplished by us, especially those we are accustomed to fulfill at the festival of the passion of the Savior with fasting, vigils through the night, and attention to the divine words? The writer referred to [Philo] gave in his own writing a description exactly agreeing with those things that are observed until now by us alone. He narrates the vigils of the great festival, its exercises, the hymns we are accustomed to recite, and how while one sings the Psalm decorously in time, the rest listen attentively in quietness and join in singing the refrains of the hymns.[28]

Eusebius claims (certainly incorrectly) that the description is of Christians because they alone observe the customs that Philo describes. That seems to refer to the all-night vigils and would not include the responsorial singing (which Jews also did), but it is notable that this manner of singing (that is, responsorial) is the only aspect of the musical practices that he singles out for mention as done by Christians. Eusebius's words are a testimony to responsorial singing being the common form of Christian practice in his day. He underscores the attentiveness of the congregation in listening to the one who sings the lead and their participation in singing the ending of the psalms.

Some information about pagan practices fills out the background.[29] Literary sources once more do not tell us much about the manner in which singing was done; the treatises that were produced "On Music" mostly deal with the technical aspects of music. There is a first-century pictorial representation, however, that provides a suggestive parallel to Philo's description of the Therapeutae. The scene comes from a wall painting at Herculaneum, one of the cities destroyed by the eruption of Mt. Vesuvius in AD 79.[30] It depicts a temple of the Egyptian goddess Isis. In front of the temple an attendant kindles a fire on the altar. At the head of the stairs two figures each hold a *sistrum* (a metal rattle used in the cult of Isis) and at the bottom of the picture two more figures each hold a *sistrum* and one person plays an *aulos* (a pipe). Between the altar and the temple there are arranged two choruses, each containing about twenty persons. As far as can be made out from the heads for which details are given, the chorus on the spectator's left is made up of men and the one on the right of women. A director stands between them, apparently leading them in song. The arrangement of the singers suggests some sort of antiphonal or alternating song, although unison singing cannot be excluded. The practice of the Therapeutae described by Philo, therefore, would fit the cultural context as to manner of singing.

Returning to the Christian sources, we can now bring the evidence for church practice back closer to New Testament times with some confidence that the allusions do indeed refer to what was actually done in church. We do not have explicit reference to antiphonal singing in early Christian sources, but it may be that Pliny the Younger is referring to such soon after the New Testament period in the early second century. Origen in commenting on the Song of Solomon speaks of two choirs answering each other, one composed of the bride and her maids and the other of the bridegroom and his companions. Presumably he offers this explanation because he is familiar with such a practice of male and female choruses singing antiphonally, but we do not know if he was acquainted with this practice from churches.[31]

Responsorial singing is confirmed by sources widely separated geographically at the end of the second century. We may note the words of Tertullian from Carthage in North Africa at the beginning of the third century: "The more diligent in prayer are accustomed to add to their prayers the "Hallelujah" Psalms and such other Psalms, at the closing of which the company responds."[32] Clement of Alexandria in Egypt at the end of the second century criticized the hypocrisy of some church members by making a contrast between worldly and Christian singing:

> After having paid reverence to the discourse about God, they leave within what they have heard. And outside [the meeting] they foolishly amuse themselves with impious playing and amatory quavering, occupied with pipe-playing and dancing, and intoxication, all kinds of trash. They who sing thus and sing in response are those who before hymned immortality.[33]

Clement does not say how they "hymned immortality," but his specifying "sing in response" in reference to the worldly singing is likely suggested by the parallel practice of responsorial singing in church. At least, Clement implies that they had all participated in the church's singing.

Congregational Singing in the Early Church

Clement makes another statement that refers to the unison or group singing of the Psalms, whether by Jews or Christians or both is not absolutely clear. In describing the singing at Greek banquets he mentions as two alternatives singing all together "with one voice after the manner of the Hebrew Psalms" or taking turns in the singing.[34] The implication seems to be that the usual manner of rendering the Psalms known to Clement was for the whole group to join in singing them. I think that we can add testimony from the beginning of the second century for this unison congregational singing.

Even as Philo drew on pagan musical practice to describe the activities of a Jewish religious group, so a Christian author nearly a century after Philo, Ignatius of Antioch, at the beginning of the second century drew on that practice in alluding to Christian practice. He is exhorting to unity, but seems to employ Christian musical practice as well as a pagan musical illustration to make his point:

> For your deservedly famous presbytery, worthy of God, is attuned to the bishop as strings [are] to a harp. Therefore by your concord and harmonious love Jesus Christ is being sung. Now all of you together become a chorus so that being harmoniously in concord and receiving the key note from God in unison you may sing with one voice through Jesus Christ to the Father.[35]

Ignatius uses a musical instrument as an illustration, a common illustration in other Christian authors, but Ignatius, like them, speaks of the church's practice as only vocal music, singing.[36] The unity of the church makes it like a chorus that sings with one voice. I take it that the illustration reflects actual church practice—the whole church singing in unison. The pagan background of his imagery is a chorus gathered around an altar, as is clear in another of Ignatius's statements: "While an altar is still ready, so that by becoming a chorus in love, you may sing to the Father in Christ Jesus."[37]

It probably goes without saying in this context that the singing in the early church was unaccompanied by instrumental music. This fact is recognized by nearly all historians of church music and of Christianity in the ancient and early Medieval periods. I could say "by all of the historians," but I cover myself in case of possible exceptions. The fact of early Christian a cappella music nonetheless needs to be stated, because so much of what is styled "Christian music" today is instrumentally conceived. Classic church music, however, is vocal music and was so until quite modern times. Even when organs were present, the music initially was primarily vocal.

There is no evidence for the use of a musical instrument in the congregational assemblies of early Christians. A musical instrument did not accompany the congregational singing. The only instrument used was the human voice. When the musical instruments of the Old Testament were applied to Christians, the instruments were interpreted as the human body. Clement of Alexandria is typical in his comments on Psalm 150:

> The Spirit, distinguishing from such revelry [at pagan banquets that he has referred to] the divine service, sings, "Praise him with the sound of the trumpet"; for with the sound of trumpet he shall raise the dead. "Praise him on the psaltery"; for the tongue is the psaltery of the Lord. "And praise him on the lyre." By the lyre is meant the mouth struck by the Spirit, as it were by a plectrum. "Praise with the timbrel and dance," refers to the church meditating on the resurrection of the dead in resounding skin [the timbrel was made of skin stretched tight on a frame]. "Praise him on the chords and organ." Our body he calls an organ, and its nerves are the strings, by which it has received harmonious tension, and when struck by the Spirit, it gives forth human voices. "Praise him on the clashing cymbals." He calls the tongue the cymbal of the mouth, which resounds with the pulsation of the lips. Therefore he cried to humanity, "Let every breath praise the Lord," because he cares for every breathing thing which he has made. For a human being is truly a pacific instrument; while other instruments, if you investigate, you will find to be warlike, inflaming to lusts, or kindling up amours, or rousing wrath.[38]

Many other passages could be quoted that take a similar approach. The interpretation of the human body as an instrument of music is found in Judaism in Philo and the Dead Sea Scrolls also. Early Christians understood the human body to be the only instrument God approved for use in his praise.

As a modern correspondent of mine put it, "The voice is the only instrument created by God."

Different from this allegorical approach to the instruments of the Old Testament taken by the school of Alexandria, the school of Antioch took the historical approach of distinguishing the covenants. Theodoret of Cyrhus in Syria is quite explicit:

> Question: If songs were invented by unbelievers to seduce men, but were allowed to those under the law on account of their childish state, why do those who have received the perfect teaching of grace in their churches still use songs, just like the children under the law?
>
> Answer: It is not simple singing that belongs to the childish state, but singing with [accompanied by] lifeless instruments, with dancing, and with clappers. Hence the use of such instruments and the others that belong to the childish state is excluded from the singing in the churches, and simple singing is left. For it awakens the soul to a fervent desire for that which is described in the songs. (*Questions and Answers for the Orthodox* 107)

To summarize, early Christian, Jewish, and pagan sources indicate the following forms of vocal rendition: (1) solo, (2) responsorial of two types—with the community responding either by repeating what the leader has sung or singing a set refrain, (3) antiphonal, and (4) unison or group. Solo performance is largely absent from the Christian sources, except in settings other than the Sunday service for the Lord's Supper. The other options, I would repeat, are all forms of "congregational singing." They each (responsorial, antiphonal, as well as unison) involve participation by the entire congregation, even if not all at the same time. They required close attention by everyone to the words and to the part of others as well as one's own. And that would be the point of the New Testament references to singing and its purposes of instruction, edification, reciprocal concern, and mutuality.

The usual manner of congregational singing in the present, with four-part harmony, occasional voice leads, and western or African style melodies are obviously different and culturally conditioned. But the essential of congregational participation with all the people singing most or some of the time and even such an incidental as a song leader have very ancient roots indeed. And we can aspire to a similarity in spiritual content and purpose in what is sung.

*Originally printed in *Acta Patristica et Byzantina* 15 (2004), 144–59.

Chapter 24 Endnotes

1. This paper began as a lecture for the Lita Witt Foundation at the Preston Road Church of Christ, Dallas, TX, May 21, 2000; repeated with modifications at the University of Pretoria, South Africa, Nov. 7, 2001 (published in *Acta Patristica et Byzantina* 15 [2004]: 144–59); and revised and expanded for the symposium "Ascending Voice" at Pepperdine University, June 5, 2007.

2. Mishnah, *Pesahim* 5.7; 10.5–7.

3. The reflexive was often used for the reciprocal pronoun, as in Eph. 4:32 and Col. 3:13.

4. Pliny, *Letters* 10.96.

5. See discussion and notes in my *Early Christians Speak*, 3rd ed. (Abilene: ACU Press, 1999), 79, 81–82, 88. "Alternately" could be translated "in turn," "mutually," or "reciprocally."

6. Basil, *Letter* 207.3, 4. Dated about 375. The translation is also found in my *Inheriting Wisdom: Readings for Today from Ancient Christian Writers* (Peabody: Hendrickson, 2004), 242.

7. Everett Ferguson, "Praising God with 'One Mouth'/'One Voice,'" in *Renewing Tradition: Studies in Texts and Contexts in Honor of James W. Thompson* (ed. Mark H. Hamilton, Thomas H. Olbricht, and Jeffrey Peterson; Eugene: Pickwick, 2007), 3–23.

8. John Cassian, *Institutes* 2.5; the practice is further regulated in 2.12.

9. Tertullian, *Apol.* 39.18.

10. Theodoret, *Church History* 2.19. "Flavian and Diodore were the first to divide choirs into two parts, and to teach them to sing the Psalms of David antiphonally. Introduced first at Antioch, the practice spread in all directions, and penetrated to the ends of the earth. Its originators now collected the lovers of the divine word and work into the churches of [that is, dedicated to] the martyrs, and with them spent the night in singing Psalms to God."

11. Socrates Scholasticus, *Church History* 6.8.11. "We must now, however, make some allusion to the origin of this custom in the church of antiphonal singing. Ignatius, third bishop of Antioch in Syria from the Apostle Peter . . . saw a vision of angels hymning in alternate chants to the Holy Trinity. Accordingly he introduced the mode of singing he had observed in the vision into the Antiochian church; whence it was transmitted by tradition to all the other churches. Such is the account we have received in relation to these antiphonal hymns." Earlier in 6.8.2 he uses the same word for antiphonal singing to describe the musical practices of the Arians.

12. Other references from the fourth century cited for antiphonal singing are the following: Gregory of Nazianzus, *Songs* 18; Ambrose, *Hexaemeron* 3.5; Augustine, *Explanations of the Psalms* 26 pref. A notice of the introduction of antiphonal singing at Milan by Ambrose is given by Paulinus, *Life of Ambrose* 4.13, and Augustine, *Confessions* 9.7.

13. *Apostolic Constitutions* 2.57.6.

14. *Homily* 36 *On 1 Corinthians* 14:33. Other references from the fourth century given for responsorial singing include Chrysostom, *Commentary on Psalms* 137; Athanasius, *Defense of His Flight* 24.

15. Joseph Bingham, *Antiquities of the Christian Church* (London: Bohn, 1845; repr. of 1708, 1722 edition), bk. 14, ch. 1, 680–83, citing Hilary, *On the Psalms* 65; Augustine, *De Verb. Apost. Serm.* 10; and the Chrysostom passages that I translate as referring to responsorial singing.

16. Ambrose, *On Psalm* 1, *Exposition* 9. Translation by Erik Routley, *The Church and Music* (London: Duckworth, 1950), 129.

17. Basil, *Homilies on the Psalms* 1.2.

18. *Commentary on Psalms* 65.10–15; cf. his *Commentary on Psalms* 91.2–3.

19. *On the Utility of Hymn Singing* 13.

20. John Chrysostom, *Commentary on the Psalms* 150.6.

21. See further below and my "Toward a Patristic Theology of Music," *Studia Patristica* 24 (1993): 266–83 (269, 273, 276–77), to which add Gregory of Nyssa, *Making of Man* 9, on the body as an instrument used by the mind; also my "The Active and Contemplative Lives: The Patristic Interpretation of Some Musical Terms," *Studia Patristica* 16 (1985): 15–23.

22. John Chrysostom, *Homily on Psalm 145* [English 146]. Cf. Basil, *Hexaemeron* 4.7 (PG 29.93C), "mingled voice of men, women, and children."

23. Babylonian Talmud, *Sotah* 30b.

24. Is the congregational repetition of everything because the minor might speak indistinctly and it was important for everything to be clearly understood?

25. Alternatively, instead of referring to the dances ("varied movements"), we could translate "the stationary choral songs well arranged with versatile strophes."

26. Philo, *On the Contemplative Life* 10.80; 11.83–85, 87–88. For Philo's treatment of music in general, see my "The Art of Praise: Philo and Philodemus on Music," in *Early Christianity and Classical Culture: Comparative Studies in Honor of Abraham J. Malherbe* (ed. John T. Fitzgerald, Thomas H. Olbricht, and L. Michael White; Leiden: Brill, 2003), 391–426 (417–22 on the Therapeutae).

27. This is the interpretation that my translation assumes, but *antiphonos* ("answer in response") may not have yet had the technical sense of answering choruses. The wording may refer only to the contrasting pitches of male and female voices. Philo elsewhere in *Life of Moses* 1.180 and 2.256–57 also refers to the choruses of men and women in Exodus 15, where he seems to describe the men and women singing together with the low voices of the men and the high voices of the women blended into a harmonious melody.

28. *Church History* 2.17.21–22.

29. A brief introduction to the available sources on music (especially singing) in pagan clubs and associations is now available in Stephen G. Wilson, "Early Christian Music," in *Common Life in the Early Church: Essays Honoring Graydon Snyder* (ed. Julian V. Hills et al.; Harrisburg: Trinity Press International, 1998), 390–401, although he (to my mind incorrectly) downplays Jewish evidence in favor of pagan evidence relative to Christian practice. Wilson notes (399–400) that for the associations the evidence points to communal participation rather than solo performance; where the singular (*hymnodos*, hymn singer) is used, it refers to a member of a group.

30. A black and white reproduction is found in my *Backgrounds of Early Christianity*, 3rd ed., 2nd printing (Grand Rapids: Eerdmans, 2004), 273.

31. Origen, *Commentary on the Song of Songs* 1.1.

32. Tertullian, *On Prayer* 27.

33. Clement of Alexandria, *Instructor* 3.11.80.4.

34. Ibid., 2.4.44.

35. Ignatius, *Ephesians* 4.

36. Examples collected in my *A Cappella Music in the Public Worship of the Church*, 3rd ed. (Fort Worth: Star Bible Publishing Co., 1999), 43–58, and further bibliography given through the book.

37. Ignatius, *Romans* 2.2.

38. Clement of Alexandria, *Instructor* 2.4.41.4–42.1. Translation from the *Ante-Nicene Fathers*, Vol. II, 248–49.

www.ingramcontent.com/pod-product-compliance
Lightning Source LLC
Chambersburg PA
CBHW030433300426
44112CB00009B/988